BEYOND THE WAVES

My Royal Navy Adventures

By

ANDREW HEASMAN

Beyond the Waves: My Royal Navy Adventures

COPYRIGHT

Published in 2017 by Seahawk Publishing UK.

Copyright © ANDREW HEASMAN.

First Edition

ISBN-13: 978-1976565014
ISBN-10: 1976565014

Printed by CreateSpace, an Amazon.com Company.

The author has asserted their moral right under the Copyright, Designs and Patents Act, 1988, to be identified as the author of this work.
All Rights reserved. No part of this publication may be reproduced, copied, stored in a retrieval system, or transmitted, in any form or by any means, without the prior written consent of the copyright holder, nor be otherwise circulated in any form of binding or cover other than that in which it is published and without a similar condition being imposed on the subsequent purchaser.
The people and events portrayed in this book are as remembered, perceived and/or experienced by ANDREW HEASMAN. However some of the names and places have been changed for privacy and legal reasons. The author takes no responsibility for the accuracy of events and dialogue retold to him by third parties, friends, or family.

Available on Kindle and other devices.

Cover design by Pro_Ebookcovers.

Beyond the Waves

My Royal Navy Adventures

Table of Contents

COPYRIGHT 2

Table of Contents 5

DEDICATION 9

FOREWORD 11

CHAPTER 1 15
   New beginnings 15

CHAPTER 2 23
   HMS Raleigh – Early Days 23

CHAPTER 3 30
   Initial training 30

CHAPTER 4 44
   HMS Raleigh – Part 2 44

CHAPTER 5 55
   HMS Collingwood – Technical School 55

CHAPTER 6 64
   Freedom of Fareham 64

CHAPTER 7 71
   Talybont on Usk 71

CHAPTER 8 81
   Sea Safety Training 81

CHAPTER 9 92
   HMS Scylla 92

CHAPTER 10 106
The Sea Journal 106

CHAPTER 11 114
Norway bound 114

CHAPTER 12 124
Standing Naval Force Atlantic 124

CHAPTER 13 134
Heading west 134

CHAPTER 14 143
Mainland USA 143

CHAPTER 15 150
The Return Leg 150

CHAPTER 16 155
HMS Collingwood – Application School 155

CHAPTER 17 165
ARE Helston 165

CHAPTER 18 178
HMS Royal Arthur 178

CHAPTER 19 187
HMS Invincible – A/POWEA (OC) 187

CHAPTER 20 196
European Deployment 196

CHAPTER 21 208
Eastern Mediterranean 208

CHAPTER 22 217
Pre-Deployment Preparations 217

Beyond the Waves: My Royal Navy Adventures

CHAPTER 23	224
Orient 92 Begins	224
CHAPTER 24	236
Across the Indian Ocean	236
CHAPTER 25	243
The Far East	243
CHAPTER 26	255
Back to the Indian Ocean	255
CHAPTER 27	262
The Middle East	262
CHAPTER 28	267
The Holy Land and our homeward journey	267
CHAPTER 29	276
The beginning of the end…	276
CHAPTER 30	282
Postscript	282
Multimedia Bonus	289
About the Author	291
Contact the Author	293
Future Releases	295

DEDICATION

To my Mum and Dad:

"Thank you for making me what I am today. Without you, none of this would have been possible."

To my wife, Heather:

"Love you always."

To my daughters, Phoebe and Sophie:

"See – Daddy did do exciting things..."

FOREWORD

It is a bright sunny day; the sky an azure blue, a scattering of fluffy white clouds above. As you casually stroll along the beach, the grains of white sand shift beneath your feet. To your left, the gently lapping waves of the ocean, and to your right, a lush green tropical forest, alive with the sound of birdsong. The heat is oppressive, pushing down on you, restricting your breathing.

Ahead, you see something obstructing the otherwise immaculate sand. What could it be? As you get nearer, amid the usual debris of frayed ropes, left-footed flip-flops, plastic water-bottles and seaweed, you see a strange, almost alien-like sculpture. It is a piece of driftwood. You move closer. You touch it, handle it. It is smooth, warm, bleached white by constant exposure to the relentless sun. It is cracked from the battering of the waves; all bark and leaves, and remnants of a former life stripped to reveal an inner skeleton.

Where did this driftwood come from? Was it from distant shores, beyond the waves, or was it from the forest beside you? How long had it drifted on the tides? How had it looked before being stripped bare? If it could talk, what stories could it tell; what sights would it have seen?

The tree that it used to be is long gone, but the driftwood remains, testimony to its former past. It is the tree's legacy to the future.

You might equate my life to that of the tree, and this book, my memoirs, to that of the driftwood. I have been a soldier, a sailor, a police officer, and a diver, but when I am gone, there will be nothing left of me other than memories, and these will fade and disappear with time. By writing my memoirs, future generations will have a lasting record of my life, my experiences, and my thoughts. This will be my legacy to my family, my daughters and all future generations.

As a wise man once wrote,

"Language allows us to reach out to people, to touch them with our innermost fears, hopes, disappointments, victories. To reach out to people we'll never meet. It's the greatest legacy you could ever leave your children or your loved ones: The history of how you felt."
~ *Simon Van Booy*

What prompted me to write my memoirs, and why choose to write them now? Well, a number of factors have aligned to bring me to this point in time. This will be a legacy for my family. At the time of writing, I have entered my 50's, but my daughters are 7 and 5 respectively. We were watching an item on television the other day about the Royal Navy when I told my eldest that I used to serve in the RN too. She replied,

"No you didn't. You're Daddy. You just stay at home all day!"

This shows two things. Firstly, children do not appreciate the role of a stay-at-home parent; cooking, cleaning, tidying-up, taking them to and from school etc. And secondly (and more seriously), at that age, they are only interested in the present. Who cares what you did in the past!

However, as they mature, they will reach an age where they will want to know more about their family. With me being that much older, I may not be around to tell them about my past, but by leaving a record of my experiences, written in my own words, they will be able to understand what made me the person I am today.

Over the past few years, I have been researching my family history and, to date, I have traced over 1000 relatives. Although it is great to have these records, to know where I originated from, they are merely facts-and-figures; there is no way of understanding what these individuals thought, or what it was like to live in their era. For those who follow me, these memoirs will add more substance to their family research.

Having had many roles, I could have written an autobiography covering *everything*, but I chose to write in the form of a memoir, split into volumes to cover the different chapters in my life. As a diving instructor, I often told snippets of my story to the customers as they always wondered what led me to end-up in some tropical location living-the-dream. Many would say,

"Oh, you've definitely got to write a book about all of that."

I would always reply that maybe I would at some point, but it never really happened. Not until now. Now I am fulfilling that promise and, at the same time, ticking off a bucket-list-item by writing and publishing a book.

Who should read this book? The simple answer is anyone, and everyone. Yes, it should be read by my family and friends, and those who know me. It should also be read by those who served in the Royal Navy alongside me. To them, it will ignite memories of things they will have experienced, places they may have visited, and incidents they may remember. Please remember though, these are *my* memoirs, as seen through *my* eyes. Each individual will see things slightly differently, and have a different perspective on them. Also, for privacy, any people I mention in this book will be referred to by either a nickname or their surname. In some cases I may change names completely if I see fit. However, if you were there, you will know who you are.

This is also for those who served in the Royal Navy (or any other armed-services), either before or after the period I am writing about. Some things will remain the same as when you served, others will have changed, but by reading this book you will be able to compare and contrast with your own experiences.

For those readers who enjoy travel to far-flung places, or who dream of such travel, this book is for you. Read it in the context of a "travelogue" and enjoy the descriptions of my voyages around the globe.

For historians interested in social-history, or the history of the Royal Navy, you should also read this book. It may not be a story of exciting wartime action, but it is a true and honest account of life for the thousands of navy personnel who served between conflicts in the 1980's and 1990's.

And for those who enjoy a good biography, or who are just curious about other people's lives, this book should provide an entertaining read and a bit of escapism.

As you can see, this book can be everything to everyone depending on what you, the reader, want to gain from it.

My introduction is now complete, so let me transport you back-in-time to the middle of the 1980's, to an era very different from now. Let us begin our journey and experience together my time in the Royal Navy...

CHAPTER 1

New beginnings

MAY 5th 1986.

This is a date forever etched into my memory, for this is the date that I joined Her Majesty's Royal Navy. The day dawned bright but cloudy in South Harrow. I was awake early, but it was surprising I had slept at all as I was full of nervous energy. I was already packed from the night before, prepared and ready to tackle anything that was thrown in my direction. But I was scared! I was scared of facing the unknown, of entering into a world that I had no experience of. This same scenario was undoubtedly being replayed in different houses up and down the country as other people's sons prepared to embark on their first day in the Royal Navy. We did not know each other, but within hours, we would be best mates, bonds would be formed that would last throughout our lives; we would be *shipmates*.

I ate a quick breakfast.

"You'll need energy for the journey down," my mum said.

Then I donned my best clothes and polished shoes, and waited nervously for the off. This was the 1980's and the first day at work was a "formal" occasion worthy of dressing-up in a suit and tie.

I travelled into central London on the underground, as I had done many times before, the distinctive smell of "The Tube" ever present; only this time I was accompanied by my mum and dad. We arrived early at Paddington Station and joined the throng of people waiting for trains, watching the ever-changing notice-boards as times and locations were updated. Eventually my train was called. I said an awkward good-bye to my parents and set-off for the platform. I did not look back, but I heard later that my mum was in tears, upset at losing her eldest son to the navy. Little did any of us know, but my brother would soon follow the same path as me.

I found a seat, put my bag in the storage area, and sat down, ready for the long journey west to Plymouth. I looked around the carriage. There were lots of people in it, some young men who looked equally as scared as me. Would they be joining the navy too? Logic would say to start a conversation, to ask them, but British reserve being what it is, we could not break the unwritten rule of all rail travellers by actually talking to a stranger. Instead, we all sat in silence, avoiding eye-contact. In fact, to this date, I cannot remember if any of them were fellow recruits as the arrival in Plymouth was a bit of a blur.

The train started edging forward, snaking its way along the track, through the suburbs of London, and out into the green fields beyond. This was to be my last view of London, of home, for the next month and a half. I did not know it yet, but there would be no contact with the outside world, no shore-leave, and no trips home for the first half of the basic-training phase.

The journey to Plymouth was uneventful, punctuated only by toilet-breaks and sandwiches. The world outside the carriage windows flew by at what seemed a million miles an hour. But it did give me time to reflect on how I had come to be in this position in the first place.

A few months earlier, I had been working for the NatWest Bank in Pinner, and then in Harrow. I had been there for the best part of 18 months since I had left college, but it was intended only as a stop-gap job until something better came along. It just got extended a little bit longer than planned. I worked behind the scenes in the machine-room, putting cheques and credit slips into the computer system. It was a mundane job, but it did pay well.

At the same time, I had joined the Territorial Army in Harrow. I was a signaller in the 31st Signal Regiment, 47th Squadron Radio Relay. This was my first experience of a military lifestyle, but in reality it was more of a hobby than a job. The Territorial Army was a totally different beast in the 1980's to that which exists nowadays. Recently, the TA have been deployed to the Afghanistan and Iraq warzones, and constituted a large proportion of the soldiers fighting in these conflicts. But in 1985, there was hardly any chance of getting sent abroad with the TA. They were nicknamed "The Weekend Warriors" and that is exactly what we were. We would arrive at the TA Centre on one evening each week to learn or practice military skills relating to our roles within the army. This might be marching, fitness, or weapons drills, but was more likely to be "tweaking" radio sets, or learning to use code-books to send messages. Then on one or two weekends each month we would either travel to the Aldershot area to play *war-games* with other army units, or spend the whole weekend at our TA centre, supposedly doing "training." This was the better option because it really consisted of doing a couple of hours of work, then spending the rest of the time in the subsidised bar getting drunk. It was more of a social-club than a job. Not only was it great fun and a good laugh, but they paid us to do it too! Definitely a "win-win" situation.

I had always been destined to join the armed forces or to join the police service. Ever since I could remember I had been fascinated by stories of war, of soldiers, of sailors, and of the police. As a child, I would play with my friends, fighting pretend battles. The local building sites became our bombed houses; the sewer pipes and drains our Vietnamese insurgent tunnels. We would climb trees, build camps, and fight our make-believe wars. Health and safety was non-existent in those days, it was normal to be out playing for hours at a time, our parents having no idea where we were or what we were doing. It made us adventurous. It made us brave. We made mistakes, got hurt, got dirty, but we learnt from this, which made us stronger. The modern world is totally different to what it was then. As a parent, I would not even consider letting my daughters go off on their own to play, out of my sight, away from the house! You do not know who is out there! It was no different in the 70's and 80's really, except people were not brought up in a state of fear. It was still as dangerous, but people just got on with it, they were more trusting of the community around them.

Throughout my childhood, television was a major influence, pointing me towards my future careers. It was a time where you watched World-War-Two films on a Saturday afternoon (glamorised as only Hollywood could do). TV programs consisted of things like "Allo, Allo," "Escape from Colditz," "The Sweeney," and best of all, "The Professionals." Who would I be today in my adventures? Bodie (ex army) or Doyle (ex police)? It is not surprising, then, that when it came to choosing which job I wanted to pursue, I was torn between the forces and the police.

Then, in 1982, the Falklands War erupted! To a 16 year old who loved the military, this was like manna-from-heaven. The reports were on all channels, at all times of day, live from the front-line. To me, it was as close to being there as I was likely to get. From the comfort of my armchair I watched as our brave forces personnel fought the war against Argentina. But this was no made-up, sanitised, Hollywood film; this was real life! I saw the real effects of war, the injuries and death caused by such conflict. The outstanding image I have is of a soldier on a stretcher being brought ashore from a burning, bombed troop-ship; his stump of a leg raised above the stretcher, tattered, smoke-blackened bandages hanging off the remains of what once had been his knee! This was something of a reality-check to me. But did it put me off the idea of joining-up? No, if anything, it reinforced my ambition to do so.

My first attempt at a military career came whilst I was at college. I decided I wanted to become an Army Officer, so off I went to Woolwich, home of the Royal Artillery. I must have had some potential, because over the course of the next year, I attended numerous interviews, selection-boards, and assessment weekends, all of which operated on a knockout basis. If you failed at any stage, you no longer continued in the process. This culminated in me attending the AIB, the final selection stage before going to Sandhurst. Needless to say, I failed. But, in retrospect, I was very young, very naive, and not ready for that sort of responsibility at that stage in my development. But it was an experience, and one I am proud to have given a go. My fellow candidates were all sons of high-ranking army officers (Captain this, or Brigadier that), so in some respects, it is no surprise that I failed. The army in those days operated on a "who-you-know" basis rather than a "what-you-know" one. I am sure that the experience of going through this selection procedure helped me greatly in subsequent applications to the navy and the police.

So, back to 1985... I decided to hedge-my-bets when deciding which future career to pursue after my job at the bank, so I applied to the Royal Navy and the Metropolitan Police at the same time.

The Metropolitan Police was easy. I visited New Scotland Yard in London to have a chat with the recruitment team, and to make my application. A little later, I visited the Hendon Training Centre to complete an assessment day and interview; and then it was simply a case of waiting for a decision to arrive by letter, in the post. There was no email or internet at this point (at least it was not as widely available as it is now); everything was done with paper and snail-mail. So I waited patiently...

In the case of the Royal Navy, I went to the Royal Navy and Royal Marines Recruitment Office in High Holborn, London. I had no appointment, but I spoke to a recruitment officer who told me all about what they offered. They asked me,

"So, which part of the navy do you want to join, then?"

Up until that point, I had not really thought about it! I just wanted to join the navy; I did not know that you could actually choose a job within a job. The Royal Marines had always interested me, but after talking to the recruiter, the fitness requirements seemed to be way beyond my capabilities. So we talked "navy."

"Well, I don't fancy being an officer," I said, having been put-off the idea by my experience with the army.

"But I've got 13 O-levels and 3 A-levels, so what would you suggest?"

From that point on, my fate was sealed; the recruiting officer steered me towards the role of an Artificer. A what, I hear you cry? An Artificer (or "Tiff") was what the navy referred to as an engineering apprentice. The details were given to me and I was sold on the idea. I left the office happy that I now knew what I wanted to do, but things were not set in concrete just yet. I had the small matter of passing the initial selection exams in Maths, English, and Science; and also passing the fitness-test. A week later, and this was done. I left the Recruitment Office clutching my acceptance certificate for the Royal Navy, with a huge cheesy grin on my face. I had just joined the navy... In fact, I hadn't. The formal attestation did not happen until day-one of training in May 1986, but as far as I was concerned, I was now *IN*.

A few days later, I received a letter telling me I had also been accepted for the Metropolitan Police! That was typical. What should I do? In the end, the decision was easy. I could join the police and end-up dealing with drunks, violence, and domestic situations; or I could join the navy, gain qualifications in engineering, travel the world, and have fun. It was no contest, so I wrote to the police saying, "Thank you, but no..." And I awaited a letter from the navy detailing my joining routine and start date. It arrived a week or so later, and May 5th 1986 was to be the big-day.

The train had been juddering along the tracks for what seemed like hours. I had no idea where we were, but I was starting to get a bit frustrated with the time it was taking. I just wanted to get on with my life, and become a sailor.

As we passed through the Teignmouth area of Devon, the track passed parallel to the south coast. I could taste the salt in the air, and I saw the flat, grey sea out of the carriage windows; it felt like I could almost touch it if only I was to stretch out my arm. I now knew I was nearly at journey's end. I still had butterflies in my stomach, only now that I had almost arrived, they seemed to be the size of giant moths!

The next few minutes were a blur of preparing my bag, straightening my tie, and putting on my jacket (I had to create a good first impression, didn't I?). As we slowly crept into Plymouth Station, I looked out of the window to see a man in smart naval uniform stood by the platform's exit gate, holding an official looking clipboard.

This was it. Almost bursting with nerves, having what felt like a lump the size of an egg stuck in the back of my throat, and all of a sudden finding I was desperately in need of the toilet, I got out of the carriage and approached the navy man.

"Name?" he said, in the most official voice I had heard up to this point in my life.

I told him. He ticked me off on his list.

"Stow your bag in the bus and take a seat."

He pointed to a relic of a coach from the 1960's. There was no "Welcome to the navy," no hint of a smile, and no sign of friendship. I did as I was told, and waited as the bus slowly filled-up with equally worried looking men and boys (some looking so young that they could barely have left school). Was this how it was going to be for the next few months? A feeling of dread started to descend! What had I done? Was it too late to go home?

The sailor got on the bus and sat at the front. He did not speak to us, and we were too scared to speak to him, so we remained in silence, a stalemate, as the bus drove us through Plymouth, and onto the Torpoint Car Ferry. Minutes later we arrived at the main gate of HMS Raleigh, the Royal Navy recruit training establishment.

CHAPTER 2

HMS Raleigh – Early Days

At the main gate, I got off the bus, grabbed my bag, and we all formed a makeshift line, as only civilians can do. Before us stood the imposing figurehead of Sir Walter Raleigh, looking down on us with contempt, and watching over the main entrance of this shore-base as a father watches over his children; protecting. This was to be my first encounter with "traditions" in the Royal Navy. The navy runs on them. Each shore-base is regarded as a land-locked ship, and as such, each has its own figurehead, just like every ship used to have in days gone by.

HMS Raleigh was the only basic-training establishment for junior rates joining the Royal Navy, at this time. Everybody who joined-up passed through this base, unless you were an officer, in which case you went to Dartmouth instead. It had been in existence since about 1940, but was totally modernised in the 1970's before taking responsibility for new entry, WRNS (Women's Royal Naval Service), and artificer initial training in the 80's. The base itself covered an area of 239 acres, spread-out over the gently undulating hills of East Cornwall, and set on the shores of the River Tamar. This was to be *home* for us over the next 4 months.

Having been handed-over to the training staff, I was ushered into a bland, formal-looking classroom, and told to sit down with the rest of the group. There proceeded to be a stream of people standing before us in smart uniforms, welcoming us, and telling us a little of what to expect over the next few weeks. To be honest, who they were and what they said was completely lost on me; they were just faces talking incoherently.

Next, papers were handed-out to everyone. It was explained that these were our contracts with the Royal Navy, and that we were about to sign them.

"Alright gentlemen, just to be clear, you are signing-up for 22 years, OK?" the officer told us.

"Surely they must have got that wrong," I thought. "I didn't remember agreeing to this when I spoke with the recruiting officer in London." But he did hasten to add that there was a cooling-off period in which we could leave if it did not suit us (called PVR or premature voluntary release).

"However, as artificer apprentices, you are required to give eight years return-of-service to account for all the time and money that we are about to spend on your training," the officer continued.

So, on day-one, I was already feeling pressured; pressured into signing the papers, pressured from the responsibility of giving the next 8 years minimum to the navy; and pressured from potentially having signed away the next 22 years of my life. However, it was not just pressure, it was also excitement and anticipation of what I was about to embark upon. With hardly a moment's after-thought, each and every one of us signed on the dotted line, and then swore an oath of allegiance to Queen and Country. I was now OFFICIALLY in the Royal Navy. I was an "Artificer Apprentice."

Shortly after this, the training Petty Officer walked us through the base towards our accommodation and training blocks. It felt like a maze as I meandered around the complex of 3-storey, interconnected buildings, each positioned around a series of quadrangles. The lower levels were built of red brick, but the upper floors were white in colour, broken-up by equally spaced, square windows. The white facade looked like it was made of plastic, and the overall impression was one of a modern designed, futuristic space station!

From behind closed windows I could hear muffled cries of, "Sprogs" and, "Tiffs." Somehow our arrival had been expected, but what we did not anticipate was the apparent animosity of the other trainees towards us. We were later to find out that artificers were not the most popular ratings in the navy. Others were jealous because our branch apparently got accelerated promotion and increased pay, but what they forgot to consider is that we had to work for this, it was not given for free. Outside of basic-training, this feeling was virtually non-existent. Yes, you might get a bit of *banter* about it on ship, but nothing nasty. And yet here, the recruits appeared to hate us, so much so, that when marching through the quadrangles over the next few months, we would be regularly spat-at, out of the accommodation block windows! But this was yet another "tradition" of the Royal Navy. These new recruits would not have known anything about artificers if their own training staff had not purposefully encouraged them to show aggression towards us. It was a rite-of-passage that all artificers had to endure and overcome; as had every other artificer in years gone by. Tradition!

At the accommodation block I was introduced to another figurehead by the name of Fisgard. I was now part of Fisgard Squadron. We were duly separated into 4 classes within this squadron; me being allocated to Warsop Division. We were to get to know this particular figurehead very well over the coming weeks because one of the punishments we were to endure was to apologise for whatever failing we had committed, by begging forgiveness of the statue (in a very loud voice). It sounds a strange thing to do, but the punishment was one of humiliation because the figurehead was adjacent to the WRNS building, and no "macho" sailor wanted to act stupidly in front of a group of wrens, did they?

If anyone in our group was under any illusions that our first day would be nice and relaxed, they were sorely wrong! Our training staff introduced themselves to us (I cannot remember their names, but under no circumstances should they ever be referred to by anything other than "STAFF"). We were shown our accommodation area (known as the messdeck), with our beds already allocated to us; and then issued all of our personal uniform and equipment.

The messdeck was a huge communal room with beds positioned in a series of rows running the length of it. There were about 40 beds in total, each with a small metal, waist-height locker next to it. It was sparsely decorated, painted a beige colour, with nothing to distinguish it from any of the other messdecks in the building. Our class consisted of only 15 to 20 men; the bulk of the room remaining unused. It later became apparent that our entire entry was the smallest they had ever had! Somewhere along the line, certain recruitment offices around the country had been given the wrong starting dates for our training, and so lots of potential apprentices were sat at home waiting for the next intake in September!

We were lectured on the rules that we had to adhere to whilst in basic-training. There were many of them, many now forgotten, but the key ones were:-

If any training staff told you to do something, you *jumped* to it, you never answered back, and you never questioned an order.

When in uniform, you had to "double" everywhere, either individually, or as a squad. This meant marching at double-speed, or "running" to those who have never served in the forces.

Class leaders and deputies would be allocated in due course, and everybody would be tested in this leadership role. These leaders were to be treated the same as you would treat any member of the training staff (sort of). You were never to argue or talk back to them.

Everybody had to shave first-thing in the morning (even those who had nothing to shave off); and those "hairy" people who grew beards at a rapid rate of knots were to shave twice daily!

If ordered to be at a specific location at a set time, you were to ensure that you arrived 5 minutes early ("Navy time was five minutes early" as they drummed into our heads).

The day would start at 0630 hours unless told otherwise (There were many groans at this rule. Many did not even know that this time existed!). But that meant you were ready to GO at this time; washed, shaved, in uniform and wearing boots. Obviously, that meant getting-up quite a bit earlier; normally about 0530 hours.

There were many, many other rules, but the major point impressed upon everyone was that if ANY of these rules were broken (and they would be, over the coming weeks), not only would the culprit be punished, but the whole class would be given the same punishment, innocent or not! The idea behind this was to nurture a feeling of teamwork, everybody being in-the-same-boat, together. It also ramped-up the pressure on us, knowing that if we messed-up, others would be punished too.

The rest of this first day was spent trying on uniforms to ensure they fitted, but more importantly, it was an opportunity to dress like *real* sailors for the first time; it was an ego boost, it was the start of our "belonging" to the navy family. We printed our names on each and every piece of kit or uniform in black gloss paint. It looked very amateurish, with some letters faint, while others were blobs. And then began the never-ending job of polishing our boots (yes, even on our first evening). I had no idea how to "bull" boots properly, I had not had my training on this yet, but I had a go, keen to impress the staff next morning.

But, whilst doing all of this, we talked, and talked, and talked. Our group was an eclectic mix of people from all over the country. We had "Mac" and "Eddie" from Scotland, "Frankie" from Luton, me and "Seth" from London, "Paddy" from Northern Ireland, "Shep" from the midlands, and "Cudders" from Devon; not to mention others from all places in-between. We ranged in age and experience too. Me, Frankie and Mac were the elder statesmen of our group (me being the grand-old-age of 20), and Frankie and Mac had both been in the Royal Navy a short while already, before transferring over to the artificer branch. We started our bonding process that would continue throughout the next few months. Our roles within the group began to become apparent; who was to be the class-joker, who were the natural leaders, who was going to last the full 22 years, and who was not going to make it through the basic-training phase.

In amongst our group, we had a sprinkling of trainees from the Royal Brunei Navy. These were soon to become officers back home, but were training with our intake due to a deal made between both governments. Their English was very poor, but they were decent lads, keen to learn. They stuck mainly to their own group, and so, even from day-one there was a barrier segregating them from the rest of us.

Full of excitement, and brimming with new found energy at the thought of what was to come, and newly made friendships; I turned-in and got some rest, knowing that I would have to be up at some unearthly hour. It turned-out to be a long night for some. There was the sound of suppressed sobbing coming from somewhere in the room! I never did find out who it was, but considering the age of some of our group, and the fact that they probably had never been away from home, it was not surprising really. Had this happened later in our naval careers, there would have been a lot of jeering and mickey-taking of the poor, homesick lad, but being as it was our first night, it was put to the back of our minds; sorry for how our "shipmate" was feeling, but equally glad that it was not ourselves who was so upset.

And so to sleep...

CHAPTER 3

Initial training

The following morning arrived with a shock! I was awoken to the sound of "Reveille" being played on a bugle very, VERY loudly. In our semiconscious condition, we all stood around in various states of undress looking for the culprit, only to realise very quickly that it was actually a recording being played over the block's PA system (which just happened to be directly opposite my bed!). Over the next few weeks, the training staff subjected us to this early morning ritual each day. Occasionally they would change the broadcast to a carefully selected song or to the self-titled opening lines from the film, "Good Morning Vietnam..." Once or twice we even had to endure a cockerel crowing at us! It all depended on how sadistic the training officers were feeling on that particular day.

After my first breakfast in Trafalgar Galley (where we were advised to eat as much as possible as we were going to need the energy!), the first port-of-call was at the base's hairdresser. Forming an orderly queue in the corridor, each of us nervously shuffled our feet and fidgeted, knowing what was about to happen. One by one, we entered the room and were asked,

"Do you want a short back and sides, or a crew-cut?"

It did not matter what you replied as everyone left with a crew-cut anyway! I had just been in the army, and so I had had a grade 3 crew-cut a couple of days earlier, in preparation.

"Sit down," the barber said to me, with a smile on his face.

He proceeded to turn my grade 3 into a grade 1 by trimming the smallest amount of hair you could imagine. I got up to leave, but he cleared his throat as if to say, "You've forgotten something," and held out his hand. He wanted money. Yes, I actually had to pay for the privilege of having my hair cut!

One person, whose name I do not recall, had a beard and a full head of greasy, tangled, shoulder-length hair. He entered the room, emerging a few moments later with no hair, and crying uncontrollably! He left immediately afterwards, handing in his notice as he could not handle the "stress" of the haircut. Over the course of our time at Raleigh a number of others were to leave voluntarily, and the reasons varied from not coping with the lack of sleep, to not liking discipline, to not being able to deal with ironing uniform! Talking to the training staff later, they explained that our initial training was split into two sections. The first 6 weeks was a constant building of pressure on us recruits, followed by a more relaxed second half of the training. The idea was to push each trainee to their limit, and beyond, in phase one; to see how they dealt with stress, and to weed-out those who were not suitable to be in the Royal Navy. The staff claimed that they could tell who would stay and who would go within the first couple of days, but that sounded a bit like bravado on their part.

And so the first phase of our training began in earnest...

That day, our class began to learn the intricacies of DRILL. To start with it was simply learning how to stand still; at attention, at ease, and standing-easy. This was done in the privacy of the enclosed quadrangles, away from the prying eyes of the other recruits, as we were not fit to be seen in public just yet. Then we advanced to actually moving as a squad, in time with each other. This was essential in order to move around the shore-base as we had to march at-the-double everywhere. The initial stages of learning this were hilarious.

"Squad...squad, attention," the Petty Officer roared.

"Move to the left in threes...Left turn."

"Stop, stop, stop. Wilson you fucking idiot, your OTHER left...!" You could see the exasperation in the PO's face.

It was unbelievable how many people did not know their left from their right! In some cases, it was common for them to write "L" and "R" on their hands to help. When marching, there was a phenomenon known as "tick-tocking." Normal marching should be an exaggerated walk whereby your arms swing in opposite directions to the leg on each side of your body. But with "tick-tocking," your right arm and leg both go forward together, as do your left. It looks so awkward, but so funny too. Try it yourself, it is actually very hard to do, and yet certain people were *masters* at this skill! It was caused by trying too hard, by over concentrating, and it was very common.

The drill instructors were called "Gunnery Staff," and they were the most officious people you could imagine. For some reason, most were short. They wore their caps pulled hard down over their eyes, and their uniforms were always immaculate; their boots gleaming like mirrors. They carried a pace-stick under their left arm which was supposed to be used to measure the length of a stride when marching. However I never saw one actually used; it was always just for show. They had what can only be described as a very "special" way of giving commands. It was always screamed at you, usually in a high-pitched squeal, and you could never understand a word that was said! Over the course of my training, I tended to associate certain pitches and lengths of unrecognisable commands with its actual meaning. It was a skill in itself to understand what was being shouted, let alone actually perform it.

God help you if you ever did anything wrong on the parade ground! The gunnery staff would walk up to you, stand with their nose about 3cm from your face, and hurl abuse at you. Every other word was a swear word, and you would be called every name under the sun. You could almost feel their stare boring into your eyes, and the shouting was so loud that you would think your eardrums would burst! They used to strike fear into most recruits. Some dreaded the sessions on the parade ground, but I loved it, it was so funny, I struggled to keep a straight face half the time. I remember one occasion. The Gunnery Petty Officer was shouting at somebody for failing to stop on the correct command, and I was struggling not to laugh. He walked up to me and stood face-to-face.

"What the fuck are you grinning at, you fucking numpty?"

This set me off even more, trying my hardest not to burst into hysterics. The PO was so close that I could feel my face being splattered in his spittle as he shouted at me. And yet, I could see in his eyes that he was struggling not to laugh along with me. It became an impasse. Who would give-in first? Who would succumb to the giggles? The next thing I know is that he had walked away, shouting at the top of his voice,

"Get down now. 40 press-ups. GO."

My punishment had been delivered, and he had managed not to lose-face in front of the squad. But from then on, on the parade ground, all of the staff called me, "Smiler."

During the remainder of my time at Raleigh, our sessions of drill continued. With more practice, we became more skilled. I learnt new techniques; marching line-abreast, slow marching (for funerals), marching with rifles (bayonets fixed), and so on.

Each of us took command of the squad, giving the orders instead of the gunnery officers. And yes, we too, found that our voices were squeaky and incoherent. The parade ground was positioned to the rear of the base, nestled between the River Tamar on one side, and the rabbit-warren of Raleigh to the other. Standing in the far corner of the parade ground, we directed the squad using voice command alone. Projecting your voice over this sort of distance in the open-air was not easy; many a time I would return to the accommodation blocks with a strained chest, rasping voice, and sore throat. But as a potential senior rate, this was something I had to learn; command-and-control."

Every Friday was a Passing-Out Parade for one group or another, and all classes had to attend, parading in "best uniform" in front of other people's families. This was why we had learnt drill so often; this was the culmination of all our efforts; and at some point in August we would be parading in front of our own families, at our own Passing-Out Parade. This was our motivation. But, being August, we had to learn to march and parade in hot weather! This was a totally different skill. Heat drained you, it dehydrated you, and ultimately, it made you collapse. So learning the "correct" way to collapse, safely, onto one knee, was essential. We practiced during lunch-breaks at "Standing Still" in the midday sun for hours at a time. The blood drained into my feet until I could feel only pins-and-needles, my head felt like it had been sliced open as my cap dug into my forehead; and there was the forever-present urge to twitch, to fidget, and to move about! We saw what happens if you do collapse, how you are dragged off the parade ground unceremoniously, your gleaming toecaps scraping on the hard concrete, never to be the same again. We even saw a member of the Guard-of-Honour collapse, falling forward such that the tip of his bayonet sliced the back of the leg of the man in front!

And so we practiced and practiced our skills at drill until we were experts (or so we thought). Would we be ready for our Passing-Out Parade come the big day?

One thing that was constant during all of my training, but especially in the early days at Raleigh, was the innumerable hours that I spent cleaning; cleaning my accommodation, cleaning my uniform, and cleaning myself.

We had been given demonstrations and advice on the art of "bulling" boots. This was the technique used to achieve the high-gloss finish that you see on the toecaps and heels of military boots. We were shown how to use an iron, and the specific methods used to iron each and every item of our uniform. I say "specific" because it was exactly that; it was a step-by-step method, never to be adapted, used in order to achieve uniforms with creases in the correct places, and folded to a specific size. Every bit of uniform had to be ironed and folded to a set "Kit-Book" size. The kit-book was issued to us at the start. It contained valuable information about seamanship skills, but it was not intended to be read, it was purely used as a measure of the size that everything had to fit into. And I mean everything! Great big raincoats had to be folded down to this size, compressed under the weight of a locker, until it fitted to the millimetre! Even our socks had to be individually folded around a cardboard former so that they were square, ironed, and displayed such that six socks, when positioned correctly, fitted exactly into the kit-book dimensions. Attention-to-detail was the order of the day. Get the little things right, and the overall effect would be achieved.

To tidy our rooms, the Leading Hands demonstrated the technique of using a broom! Believe it or not, there is a right and a wrong way to use one. We were shown how to polish floors (or decks as they were called). We were given tips by the training staff on how to make our lives easier. It was a lot to take in, but the real learning took place by trial and error. No sooner had we been given the information that we needed, than the inspections started. We spent hours every day washing and drying uniform; the training staff very kindly ensuring that we changed uniform at least two or three times a day just to make sure we never ran-out of dirty things to wash! Any spare moments that we had (not that there were many), were spent polishing boots, hour after hour, day after day. It was relentless.

Some inspections were scheduled, so we had time to prepare, but others were sprung on us at a moment's notice, building-up the stress levels. No matter how good you were, the training staff would find something (or in most cases, *lots* of things) to fail you on. They would take great pleasure in throwing your carefully prepared and presented uniforms all around the room, so even if it was up to the required standard, they ruined it on purpose so you had to re-do everything each time. It was very demoralising, it felt like you were banging your head against a brick wall, but you had no time to worry about it, you had to prepare for the next set of inspections. The best attitude I found was to regard all of this as a big *game*. The training staff were trying to break you, to get you to quit; so by treating everything in this manner, never taking anything personally, you were always one step ahead of them. They could never win. This way of looking at things worked for me, but some of our class struggled with the constant rejections and failings. Some left; but most remained, with the rest of us helping to get them through these dark times.

Remedial inspections were a daily occurrence; remedial boot inspections, remedial room inspections, remedial kit musters! It went on and on. I became the boot inspection "King!" I seemed to have remedial inspections every day! But I learnt; I put in the hours, often working until 2 or 3 in the morning to get my kit right. And despite the lack of sleep, despite the constant pressure of failure, I improved. Often we worked as a team, which was the aim of Royal Navy training. Some in our class were brilliant at boots, others like myself, loved ironing; so I would do someone's shirts, while they bulled my boots. TEAMWORK, it was the basis of all Royal Navy life. We were learning an important lesson. But we also learnt a few shortcuts. We tried any techniques we could find to make things simpler. With the number of kit inspections we had to prepare for, the easy option was to get a second issue of kit, prepare it, and reserve it for inspections only; it was never worn. Various methods to speed-up the boot bulling process were tried, most of which did not work! We tried melting polish onto the boots with a flame. We tried using wipe-on liquid polish. One person even tried painting his boots with black gloss paint! But no matter what we tried, the only method that worked was lots of patience, lots of elbow-grease, and layer after layer of Parade-Gloss applied with a delicate touch and a soft yellow duster. There were NO shortcuts on this one, unfortunately.

For room inspections, a few drops of AFFF (foam used in fire extinguishers) added to the floor-polish worked wonders; they literally gleamed after this. But the big lesson we learnt was "The-Art-of-Bullshit." If it shines, polish it. If it can be arranged in straight lines, or at 90 degree angles, do it. If the overall appearance is one of a perfect finish, then the theory goes that the inspecting officer will be baffled by the shiny things, and overlook any minor errors. However, as time went by, inspections became less frequent, but more intense. It was not unknown for us to prepare our kit and rooms late into the night, and then to sleep on the floor next to our bed rather than have a last minute panic next morning. The inspecting officers became more paranoid too. By this stage, they expected the obvious things to be above standard, so they looked at more obscure areas to find faults with. On one occasion, the inspecting officer removed an air-conditioning vent-cover to inspect inside the ducting. Another time, they removed countersunk screws from a stainless-steel kitchen counter to check inside the screw hole for dust! Attention-to-detail was required, and expected.

Of course, should anyone fail at any point, not only did you get the privilege of re-taking the inspection, but you also had other punishments. Some were menial, others embarrassing, but most were physical. The main one was called "The Fire School Run." To the west of the base was the fire fighting school, situated at the top of a low hill, well away from the main areas of the camp. It was probably about half a mile away (although it felt much further), following a narrow path over the undulating terrain. The punishment was for the whole class to run, as a squad, to this area and back as quickly as possible. Remember, the whole class gets punished for one person's mistake. It does not sound like much of a punishment, I hear you cry. Well, at our worst, we were doing this run up to six times a day, missing meals quite often, in addition to other physical activities. We would do it in all weathers, often not wearing the correct uniform for the conditions. We even did it once straight after a Friday Passing-Out Parade, complete with best uniform and highly polished boots. Needless to say, the bulled toecaps did not survive this little jaunt, and many a tear was shed as we started the laborious task of re-polishing them from scratch for the millionth time!

Punishments might come at any time, day or night. We were once awoken in the small hours of the morning to lots of excited shouting!

"Everybody up...NOW!" the PO shouted. What was going on? We had no idea.

"I wanna see all of you running round the quadrangle with your mattresses on your backs in 30 seconds. GO, go, go...move it!"

Maybe the training staff had been ashore for a few drinks, and on return thought it would be funny to get us up and running; who knows?

On other occasions, people who had not shaved to the required standard were made to shave in front of everyone, in the quadrangle, using a blunt razor and ice-cold water! And on many occasions we had remedial drill sessions in the rain, or extreme heat!

However, everything that we endured was done for a purpose. We may not have known the reason at the time, we were not thinking straight due to lack of sleep and constant physical and mental stress, but it was always there; making us better, making us fitter, making us future leaders, and making us strong. We were being formed into tough naval ratings just as many others had done before us.

The area around HMS Raleigh was beautiful. The narrow country lanes; the leafy trees on either side reaching up into the sky, spreading their branches and forming a canopy above your head so dense that it formed a tunnel. The open fields, dotted with white cotton-wool sheep; and the gently undulating hills that seemed to go on forever. An idyllic scene for many, but not for us...

The only time we got to experience this area was during the dreaded *squad runs*. I will admit that I was not fit when I joined the navy. I did a bit of exercise now and then, and thought I would be able to get-by, but how wrong I was!

The extent of my vision was limited to the 2m of road directly ahead of me as I ran, shuffled, and staggered around the lanes surrounding Raleigh. Occasionally I would look up, only to see the rest of the squad extending their lead over me, the gap between us becoming an unsurpassable chasm. At the outset we had marched through the gates of Raleigh as a united squad, a unit. We turned right, and increased speed to a steady jog. No problem so far, I thought. We ran a bit, marched a bit, and ran a bit more. Gradually, the pace took its toll on me, and on others. I started to drift off the back of the group. I was gently encouraged to keep-up by a few choice words and shouting from the PTI's (Physical Training Instructors).

"Come on Heasman, you lump o' lard; keep up with 'em. It ain't like they're going fast or nothing!"

"Has someone tied your blood boots together? Stretch those legs. Put some fucking effort in."

But it was to no avail. It may have only been a 3 mile run, maybe 5, or even 10; it mattered not to me, I was alone in my own little world of pain! My feet felt swollen inside the combat-boots that rubbed at my ankles. With every step, my thigh muscles screamed in agony, on the verge of locking-out with the onset of cramp. My heart was pounding so hard, I swear I could see it through my chest, and my lungs took on the sound of a steam train, huffing and puffing as I struggled forward. If I could have seen my face, it would have been puce in colour, and my whole body was dripping in sweat. Not a pretty sight I'm sure, but at that particular moment, it was the last thing on my mind. All that mattered was putting one foot in front of the other. I would NOT give up; I would finish this run, one way or the other. And so I chanted a mantra in my head,

"Left, left, left right left... breathe. Left, left, left right left."

In America they would be singing chants as they ran, but not us; we were British, we did not do that sort of thing! And yet, in my head, that is exactly what I was doing.

As we neared the main road leading back to the main gates, I looked ahead to see the squad stopped, waiting. We formed a group again, and marched triumphantly back through the gates. Nobody outside our group need ever know that we were not as smart and fit throughout the whole of the run as we appeared to be now.

Fitness training was a daily chore during my time at Raleigh. It came in many forms, some were fun, playing basketball, or 5-a-side; but others were more structured, formal, stressful. I had a number of Fitness Tests, one at the start to gain my current fitness level, and then again at regular intervals, to judge my improvement; or lack of it. It consisted of a one-and-a-half mile run in a set time, followed by sit-ups, press-ups, burpies, and a number of other exercises, each being done for a maximum effort over a minute. As with the squad runs, I struggled at first; but with increased practice, and increased fitness, I slowly got better. I look back on those days now, and I do not recognise myself. Since then, I have taken my fitness seriously; even now, aged 52, I still run 4 times a week. At my peak, I ran marathons; my best time being 3 hours 5 minutes for the 26 mile course. So looking back, seeing how bad I was, is like looking at a totally different person!

As we progressed through training, we took on the challenge of the Raleigh Assault Course. My first attempt at it was bad! I had no technique over the obstacles; just using brute-force and ignorance. I ended up with cuts, grazes, bruises, and dented pride as I managed to fall off everything put before me. But with a lot of guidance from the PTI's, and hours of practice, I became reasonably proficient at it. It was all about technique. Put a 4m wall in front of me, and I would show you the easiest way to scale it. Put a stream of flowing water and a few sewer pipes before it, and I would leap like a gazelle over the boulders, barely getting my boots wet. Throw a rope cargo-net at me, and I would crawl under it or climb over it. Nothing was a problem. Nothing that is, except "The Leopard Crawl!" This was a nightmare! The idea was to crawl across a single length of hemp rope strung between two poles without falling off, and staying on-top of the rope (not dangling beneath it). Technique was everything; you needed to throw one leg forward and down, to act like a pendulum, and then use your other leg to push you forward along its length. Eventually, despite rope-burns across shoulders and sore groin areas, I managed it; I was elated.

With this new-found confidence, we gave demonstrations of our skills in the gym to the Captain of HMS Raleigh; performing ropework displays (hanging upside-down on a rope, holding position by legs alone, no hands); circuit-training, and gymnastics (mainly springboard work, and vaulting over the gym horse). We were good. We were fit, at last.

But then came my nemesis! The Royal Navy Swimming Test. Since the Falklands War when they found that lots of sailors could not swim, the swimming test became compulsory. I hated swimming, I still do (which is perhaps surprising seeing as I have been a SCUBA diving instructor over 10 years). It consisted of swimming a couple of lengths of the pool in thick, denim overalls; treading-water for a set time, and jumping off the high-board. My first attempt was pathetic. I failed dismally. Standing atop the 5m board, looking down at the water, my heavy, water-sodden overalls dripping, and my whole body shaking with fear; I remember the instructor shouting out,

"Don't look down."

Good advice I'm sure, but he was stood at the side of the pool 5 meters beneath me at the time, and the natural instinct was to look at who spoke! Not good!

With many remedial swimming lessons, and my skin permanently smelling of chlorine, I finally passed the test. I was chuffed with myself, my biggest challenge to date now complete. But this was also the source of my nickname during training; the first of many during my various careers.

From that day forth, I was forever known as, "The Brick."

And so I had reached the end of the first stage of my training at HMS Raleigh. Six weeks down, only a few more to go. As a reward, I was given a weekend leave-pass; I could go home for a couple of days. I had not spoken to my family over the last few weeks (remember, this was before the age of the mobile phone), I had not had any time-off, not even seen any TV, so I had no idea what had been happening in the outside world; this was my chance to catch-up.

We had to wear our second best uniforms (number 2's) on the journey home, so on arrival at London's Paddington Station; I walked through the crowd of people exiting the train, looking for my mum and dad who had come to meet me. I was wearing a white-topped peak cap and a smart black tunic with shiny silver buttons, and I stood-out like a sore thumb! But could my parents spot me? No! They walked straight past.

"Oh, my God. Sorry Andrew, we didn't recognise you. You've lost so much weight." they said.

"But surely the uniform alone would make me pretty obvious?" I thought.

And so began a couple of days away from the Royal Navy. Would we all return? Would anybody decide that life away from the job was more tempting than the prospect of the next phase of training? We would have to wait and see...

CHAPTER 4

HMS Raleigh – Part 2

On returning from our mid-term break, it was like walking into a different world. The training staff were more human; they spoke instead of shouted. There were fewer inspections, less beastings, and more academic and technical training. It was as if the staff had rejected those without potential, and they could now concentrate on teaching the rest of us about "proper" navy skills. We started to learn about things that we would use aboard ship.

We tackled the gas-chamber, learning what it was like to feel the effects of CS gas. Stood in a sealed room full of swirling, white noxious fumes, we breathed through our respirators, safely. As I approached the Petty Officer in-charge, I removed my mask and shouted,

"Apprentice Heasman. Service Number D206...cough, cough...906...Q. Cough, cough, cough..." before exiting rapidly through the side door, into fresh, cool air.

I left that lesson with skin-irritation, my eyes streaming, and coughing-up mucus and phlegm; safe in the knowledge that my respirator would protect me from having to suffer these effects (and worse) in the future.

We did some basic fire fighting. At this stage, it was only learning to operate the huge "number-3" sized hoses that, when fully charged with high-pressure water, could lift a man off his feet if not handled correctly. We tackled small fires, smothering them in layers of foam. And we fought electrical fires with CO_2 extinguishers. All the time though, we were dwarfed by a series of charcoal-black, metal boxes; each the size of a 3-storey building, with ladders to entrances set at various heights. They stank of oil and fire; and we were intrigued, if a little intimidated, by them. What were they for? Eventually one brave soul plucked up the courage to ask.

"What are those black boxes for, PO?" he said.

"They're to train people in advanced, onboard fire fighting. Don't worry; you'll all get to tackle them when you come back on a Sea-Survival course just before you join your first ships." He replied. We were all a little scared by this prospect, but having just completed our first taste of fire fighting, we were equally excited.

As part of this pre-deployment training, we would also be subjected to the HAVOC simulator, although at this time it was still being built. That pleasure would have to wait a while. It was designed to simulate a sinking ship, damaged by explosions and fire, and flooding from below. For now, our class would have to suffice with practicing the skills of damage-control (preventing water from entering splinter holes, and shoring-up decks and deckheads); by pretending our classroom was a sinking ship. It was not exactly realistic, but good enough for now.

As was every boy's dream, I got to play with guns! Firing, cleaning, and assembling these weapons was an essential job for all sailors. The main weapon we used was the SLR (self-loading-rifle). It was big, bulky, powerful, and accurate. Once you had fired it, you knew about it from the bruising on your shoulder as it gave you a "kick!" The secondary weapon that I had to become proficient with was the SMG (sub-machine-gun). This was smaller, lighter, and not very accurate. On the ranges, you were lucky if you could hit a human-sized target at all; but it was good at spraying lots of bullets around in a short space of time. And finally, I had to shoot the 9mm pistol. This was horrible! The top-slide ripped the skin from your hand between the thumb and first-finger! It had a massive "kick," and you were lucky if you could hit the range wall, let alone a target. You would have been better off throwing the pistol at an enemy if you ever came to use it! This was the fun side of training at Raleigh; it was relaxed, it was interesting, and you could see the purpose behind it. I was now really enjoying my time in the Royal Navy.

As we progressed through the second part of our training, we moved on to adventure-training to be conducted away from the base on the moors of Bodmin and Dartmoor. We were being let loose into the big wide world...

We had been lucky with the weather so far; it was a lovely sunny day, warm, but not stiflingly hot, with a gentle breeze from the south. Our whole entry was aboard a rickety old coach heading into the depths of Bodmin Moor. We had passed near to Cardinham, and had just gone through Maidenwell, heading along a narrow country lane which was as straight as a roman road. We were in good spirits, laughing and joking; it was as if we were on a school outing, our first bit of training away from the confines of Raleigh. We were excited.

Ahead, in the far distance, I noticed what appeared to be three or four snow-capped mountains rising above the rolling green of the countryside.

"Hey, Andy, what do you think they are ahead?" someone said.

"Dunno. Look like mountains to me," I replied. "Looks like snow on the tops don't it?"

"Nah can't be, not in this heat. Must be something else."

As we got nearer, they formed into a series of peaks, very *steep* peaks; they were ochre and white in colour, and they loomed over us.

The coach came to a halt at the foot of one of these mounds. I nervously exited it and looked around at the site. There was a semi-circle of what we were told were slagheaps from an old mine. At their base was a small lake, and to one side, a few derelict buildings covered in moss and lichen. No sooner had we got our bearings, than the training staff were shouting at us to sprint up-and-down each of these heaps! We had not expected this, so it came as a bit of a shock; but off we went, keen to impress, and running at full speed, we arrived at the foot of the first hill. It was at this point that I realized these hills were made of a sand-like material! No matter how hard or fast you ran, for every two steps you took up the hill, you slid back one! And those ahead of me would inadvertently kick this sand onto my head, which I would duly inhale as I gulped for air! By a combination of using other people's footsteps, and clawing at the dirt with my bare hands, I eventually mounted the summit of the first hill. Had there been time, and I was not sucking in lung-full's of air, the view would have been glorious; but this was just one of four mountains to climb, so down I slid on my backside, the sand entering every crevice of my clothing and body. From hill two onwards, I took a much steadier pace, not so much through choice, as by necessity, as I was exhausted already, covered in dirt from head to foot, my lungs screaming for air, and my legs in complete agony from the constant climbing and sliding.

Finally, we reached the end of the climbs and staggered towards the trainers who were stood by the lakeside. By now, the lake had taken-on the appearance of a huge, cooling bath; all we wanted was the chance to wash all the sweat and dirt off, cool down in the calming waters, and quench our parched throats. They must have taken pity on us because they did allow us to get clean, but they did add,

"Whatever you do, don't drink the water. It's full of arsenic; some sort of by-product of the mining! Oh, and **welcome** to the Cardinham Exped..."

Over the next few hours, we erected our tents and ate some food in preparation for the next task to be thrown at us. We did not have to wait too long. It came in the form of an obstacle course, set amongst the buildings and natural features surrounding our campsite. I set-off at a slow pace, tackling the slag-heap for a second time, and then onto a rope-climb up and down a low cliff (part of the opencast mine). There followed some running through a rocky stream, and then I entered what appeared to be a tunnel. This was actually the flue from a chimney at the mine. It was about 50m long, built of bricks, and so low that you had to crawl through it on hands and knees! So there we were, crawling through the darkness, one following the other like a herd of elephants holding onto each other's tails. Some were a bit scared of the dark, confined spaces, but they could not turn back, they could not turn around, they had to go on regardless! Halfway along, there was a horrible, sickly smell that became over-powering the closer I got to its source! It stuck in the back of my throat making me gag and choke! I did not know it at the time, but from my days in the police force in later years, I would instantly have recognised it as the stench of death! We gradually edged forward until, one-by-one we climbed over a soft, spongy mass of flesh, bone and hair! Many of us were holding our breath at this stage, so the sooner we could get over it and escape, the better.

After the race was over, the training officers approached us with a huge grin on their faces.

"How did you find the dead sheep, then?" they asked.

It seemed that the smell came from a decaying carcass left midway along the tunnel! Whether it had just wandered in there to die, or whether the training staff had purposely placed it there, we will never know; but from the look on their faces, I know which one I would believe.

The next day brought the start of a 2-day navigation exercise across Bodmin Moor. Having been split into teams, we had already planned our route, taking into account various marker points that we had to reach in sequence, along the way. We had a deadline in which to arrive at the overnight camping area, and would then continue with the "NAVEX" the following morning. We set-off, full of energy and excitement; this was the first time that we had had any freedom as none of the trainers were coming with us. How difficult could it be? Follow the compass bearing, hit all the waypoints, and then camp overnight; no problem! We found the first couple of markers easily, both being piles of rocks on the summits of hills. The third point could be seen from cairn number two; it too was on the peak of a hill. All we needed to do was walk in a straight line across the valley, and up the other side. However, as we neared the valley floor, each step we took got progressively wetter! We were entering into a bog!

"That's not on the map, I'm sure!" I said to everyone.

My feet and lower legs became quickly sodden, and lifting each foot became a major effort as I fought against the suction of the foul-smelling mass of grass, mud, and peat.

"Come on, this is getting ridiculous," I said. "Let's change course and go over there, to the right. We might be able to skirt the bog entirely."

It added quite a bit of time, and used a lot more energy than planned, but we did get to the next marker safely.

And so continued the rest of day-one; trekking from point to point, effectively traversing the eastern side of Bodmin Moor. We were always fighting against time, and as the wet clothes, heavy backpacks, and soaked boots started to rub, we got more and more demoralised! Were we going to beat the time limit? It was not looking good. By the time we reached the overnight campsite, we were exhausted, dead-on-our-feet, barely able to place one foot in front of the other! We were dehydrated, and in dire need of water and food. We physically had to drag one of our team up the last hill as he was dizzy and on the verge of collapse! We were in a bad way!

But on arrival, the trainers gave us plentiful supplies of water, we started to cook some food, and we began to recover. However, our feet were a complete mess! Each of us had blisters, some had blisters on blisters! My socks were wet from the bog, but also covered in warm sticky blood. And as feeling started to return to my lower extremities, the pain started to kick-in. The training officers called in a medic, and we sat in a line on the edge of a grassy ditch, as he injected each blister with a syringe of iodine, and then bandaged us up. It was as if liquid-fire was being forced under the skin. "Surely they would not make us do the second half of the hike next day?" I thought.

I was wrong! Day-two dawned, and the trek continued. The first hour was absolute agony, my feet screamed-out in pain with every step. But eventually, my lower legs went numb, and I continued, step by step. In some respects, day-two was easier despite this hindrance, because I knew what to expect. By the end of the day, we collapsed into the seats of the coach on our way back to Raleigh; sore, exhausted, but exhilarated at having walked the entire circumference of Bodmin Moor over the last two days. We were proud of our achievement. At this time, I had no idea that a few years later I would be back on Bodmin; tackling the same route in reverse, on my Leading Hand's Leadership Course. This time though, I would be completing the whole thing in less than 12 hours!

A few days later, I woke to find that the blisters I had acquired on this expedition had become infected! The little toe on my right foot was so swollen that it was the size of my big toe! I was rushed to the Sick-Bay where they discovered that the poison was tracking up my foot into my leg; it was sepsis! I watched as the doctor produced a scalpel that looked like a scimitar, and proceeded to scoop out the center of my wound as if he was coring an apple. I thought to myself,

"Surely I should be feeling pain while he did this," but I was so swollen that all sense of pain was gone. Over the next 5 days, I remained in sick-bay on bed-rest. But this was the Royal Navy, and I was still a trainee, so bed-rest actually meant getting up at 0630, making my bed in a uniform manner, then sitting on a chair, leg raised, awaiting the surgeon's inspection. Not very "restful" at all!

Once I was deemed fit enough, I returned to my class to continue the final stages of my training at Raleigh. We needed to decide which area of engineering to specialise in; marine, weapons, or aircraft. I chose weapon engineering, but there was no guarantee I would get it, so we awaited our first draft orders to arrive.

In the final weeks at Raleigh, everything continued as normal; inspections, technical training, and physical training; but I did get a little spare time in the evenings. I found the NAAFI bar. I went for a few relaxed training runs around the base (just to improve my fitness). And I was given shore-leave. Admittedly, I was given a curfew of 11pm, but it allowed us all to visit the pubs of Torpoint (in particular The Harbour Lights) to let our hair down (not that I had any, having been given a crew-cut). Freedom at last; we were being treated like grown-ups. Just like Cinderella, on many a night we realised the lateness of the hour, and in our inebriated state, ran back to the main gate of HMS Raleigh, only to face the disapproving stare of Raleigh's figurehead.

And so began the seemingly never-ending preparations for our "Passing-Out Parade." We had long sessions of drill training every day, specifically practicing the manoeuvres that would be used on our parade. We drilled in the heat of the sun to prepare for the rigours we would face on the big day (assuming it did not rain). And we prepared our accommodation blocks for our biggest inspection yet; but this time it was a pleasure because our families were to be our biggest critics, and we did not mind the extra work involved to please them.

We received our draft orders. Where would we be spending the next year or two of our lives? I was lucky and was accepted as a weapon engineering apprentice (WEA), and so I would be heading to HMS Collingwood in Fareham after our period of leave. It did mean that our class would be split-up though! Friends we had made would go to other bases, and so we would be dispersed throughout the Royal Navy. Consequently, we had mixed feelings about our drafts.

Prizes were awarded for our training. I was given "The Captain's Prize" for kit, bearing, and appearance. It was a true honour; something to be proud of, and an acknowledgement of all those hours of hard graft washing, ironing, and bulling boots. I was chuffed.

The day of our "Passing-Out Parade" arrived. Our families would be here in hours, our accommodation was immaculate, our uniforms pristine, and our bags packed ready to go on leave. We were ready. But it was a sunny and hot day! Would we survive the temperatures on the parade ground? We prayed that we would...

For the last time, we formed a squad of three ranks in the quadrangle outside our block. Our movements were crisp and smart. We were bubbling with excitement at the thought of parading in-front of our families.

"Turn to the right in threes, right turn," the training PO ordered. "By the left, quick march. Left, left, left, right, left..."

And then it all started to go wrong! One person failed to hear the order (or was day-dreaming) so did not step-off in time, another started on the wrong foot, while yet another began to "tic-tock." We were a total mess. We were ordered to stop, given a few choice words from the instructors, and told to take a deep breath and calm down.

Our second attempt was much better. Those initial nerves had been banished, and all of our mistakes had been made early, out of sight of everyone. We were now feeling much more settled. A couple of hours, and it would all be over.

As we approached the ramp leading onto the parade ground the sense of occasion hit us. We puffed-out our chests, straightened our backs, lifted our chins, and concentrated hard. We were the proudest peacocks on that square as we took our place in the front row, right of center; knowing that our families could now see us, even if we had not spotted them in the crowds yet.

Over the next couple of hours we conducted the usual drill manoeuvres, as we had on numerous other Friday afternoons. We were inspected by a senior officer who asked everybody if they had enjoyed their time at Raleigh, and where they were going next. It was a standard question, eliciting a standard response. And then we waited while the rest of the parade was inspected. Most parades were 90% waiting, and only 10% conducting drill movements. The heat was unbearable; sweat was dripping down my back, soaking my crisp white shirt. My cap seemed to have shrunk, the rim digging deep into my forehead. I needed to wiggle my toes inside my boots to keep the circulation moving in my legs, fearful of falling on my face the minute we were ordered to march with numb feet. Then the first person dropped to their knee to prevent collapsing, the heat having gotten the better of them. As they stood back up, another went down. From my point of view, I was grateful that those suffering heat exhaustion were not from our class; clearly all those hours of drill training, and standing-still practice had done their job.

After what seemed an eternity, we started our march-off. We were still alert despite the heat, and our marching was sharp as we turned line-abreast to march past the senior officer, and our families. With the, "eyes-right" order, you could almost hear the sound of our necks snapping in unison for the salute. Unlike the army, it is said that the Royal Navy marches with a swagger; well on this one occasion, we certainly had that swagger. It was the perfect march-past. The parade was over.

We came to a halt at the rear of the parade area, and were kept in formation, at attention. Our families had followed us off the square, and were stood at a respectable distance, unsure whether they should wave, or run-up and hug us. It seemed they were equally intimidated by the officialdom of the gunnery officers. They did not want to upset them, or get us into trouble. But they need not have worried; we were dismissed, and were free to approach our families. After the customary hugs and kisses, and suddenly reverting back to a feeling of a mother's son, we took everyone to our accommodation block, showed them where we had been living for the last 4 months, and collected our belongings ready to go on leave. Pride is not a tangible thing, but I am sure that at that time on that day, you could taste it in the air; it was real to us, we were proud to serve in the Royal Navy.

HMS Raleigh was now in the past. I would return at various times over the next few years, but for now it was over; I was no longer a recruit, I was a weapon engineering artificer.

Time to move on...

CHAPTER 5

HMS Collingwood – Technical School

My first car was a red Metro. It was small, old, and not very powerful; but it was mine. It was in this vehicle that I arrived at the main gate of HMS Collingwood early one September day in 1986, and showed my navy ID card to the young rating guarding the barrier. This was to be my new home for the next 22 months. I was about to be inducted into the world of weapon engineering.

HMS Collingwood was a sprawling shore-base on the main road between Fareham and Gosport, in Hampshire. Originally commissioned in January 1940, it was built on the site of a local marsh. Having drained this bog, the shore establishment was expanded, and in 1979, it became home to the Royal Navy's Weapons and Electrical Engineering Branch. It was the fourth ship to carry this title, and was named after Lord Collingwood (1748-1810) who took command of the British Fleet at the Battle of Trafalgar after Nelson was mortally wounded.

On passing the gatehouse, I was faced with a straight road ahead (called the Main-Drag). Immediately on my left was a white flagpole with the White Ensign rippling in the gentle breeze; and beyond this were the officers' quarters and the WRNS' accommodation. To my right, across a grass-covered playing field, was the swimming pool and gym area; effectively a modern leisure center, with the initials SARC emblazoned across its front. Directly in front of me lay the office and administration blocks which shielded the huge parade ground beyond it from my view. The road split to pass either side of the parade square; the Senior Ratings Mess on the left, and the classrooms on the right. Thus far, all of the buildings were two-storey, red-brick constructions, surrounded by grass verges and footpaths in an open-plan, low-rise design. In contrast, immediately in front of me, on the far side of the parade ground was an area covered in neatly trimmed grass, housing 4 tall blocks of what appeared to be apartments. One of these was to be my living quarters. Each was built of prefabricated concrete panels, interspaced with panoramic glass windows. Behind these towers was the galley and "duty-muster" building; and beyond these were a large number of long, narrow, single-storey huts containing the engineering workshops. These appeared to be old and needed some repair, and were probably some of the original buildings from the 1960's.

 Having been allocated a room for the duration of my stay at HMS Collingwood (or "Collingrad" as it was affectionately known), I went to claim my bed. Each of the 4 accommodation towers was identical, and each floor of each tower was identical; navy uniformity at its best. Each floor was accessed via steps at either end of the building, with all of the rooms positioned down each long side of the rectangular floor space. The center of each floor consisted of two sets of toilets (known as "the heads"), and a shower room. There were also two small communal TV rooms; one on each side of the floor.

 Our rooms had dividing walls between them, but where there might have been a wall to separate the corridor, there was only a large curtain; noise reduction was not a major concern. Each room housed 4 people, each having their own bed, wardrobe, and a bedside locker; specifically arranged to create as much privacy as possible. Although we were still living communally, it felt semi-private compared to Raleigh's vast dormitories. It varied as to who we shared with; most had at least one other person from our original class, but we were mixed with others from the previous intake too. As a result, we were able to benefit from their knowledge and experience, even though they had only been in the Royal Navy a few months longer than ourselves.

As far as Artificers were concerned, HMS Collingwood was divided into two distinct schools; Technical School (T-school) and Application School (A-school). I was to join T-school where I would learn the academic and practical skills required of my apprenticeship. In later years, I would return to A-school where this knowledge would be applied to the specific equipment and machinery that I would encounter aboard ship. Collingwood also trained the mechanics who, in the very near future, would be working for me when I became a senior rating in-charge of a section on a ship. So, as you can imagine, this was a very busy shore-base with thousands of personnel living and working on it.

Although my primary aim at Collingwood was to acquire the knowledge needed to become an effective engineer, I was also a member of the Royal Navy too. Discipline was still paramount. I was still regarded as a "newbie," still under-training; and as such, there were rules I had to follow. Unlike at Raleigh, where we had to run everywhere, here we were required to march, either as a class or individually. We had to wear brown gaiters with our working uniform (number 8's) to differentiate us as artificer apprentices in T-school. To ensure that we were still keeping our uniform to the correct standard, we had daily inspections by our class officers, parading each morning before them. This had the added advantage that we could then receive daily-orders, duties, and information that needed passing-on to us; and the class leaders could be allocated to act as liaisons between us and the officers.

Collingwood was a bit like going back to school. It operated on a 0900 to 1700 day, working Monday to Friday. During that time, I attended both academic and practical lessons, taught by naval officers as well as civilian teaching staff. Outside of these times I was free to do what I liked, including having shore-leave of an evening or at the weekend. However, as I was still under training, I was never left idle. I would often have homework to complete, or textbooks to study. I would often have inspections to prepare for. And, of course, I always had the duty-roster to fit around. Each of us was rostered to be one of the base's duty ratings at least once a week, and usually two out of every four weekends. The duties themselves varied from accommodation block duty, to fire party duty, to gatehouse duty; the hours you worked depending on which duty you were allocated.

Gatehouse duty tended to drag and was quite boring. From 1700, you moved into the gatehouse building and then worked a shift pattern with other ratings, manning the main gate and barriers. Evening time could be quite busy, but come the small hours of the morning, the main highlight was watching the family of foxes hunting in the long grass outside of the base perimeter; trying desperately to keep your eyelids from drooping or shutting entirely. As the threat level from terrorists was raised, so the gate staff were routinely armed. This was a mixed blessing. Some of the people given loaded weapons simply should not have been anywhere near live ammunition! They did not have the mentality or maturity to be given such responsibility. On one occasion, I heard tell of a junior weapons mechanic on gate duty. He stopped a car at the barrier, asking for ID, as he was supposed to do. The car, which was flying-the-flag of the Admiral on the front wing, was easily identifiable, and the passenger was the Admiral's wife who was also recognisable. She said that she did not have her ID on her, and told the driver to move off through the gate. The armed sentry panicked, shouted a warning, and shot a few bullets into the car's engine! Needless to say, the Admiral's wife was NOT impressed, and I do not think the rating lasted too long in the navy either!

Fire party duty meant wearing a red jacket over your uniform, and being on-call in case a fire was reported anywhere on base. At least once a day there would be a fire exercise broadcast over the intercom system. This could be a long training exercise lasting over an hour, or a short 10 minute one; it was at the Officer of the Day's discretion. However, when it was called, all duty personnel had to drop what they were doing and run to the fire cart. This was a hand-drawn cart containing stand-pipes, hoses, and other fire fighting equipment. We would then drag this cart as fast as we could to the reported location of the fire, set-up the hoses, and fight it. Sometimes it was a dry-run, other times the hoses were pressurised with water; again, at the discretion of the Officer of the Day. This was the exciting part of the duty, even though you were on-edge all day, waiting for the call-to-action. The not so exciting part was operating a shift system overnight where you conducted fire prevention and security rounds of certain buildings on the base.

With all of these duties, the day after, I was exhausted! But what it did do was prepare me for the duties I would have to perform aboard ship in the months to come.

I spent the majority of my time at Collingwood in the classrooms. My first 6 months were relatively easy compared to some, because the initial lessons were designed to get everyone to the same standard in maths and science. I had A-Levels in Maths, Physics and Chemistry, so everything was just revision to me. The naval instructors were not very helpful! They seemed to be over-qualified, and were teaching the wrong subjects. Our maths teacher was actually a nuclear scientist, but he certainly had no aptitude for teaching; I knew the subject-matter and he still confused me! It transpired that I became an unofficial teacher within our group. Both during the lessons, and in small study-groups in the evenings, I helped the less able members of our class grasp the basics in these subjects. Teamwork; this is what had been instilled into us at Raleigh. It also worked on a sort of karma basis too; I helped others in the group where I could and over the course of the time at Collingwood, they tended to return the favour. This was no doubt the source of another of my nicknames in the navy. When I joined my first ship after Collingwood, I was known as "Professor."

Over the following 22 months the subjects that I studied varied from maths and physics, to subjects closer related to the engineering disciplines that I was to follow. I learnt mechanical principles, control engineering, and electronics. I learnt the basics of hydraulics, and computers. Computers in the 80's were nothing like they are now; you would not recognise the subject-matter that we learnt. To program a command involved writing out the instruction in a binary form, translating it into a code of holes that were punched into lengths of ticker-tape on massive reels. These were then fed into the computer like a film would be run from one spool to another. And the computer itself would be contained within a series of filing-cabinets filling an entire room; the capacity of which could now be handled by a single modern laptop!

I had lessons in navy-related subjects too. I studied explosives; their use and safety. I studied how ships were arranged internally; how to identify compartments from a code of letters and numbers in each section. But a vast amount of the time was allocated to the study and practice of workshop skills. I devoted hundreds of hours to learning technical drawing, operating theodolites; and in the workshops, learning how to operate pillar-drills, milling machines, and lathes. These were to be the core subjects that I needed to be an expert at. I practiced so that I could hand-file metal to within a hundredth of a millimetre. I followed technical drawings, constructing objects within finite tolerances. I cut internal threads, external threads, and tapers on the lathes. Everything culminated in my final apprenticeship test-pieces. For the hand-filing skills test, I had to build a mini bench vice. Each component of it (and there were many) had to be made from a set material, hand-crafted to within a hundredth of a millimetre, perfectly flat and square, and assembled correctly, as per the drawings. For the machining test piece, I had to build a shaft of steel, of varying diameters, internal and external threads, and a tapered spigot that fitted perfectly within a corresponding brass tapered sleeve. Looking back on it, I am still amazed that I was capable of making such objects. If asked to do the same now, I would not have a clue; you lose these skills rapidly once they are no longer used.

As with all of the subjects that I studied, I had to pass a multitude of tests, some were formal exams, others assessed on my progress during the training. Ultimately, all of these results went towards me obtaining formal BTEC qualifications in engineering, recognised internationally, which would be of benefit should I follow this discipline outside of the Royal Navy in the future.

I lay on my stomach, my left leg outstretched, my right bent at 90 degrees providing traction and stability on the hard floor surface. My left arm was immobilised due to the webbing straps that were wound around it like a boa-constrictor, connecting me to the highly polished wooden stock of the target-rifle resting lightly in the palm of my hand. As I looked down the sights of this weapon, the circular target rose and fell gently in time with my breathing. "Control that breathing. Slow, deep breaths. Relax." This mantra was repeated over and over again in my head. As I steadily let the air escape from my lungs for the last time, I gently eased the trigger back with my right forefinger. "Don't snatch at it," I told myself. "Gently..." The bullet left the rifle with a loud, "Bang." It sped through the air as if in slow-motion, hitting the target at the furthest end of the darkened range, before embedding itself into the sand behind with a muffled, "Ummmf." The spotter to my rear looked through his telescope and said,

"Heasman. Bull. Nice shot."

And that was it. I had just won the target-shooting competition at RAF Halton. I was representing HMS Collingwood against my equivalents in the army and air force, and I had just won on my last shot! I was chuffed, more so because I had out-shot the army at their own speciality. On returning to Collingwood, this was to be a major feather-in-my-cap as the forces are very competitive, and any opportunity to get one-over on the "Pongo's" (from the saying – "Where the army goes, the pong-goes!"), was greatly appreciated. It was held in great esteem, so much so that I was awarded my "T-School Colours."

But this achievement did not happen overnight. It was the result of months of training and practice which started on one of our regular Wednesday afternoon "Make-and-Mends." HMS Collingwood was very much sport orientated. Each Wednesday (and other days on occasion) there would be an afternoon of sport training. Often it was left up to ourselves to arrange football, basketball, or running; but sometimes, special sessions were arranged for us to try less popular sports. It was through this route that I first tried .22 shooting. From day-one, I loved the challenge of trying to improve my high-score, and with a natural aptitude, I soon became addicted to it. I practiced whenever possible, in the evenings as well as during school hours, and soon became quite good at it.

Collingwood was the perfect place for sports. It had its own SARC (Sports And Recreation Center) housing a large top-quality pool, sauna, and water-sports complex. It had numerous gyms and sports-courts, as well as out-doors facilities for other events. The building was also home to the base's bar and social facilities. Not only were these some of the highest quality sports and social resources in the Royal Navy, but they were also some of the best in the local area too. Come the weekend, they were made available for the general public to use. A disco (called The Bop) was put-on every Saturday night for the local girls to meet sailors (and vice versa). If you watch the film, "An Officer and a Gentleman," it will give you a good idea of the mentality of the local girls with respect to how they regarded us navy personnel. It was a laugh, it was fun...

Running became my *main* sport whilst at Collingwood. At Raleigh, I had been abysmal when it came to fitness, but on leaving, my head PTI, Staff Saynor, said to me,

"You've done well to improve your fitness level during basic-training. But you need to keep it up. Try to do at least a few minutes of exercise every day, and you'll soon get fit. Then you'll enjoy sports much more."

I was sceptical, but it was good advice, then and now. I took him at his word and started jogging. Jogging short distances led to longer routes as I improved. I took to jogging around the perimeter of the shore-base. Then jogging turned into running at speed. Combine this with the physical training sessions we had to complete during our time at Collingwood, and the numerous assault courses we had to endure, and my fitness improved drastically. We had quite a few free weekends. I went home for some, but the hassle of sitting in traffic on the M25 on a Friday afternoon for hour-after-hour became too much of a chore on occasion. I became selective of when I visited my family, which meant that I often had available time to run. So I began entering local road races; 10K and 10 milers at first, but soon increasing to half marathons. I entered cross-country races on Dartmoor, and travelled all over the south of England to compete. And I became good... The more I ran, the better I became; and the better I became, the more I wanted to compete. By the time I left Collingwood for my first ship, I was addicted to running, but I was very fit!

CHAPTER 6

Freedom of Fareham

March 21st 1987.

This was the date that HMS Collingwood received "The Freedom of Fareham." It meant that we had the right to march through the town with bayonets fixed (amongst a whole host of other rights which were embedded into local bylaws). It was an honour that the base had been selected, but it was met with mixed feelings by those of us who had been chosen to take part. As is the case with most military establishments, there tends to be resentment from the local people, often without cause, which leads to tension between the military personnel and the locals. Such was the case with us. Prior to the announcement of this parade, there had been a few arguments and fisticuffs between our trainees and local youths, most of which was alcohol fuelled. We blamed them; they, no doubt blamed us. But, as a result, we were half expecting there to be some sort of disruption or protest to our march through the heart of *their* town. We were entering "enemy" territory; entering into the unknown!

That aside, this was to be a once-in-a-lifetime occasion; it was rare to receive this honour, and so it was made abundantly clear that we had to ensure that everything went smoothly, and we performed at our peak on the day.

Over a month prior to this date, those who were to attend were nominated. I was to be part of the Guard-of-Honour; the centrepiece of the whole ceremony. Was this a good thing? Or was it going to mean extra effort, extra training, and more disruption to our already busy days? Bearing in mind the importance being placed on this parade, it was probably the latter.

Drill training at HMS Collingwood was a regular thing anyway. There was a parade every Friday afternoon (called "Divisions") where the entire base formed-up on the parade ground and marched past the commanding officer (followed by a mass escape on weekend shore-leave the moment it was complete). And so, training was conducted routinely. However, the moment our class was selected for the "guard" everything became much more intense. The Gunnery Officer made it his personal responsibility to train us!

At Collingwood we had the last REAL Gunnery Officer in the Royal Navy. Others since have been given the title, but they were not proper gunnery officers as ours was. Ours was old-school. He seemed to have been in the navy since the days of Nelson; and he was held in the highest of esteem. He was like a God; you never wanted to cross him or get on his wrong side. At the same time, he was eccentric in his ways and habits. It was forbidden to cross the parade ground at any time unless you were marching, but should you so much as step onto it, even when there was nobody around, you could expect to hear the booming voice of the Gunnery Officer yelling at you to,

"Get off my Parade Ground. Report to the drill hall NOW!"

It was as if the voice was coming from above, from the All-Seeing-Eye that was our "Guns." Sometimes he would suddenly appear from behind a bush, springing-out on you when you least expected it; so you could never let your guard down. Even off-duty, he had been known to go into town to do some shopping. Dressed in civilian clothes, he could be seen to march from shop to shop, as if still on the parade square. This was no doubt a strange sight for the locals, but to us it was an indication of his dedication to the role he performed; he was never *off-duty*.

    The Freedom of Fareham was to be one of the longest marches I had ever performed. It involved marching a number of miles through the streets of the town, forming a parade in the pedestrian town-center, and then marching off afterwards for another few miles. Add to this the fact that the center part of the parade was to be performed on a cobbled surface (which is like glass when you are wearing studded parade boots), and you can understand the need for extensive preparation. The band would be marching ahead of us; and with the narrow, building-lined streets, the sound of their music would bounce off the walls causing havoc with our timing, and marching to the beat. As the Guard-of-Honour, we would be carrying SLR rifles with bayonets mounted on the end of the barrels. These were heavy weapons, so carrying them in the same arm for hours was going to result in a lot of pain, and potentially a few dropped firearms! There were so many things that could go wrong; it was a daunting task ahead of us.

    Every day I had practice sessions; morning, noon, and evening; for weeks. I would be up early, given a special early breakfast, and be marching from 0630. My lunch-breaks were spent conducting general-salutes with my rifle. My evenings spent marching in endless circles around every side road we could find on the base. I learnt to conduct a "change-arms" manoeuvre whilst still marching, so that I could rest my arm by moving the rifle from one shoulder to the other. I built-up my muscle strength and endurance for the distance I would need to cover. We often practiced with the Collingwood Band, getting used to the tunes they would be playing, and ensuring that we could march in-time with their beat. But HMS Collingwood was a flat base, and part of the route for the Freedom of Fareham was to be up-hill! This was to remain an unknown until the day, as was marching on cobbles, as it was not permitted for us to have a dress rehearsal in the streets that we would be using.

We had prepared and prepared. We were weary from the physical and mental effort of learning our drill routines. We were tired from our constant inspections; inspections of our number-1 uniforms, inspections of our rifles, and inspections of our marching. We grew to hate the sound of the Collingwood Band. And we began to dread the prospect of the miles of marching we were about to face. We had done everything we could to get us ready for the big day, now all we could do was wait for the off...

We were dropped on the outskirts of Fareham, and with the band, the guard, and the marching masses, we took-over the whole area, filling the roads and pavements. Each of us was busy ensuring our uniform was immaculate, not a stray thread or piece of fluff to be seen. Our buttons were gleaming in the hazy sunshine, our boots like mirrors. Our ceremonial gaiters had been "blano'd" to within an inch of their lives, and each of us had a rifle fitted with a chromed bayonet.

The time had arrived. We formed-up into our respective units; the band leading, the guard next in line, and the other divisions to the rear. The guard was inspected one last time, given words of encouragement, and then the officers took their positions at the front. As the band struck up the first of many tunes, the command was given to march off. With a crisp, "crunch" of boots hitting tarmac in unison, we stepped off.

"Left, left, left right left," the Gunnery Officer called.

Everyone was in time with each other. A miracle had occurred!

We followed a meandering route through the town, taking-in residential streets as well as shopping areas. A few people lined the streets; they were intermittent, in small clusters, as if they had just turned-up to see what all the noise was about. But a few clapped and cheered; whether they actually knew what was going on I seriously doubt. And so our march continued. Occasionally, the band would change the tune they were playing, and on restarting, would find that everyone was out-of-step with them. So adjustments were constantly being made. After a mile or so, the pain in our shoulders was becoming quite severe, so our officers gave the order to change arms. Oh, the relief! Why hadn't we been taught this skill ages ago? It would have made things so much more comfortable.

After what seemed an eternity of constantly stamping our feet into the ground, the marching masses approached the town-center. As the guard stepped onto the cobbles for the first time, the inevitable happened; someone in the leading rank slipped, recovered their composure, and carried on. I guess it could have been much worse; at least he stayed on his feet. But the Gunnery Officer, in a rare moment of humanity, quietly said,

"Steady lads. Shorten your stride a little, and don't lean back so much."

It made all the difference. That was the first and last slip to occur on this parade.

Once in the pedestrian street, the guard came to a halt outside a pub, and re-adjusted position ready for the general-salute and inspection to follow. It was a relief to stop marching, but the moment I did, the blood drained to my feet. I suddenly had a feeling of light-headiness; and now that I was stationary, the heat hit me and I began to sweat under my heavy woollen tunic and cap. The crowds were 4 or 5 deep in this area; clearly the word had got around as to what was going on, and the locals had come out to gawk at *those silly sailors showing off in the High Street*. For me, it made a change to have something to look at, to take my attention during the parade. Normally, I just stared straight ahead as an officer inspected us; but on this occasion, there were lots of people to look at. Some sniggered at us, but most had huge smiles on their faces, chatting and laughing, and enjoying the spectacle. All those fears of disruption from the locals were unwarranted. Everything was going fine...

The inspection by the Mayor of Fareham came and went in a blur, as did all of the speeches. Then it was time to march off again for the second leg of the parade. My first few steps were agony! I had no feeling in my feet, my shoulders had seized-up during the inspection, and it felt like the grip on my rifle would slip at any moment! Did the public notice any of this? No, they were oblivious. They cheered as we set-off on the last stage of our endurance march; the young kids running alongside us until they got bored, or mummy called them back again. It was nearly over, just the hill to contend with!

Eventually, we reached the end, came to a stop, and were dismissed. Water was available in plentiful quantities which I downed until my belly was bloated. It had been a long day, but it was over now. Or was it? Most of the parade was free to return to base, but a select few, me included, were required to attend the Civic Reception. At the time I had been chosen, it sounded like a fun event; free food, and more importantly, free beer. I was sold. But right now; hot, sweaty, tired, with swollen feet, and feeling like my head was about to explode with migraine; it was the last thing I wanted to do!

But, like the dutiful rating that I was, I went along and mingled with all the officers and council hierarchy. I felt like a fish-out-of-water! I put on my best "official face" and played the role I was there to perform. The promises of free beer were somewhat exaggerated; I had a couple of glasses only, but as I was so dehydrated it went straight to my head. Not soon enough for my liking, the guard officer thanked us all for our efforts, and told us we were free to go. "Hooray," we thought, until we realised that there was no transport provided; we had to make our own way back to base, in full uniform! Somebody had NOT planned this part of the day very well!

Off we trotted for a well-earned rest...

CHAPTER 7

Talybont on Usk

As part of my course at HMS Collingwood, I was required to do adventure and leadership training. Collingwood had its own facilities alongside a reservoir in the Welsh Brecon Beacons at a place called Talybont on Usk. Whilst in T-school we visited this location twice and once again during A-school. It became like a second home; a base-away-from-base, a bit of a break from the routines of the shore establishment.

On my first visit, the instructors made us leave our coach in a quaint little Welsh village, nestled amongst the heavily wooded mountains. Having donned our rucksacks, and carrying our tents, we set-off following our maps. The aim was to locate the training center shown as a red dot on the side of a large reservoir. This was not too difficult a task as we were able to follow roads and tracks the whole way. Our class was in good spirits, having had a restful drive to Wales; and remembering Raleigh, and our initial race up the slag heaps of Cardinham, we had been expecting the worst! We were pleasantly surprised.

The hike was easy going, over gently undulating terrain. But we were dwarfed by the colossal mountains that obscured the horizon in every direction. This was somewhat foreboding as I knew that at some point very soon, we would be trekking up and over these behemoths. It would not be as relaxing as it was just now!

As we neared our target, we strolled along a track at the foot of two hills, the course of a stream trickling along the valley floor. There was dense forest on either side of us creating a claustrophobic atmosphere; but suddenly, before us, this opened-up to reveal a dam-wall and a reservoir of still water stretching into the distance.

According to the map, we had to cross the dam, and then follow a path along the left side of the reservoir. This path was well used, perfectly straight, and steadily climbing up and away from the water's edge. We soon lost sight of the lake, blocked by the thickness of the tree growth, and the path was becoming a tunnel as the foliage encroached on our view ahead. The smell of crushed pine-needles was ever present as we strode towards our goal.

Halfway along the reservoir's length, we came across a small stone cottage located on the side of the track furthest from the drop-off to the water. Was this where we would be staying? If so, why had we been carrying heavy canvass tents with us? All would be revealed very soon!

Suddenly there was movement in the trees to my right. Whatever it was, it sounded big, heavy, thundering through the undergrowth. What could it be? Surely there were no bears in Wales? The noise got closer, until, out of the tree-line came a man carrying what appeared to be a tree-trunk! He was tall, had a cropped hairstyle, and had muscles everywhere. Welcome to our instructor; a Royal Marine corporal, and a complete nutcase. Our hearts sank. If this was who was going to be training us, we were doomed. It was going to be a week of Hell!

It turned out that he was not half as bad as we had thought, however he did have a warped sense of fun. Whilst waiting for our arrival, he had gone for a run, up a mountain, through a forest, carrying a tree! That is what makes marines a bit *different* from the rest of us I suppose.

"Welcome to Talybont," the corporal said. Rules were given for our stay.

"Right you lot, this lovely little cottage is for STAFF only. I don't wanna see any of you 'orrible lot anywhere near it. Is that clear?" I had guessed as much!

"You lot will have the pleasure of becoming acquainted with the midges as you camp over there," he continued, pointing to the tree-line.

"You'll be away from camp on a couple of nights, so I want your tents and kit stowed away every morning unless I tell you otherwise."

"You'll need to make a fire, and your food will be supplied in the form of nutritious Rat-Packs. You'll love 'em!" he chuckled.

They were not as bad as they sounded; they contained no rats (although from the taste of some of the sachets, it could easily get confusing). It simply meant Ration Packs. They were a selection of dehydrated meals or tinned foods, plus high-energy chocolate bars and biscuits. Terrible for the waistline, but we would be burning-off this excess energy very quickly.

"Make yourself a toilet in the trees, but use your brains – if you can find 'em – don't build it uphill – piss and shit flows downwards, yeah? And make sure it's well away from my cottage – I don't wanna be breathing your stench."

With our introduction to camp-life over, we set about erecting our tents and preparing the site.

"Come on then, what you all waiting for? Move it, NOW!" he screamed. We jumped to it as if our lives depended on it.

Over the course of our many visits to Wales, we were introduced to a number of adventurous sports. Most of them were new to us, a few people had tried them before, but to the majority of us they just created a feeling of fear.

One of the first sports I attempted was canoeing on the reservoir. Some in our group had tried this before, and to the rest of us, it did not sound too daunting; so off I set to the water's edge. What I had not accounted for was the weather. On this particular day, it was icy and there was a strong northerly wind being channelled down the valley and across the surface of the water. To begin with, the canoeing was fun, if a little uncomfortable in these conditions. But a few minutes later, all feeling in my face and hands had been lost. The session was called off, and I slowly paddled back to shore, shivering uncontrollably. As I tried to exit the boat and put my paddle on the shingle shoreline, I found that my bare hands had literally frozen to the paddle shaft! Nightmare. It took a bit of coaxing and rubbing of the skin before the grip could be separated. Then it was a mad rush up the hillside to the warmth of our camp fire where copious amounts of tea were drunk to warm my inner being. Had there been better conditions, canoeing would have been exciting, especially in these glorious surroundings; but as it was, it was not the best introduction to a sport. Many may have been put-off for life, but not me.

Abseiling was never something I would have volunteered to do. I hated the idea of stepping off an object at a great height. When we were told that this was to be our activity for the day, I was scared! Would I be able to go through with it, or would I panic and not complete the task?

The class leader led the way through the woodland towards the site we were going to use. Most people were silent, locked into their own private world of fear. A few were overly chatty; their own way of coping with the stress and worry. We followed a path, deep into the forest, with a steep drop to our right. And then I saw it! Ahead was an old, disused viaduct spanning the gap between this side of the valley and the next. It was made of roughly-carved stone blocks, with three arches dropping away to the valley floor, a good 30m below. The top was covered in gravel, and there were two parapet-walls on either side to prevent us falling over the edge. In the center stood our marine instructor, a huge sadistic grin on his face. He showed us how to wear the safety harness, and how to control our speed as we walked down the leg of the bridge. Then he rigged two ropes over the side, attached himself to one, and demonstrated a textbook abseil to the floor. It looked simple enough, he had only bounced twice to cover the whole distance; what could go wrong?

Slowly, each of us edged nearer to the ropes. One at a time, our marine attached us to them and helped us to abseil. It was my turn. I was "cacking" myself! I was strapped to the rope via my harness, and I backed towards the parapet-wall. I was told not to look down, so I instantly looked! Big mistake. I clambered onto the top of the wall and leant backwards over the drop; the rope taking the strain. It felt like I was horizontal, such was the angle I was leaning over, but it was probably only about 45 degrees. At this point, the tremors in my legs started. We had been told that the first step was the hardest. I became suddenly aware of everybody watching me. Could I take the big step? I decided that as I was half over the edge anyway, I had better go for it. If I died, I died! And so, I took that first tentative step down the wall. It was not too bad, I was gaining confidence. I took another, and another; increasing speed to that of a snail. On my 5th step, I suddenly found myself hanging upside-down, spinning and swinging wildly on the rope.

"Wooaah! What the fuck..." I cried.

I locked-off so I would not fall, but I had no idea what had happened. I looked up to see the marine peaking over the wall with his grin now spread across his entire face.

"Sorry," he said. "I forgot to tell you, you were on the rope over the arch, not the leg of the viaduct!"

"Cheers mate. Thanks for nothing!" I mumbled.

I was not impressed, but I managed to get back to terra-firma, still shaking from head to foot. By the time I had clambered up the steep valley wall to the top, I was slightly more composed. Despite my fears, I actually had a second go; this time down the *leg* of the viaduct. I had survived. I was now full of pride in my achievement. However, just to let us know how simple the abseiling we had done was, the marine then climbed up on the parapet-wall, and RAN forwards down the leg of the bridge at full speed, as only Royal Marines can do. We were all impressed. We were also thankful that we had not joined the marines. And it was confirmed; this marine was a complete "nutter!"

In a similar vein, the rock climbing that I attempted was a mixture of nervous excitement and fear. There had been a lot of rain the night before, so the air was damp and clammy, with the smell of rotting leaves assaulting our senses. As I approached the rocky outcrop perched atop a grassy hill, my heart sank. It looked massive. There was no way I was going to climb that; I was not a mountaineer!

Two safety ropes had already been prepared, hanging down the cliff face, showing us the routes that we could climb. From the base of the cliff, looking up, the top seemed to fade off into infinity. Our marine attached us, one at a time, to the end of the safety rope, which disappeared over the top of the rock-face, before returning to ground level to be held by a safety officer. The theory was that we would climb unaided to the top, but that we could not fall as the rope would be under tension the whole time to prevent any accidents; I was sceptical though!

My turn arrived. I edged to the foot of the rock and looked up. I had never seen a wall of rock look so smooth!

"Alright Heasman, look for the hand and foot holds. Just use your arms and legs to lever yourself up, one step at a time, it's easy. Any questions?" the marine said.

I looked carefully, but the rock-face appeared flat to me! Surely he did not mean those barely noticeable undulations in the rock's surface?

"Err, corporal, which hand and foot holds do you mean?" I asked.

"Are you stupid or something? Those ones right in front of you."

I heaved my weight onto one of these minute protrusions, and gradually started to make progress vertically. It was slow going. After a few minutes, the cold of the rock had permeated into my fingers and all sense of touch was lost; it was like trying to hold-on wearing gloves. Then last night's rain began to escape from a crack in the rock above me, soaking the surface in a thin layer of icy water. It became glass-like and my fingers lost their grip entirely. But the marine had assured us that there was no way of falling, we had a safety rope. How wrong he was. I dropped instantly, bouncing off the rock-face, and scraping my bare skin against its rough surface. Of course, my fingers were numb with cold, so I felt nothing at the time; only later did the pain arrive. I guess I only fell about 2m before the rope took the tension and left me stranded, swinging helplessly from side to side like a pendulum. I was lowered to the ground and made to try again, which I did. But this was to be the first and last experience of rock climbing that I was to have. It was not the height that was the problem; it was a combination of being made to climb in less-than-perfect conditions, and then falling on my first attempt. It was not something I would be doing again in the near future...!

Another rock-based sport that I tried was pot-holing. This was something that none of our group had tried before. Our instructors took us to a village where we were kitted-out in thin waterproofs and "wellies," to be worn over our denim overalls, and then given miner's helmets with lamps that worked intermittently. Having trekked through the undergrowth, we came to a small cluster of boulders on the ground. Between them was a tiny hole, about the size of a manhole-cover; this was the entrance to the cave.

One by one, we dropped through this orifice, entering a world of blackness! I turned my lamp on, but it only lit an area of a few meters directly ahead of me. Everything else was lost in the darkness.

"Form a single-file line and NEVER lose sight of the person in-front of you," the marine told us. "We don't want to lose anybody down here, do we?"

Slowly we began to move forward, going deeper into the tunnel complex. Initially, the roof was way above head-height, so it was just a case of clambering over the rocks and boulders that littered the cave floor. But gradually the roof lowered until I was walking along, bent-double at the waist, constantly battering my helmet on the rock above. It was cool down there, not too cold, but chilly and damp. There was an ever-present sound of rushing water; far away at first, but increasing in volume the further I climbed into the depths of the caves. Eventually, I arrived in a chamber that opened-up so that I could stand comfortably. With all of our lamps combined, we were able to make-out the magnificence of the cave; see the stalactites and stalagmites, and see the beauty of the underworld. This must have been our goal; surely we were going to retrace our steps and go back now!?

The sound of the water was deafening in this chamber, but I could not see its source. Suddenly, the marine shouted,

"Follow me."

He walked to the far end of the cave, sat on this backside, wiggled into a crack between two walls of rock, and disappeared feet first! We looked at each other in the murky light, bemused.

"Where did he go?" someone asked.

"Dunno. Down that hole I guess. Should we follow him d'you think?"

"Maybe we better turn around and head back the way we came," someone else suggested.

"You think you can find your way out in the darkness do you?" our officer said, his voice trembling with fear.

"Nah, I doubt it, Sir. Maybe we better just follow him down there then," he replied, pointing into the darkness.

So we followed him through the crack. No sooner had my feet entered the unknown, than they were dragged by a torrent of rushing water, and I was forced onto my back to go with the flow. I had no control. I had no way of stopping. I just bounced from rock to rock, being washed over the rapids by the water that was flooding behind me. Finally, I splashed into a pool in another chamber; relieved it was over, but exhilarated, and pumped full of adrenalin. This must be the end, surely?

To my right, I saw a triangular spot of light in the distance. I followed the marine towards it. It was our exit; the light was daylight. But to get to it, I had to remove my helmet, dragging it behind me on its cable. I lay on my back, and wiggled my way head-first towards the light; passing along a 25m triangular tunnel (similar to a large Toblerone box), the width of my shoulders. This tunnel was partly flooded with water, so the only air was in the peak of the triangular cross-section; my face pushed into this air-pocket the entire way. Our slow, uncomfortable crawl to the outside world had begun. We wriggled along the tunnel, one behind the other, like a line of hungry caterpillars in search of food. Many in our group became claustrophobic; one of our officers actually had a panic-attack when his helmet got caught on a rock. But, after what seemed like hours, we all arrived safely in the welcome sunlight.

Our marine bounded-off like a mountain goat, hopping over the boulders that filled the riverbed leading away from the underworld. But the rest of us; drained from the mental exhaustion and physical effort of our trial underground, simply clambered along the river's edge, probably still in shock from what we had just endured!

The rest of my time at Talybont was a combination of hiking over the mountainous terrain; often conducting navigation exercises, either during the day, or occasionally at night; and participating in leadership tasks. Sometimes we would form into groups, a leader would be nominated, and we would be tasked with getting the group from one side of a river to the other. How you did it was entirely your choice, but usually it involved building a leopard-crawl, or a death-slide, or even a raft. No matter what method you employed, it always resulted in lots of laughs as it went wrong, and everyone ended-up getting soaked as they fell into the water. But the aim had been achieved; it developed our leadership qualities, and it built teamwork. That was the whole purpose of adventure training at HMS Collingwood. Of course, it was also there to push each individual to their limit, and beyond. Every one of us had a weakness; whether it was confined spaces, rock walls, or leaping off viaducts; but by working together, we overcame these things, making us stronger people.

Overall, Talybont was fun; I enjoyed our visits, and I looked forward to the challenges that it would throw at me...

CHAPTER 8

Sea Safety Training

In the final few weeks at HMS Collingwood I applied for my first sea draft; this would be the ship that I would spend the next year of my training aboard. Training aside, what everyone really wanted was a year of foreign travel. However, when the list of possible ships was released there were no details of their schedules. After a few discussions with various contacts I had made around Collingwood, I heard that one particular ship was soon to be joining the "Standing Naval Force Atlantic," a NATO led fleet, due to visit the Caribbean and USA; so I immediately applied for this position.

A few weeks later, our sea drafts arrived. I had been successful. I was to spend a year aboard HMS Scylla, a Leander Class Frigate. I was chuffed. Also on the draft order, it said that before joining Scylla, I was to return to HMS Raleigh to complete a "Sea Survival Course." This was a prerequisite to joining any ship afloat for the first time.

And so, in June 1988, I returned to Raleigh for a week; no-longer a recruit, and no-longer treated like dirt.

This time I was shown a little more respect, and the new trainees looked up to me like a God.

The Sea Safety (or Sea Survival) Course consisted of 4 main elements and lasted 5 days. One section of it was NBC training (nuclear, biological, and chemical). This was merely a refresher in the use of my respirator in the event of a gas attack; and required me to endure the CS gas-chamber again! As before, it was uncomfortable, with streaming eyes and noses, and stinging skin around the face; but it would be nothing compared to the effects I would encounter if ever an attack was for real.

The second section of this course was designed to prepare us, if ever we had to abandon ship at sea. I arrived at the water's edge, by the shores of the River Tamar. Before me stood a scaffolding structure with a wooden platform at its top, looming over the water beneath it. I was wearing my thick denim overalls and sea boots (known as "steaming bats"); exactly what I would be wearing if this were a real emergency situation. The training was intended to practice the techniques used to enter the water correctly and safely; and to experience what it would be like being adrift in a life raft awaiting rescue. I could already tell it was going to be a long, cold, and uncomfortable day!

Slowly I clambered up the ladder to the top of the platform. I had now donned an orange life-jacket over my overalls, and was told to inflate it. This had the effect of restricting my movements as it squeezed my chest and forced my head slightly forwards. From this height, the water beneath me looked miles away. It was choppy with a breeze creating small white-topped waves, and it looked extremely uninviting! Amid these peaks and troughs sat a fluorescent-orange inflatable life raft. It had been conveniently inflated for us, but purposely placed upside-down by the instructors. Circling this raft was a rigid inflatable boat (RIB) with two instructors aboard; and other instructors were stood on the shore with charged fire hoses at the ready! Things were looking very ominous!

Just like lemmings, each of us followed the one before to the edge of the platform, looked down, and launched ourselves into the void, before hitting the swirling grey maelstrom below. Having surfaced from beneath the dark waters, we bobbed-about like stranded turtles; the life jacket forcing us onto our backs. It was then that the fire hoses were let loose on us. The instructors bombarded us with high-pressure jets of water, spinning us around until we were dizzy, and forcing it into our throats causing us to choke. We kicked with our feet, trying to get close to the upturned raft. The first person to arrive had the unenviable task of hanging from a rope, using their body-weight to turn the raft over on top of them. And then we all clambered over the edge of the raft into the relative safety within.

Once inside, the top of the raft was inflated to create a sort of protective tent with two exits/windows. There was an overpowering smell of plastic or rubber which clung to everything; people were already gagging! We were slumped around the edges of the circular boat, exhausted at the effort it took simply to get inside; drenched in water and shivering with the cold. The smell was horrible, and was giving everyone a headache; and then the instructors started to spin the raft in circles, towing it with the RIB, and blasting it with the fire hoses. As there was no view outside, this made everyone feel nauseous; our first taste of sea-sickness! Watching each person's face, you could see them swallowing hard, trying not to be the first to vomit. But it was a hopeless task. Eventually one person could no longer hold it in, so they climbed over the mass of legs towards the exit hole, stuck their head through, and emptied their stomach contents into the water outside. On coming back into the raft, the rubber smell became infused with the stench of vomit, which set-off the next person to make the trip to the window in order to be sick. And so it went on; no one was immune. After what seemed like hours, the exercise was ended and the boat was dragged to shore. We looked pitiful as we staggered out of the boat; each with skin the colour of the grey water, specks of vomit dotted around our mouths.

Was the training worth it? Well, nobody can deny it was realistic. If ever I had to do this for real, I would certainly have had a better chance of survival. So, yes, it was definitely worth it; but it was something I would not fancy doing again too soon...

The HAVOC trainer was designed to simulate a sinking ship, damaged by shrapnel and pierced by bomb damage. Our team's task was to use the techniques of damage-control that we had learnt in order to prevent, or at the very least, reduce the amount of water taken onboard by the damaged ship. On my previous visit to HMS Raleigh this unit had not been fully built so this was to be my first experience of it. I am not sure what the letters of HAVOC stand for, but the word "havoc" was very apt; it was like being amid a scene of total devastation and destruction; organised chaos!

The simulator was a mock-up of two or three decks of a ship. It was mounted on hydraulic rams which could move the entire structure to simulate the motion of the sea; and it was built over a massive water-tank which it could pump into the simulator wherever there was a hole, at very high pressure; just the way that sea-water would enter a ship if damaged for real.

Our team waited nervously in a small compartment on the top-deck of the simulator, and each of us was allocated a task within the damage-control team. The room was what I would have imagined a real ship to look like; dark, grey-painted metal walls, floors and ceilings. Pipework running in all directions, and there were heavy metal hatches and doors.

"BANG!"

A thunder-flash was detonated in the passageway outside the compartment. The sound was deafening as it reverberated around the metal walls; the vibration felt deep within my chest. The lights went out, replaced by emergency red lighting; and smoke started to enter through the doorway. On opening the door to the passage beyond, I was hit by a wall of noise; voices shouting, screaming orders; more explosions; calls to "Emergency Stations" over the intercom system; metal hitting metal... The choking smoke was making my eyes pour, unable to see clearly where to go. And above all of this was the sound of water; fast-moving water, forcing itself into the ship somewhere beneath me! There was a sudden lurch to one side, throwing me off-balance; followed by a gentle rolling motion as the ship began to wallow in the water. I was suddenly unable to walk in a straight line anymore; bouncing off the walls from side to side. Confusion reigned...!

To all intents and purposes, this was *real*; I was on a sinking ship, and the adrenalin was pumping through my body. Yes, it was exciting, but it was scary too; what was going to happen next?

On entering the passageway, I was directed towards the hatch and ladder going into the compartment beneath me. Above the ladder was a red pipe with a gash in it; water pouring out in a powerful jet that forced me off my feet as I tried to climb down into the blackness. I was shoved through this blockage and down the ladder, with encouraging screams of,

"Get your arse down there. Go, go, go..."

I do not think my feet actually touched the rungs at all; I landed in a heap at the bottom, up to my waist in icy cold water, with the next person landing on top of me!

The sight before me was terrifying! The room was already over 1m deep in water. There were water jets coming from multiple holes in the walls; so powerful that the streams were hitting the ladder about 4m away from them. There was water erupting like a volcano from the holes in the floor. The air was thick with acrid smoke; and the whole room was moving side-to-side causing the standing-water to follow its motion, creating waves that knocked me off my feet. The sound was a mixture of people trying to shout over each other, claxons blaring, explosions from above vibrating through the walls and floors; all merging to form a physical barrier of white-noise.

My initial task was to stem the flow of water coming through the splinter holes in the walls. Easy I thought; all I had to do was hammer some wooden wedges into them until the water stopped. The first problem was locating the bag of wedges in the chaos that surrounded me. But once done, I approached a series of holes. I could not stand in front of them due to the pressure of water coming through, so I stood to one side. I grabbed a wedge, held it in the first hole and took a swing at it with a lump-hammer. It looked secure so I let go, only to see the wedge fly across the room like a bullet-leaving-a-gun, hitting someone in the lower back as they came down the ladder!

"Ooops; first casualty of the exercise!" I said to myself.

They were dragged off in agony. I continued with some urgency as the water level was rising rapidly. Gradually, the water entering through these slots diminished, but by this stage my hands were numb with cold and I could not remember how many times I had hit my fingers with the lump-hammer; judging by the swelling, quite a few! The pain would come later.

After this, I helped others tackling the floods coming through the floor. We needed to place a box-like object over the holes, and then erect an extendable acro-prop between it and the ceiling. In the comfort of a classroom, this was easy enough; but with the adrenalin running in our veins, our bodies frozen, and in a near-panicked condition, this was far from simple. I dived under the water, holding my breath, and tried to place the box in position. I emerged from the depths gasping for air, only to have a wave pass over my head and down my throat. The box subsequently slid across the rolling deck, so I had to repeat the task a number of times before it was in position and secured properly. By this time the water level had reached the ceiling; I had to float at the surface, grabbing a lung-full of air as the ship rolled. Clearly we were losing the battle against the flood.

"Endex, ENDEX. Everybody out," the order to leave the compartment was screamed. We clambered up the ladder like a group of half-drowned rats. The exercise was over!

We were duly informed that we had all "drowned," or at least, we would have done had it been for real! However, the caveat was that *everybody* failed to save the ship in the HAVOC simulator, which was what it was designed to do. Having learnt a lot of valuable lessons from this training, I moved on to the final part of my Sea Safety Course; the dreaded "Fire Fighting School."

During my previous visit to HMS Raleigh, our class had practiced some basic fire fighting; learning to use extinguishers, operating the fire hoses, and putting-out relatively small fires. But this time we were going to spend a couple of days learning much more advanced techniques. When at sea, in the event of a fire, you cannot call the fire brigade; you ARE the fire brigade! Because of this, there would be no simulations; we would be fighting *real* fires. If you did not follow the correct procedures you could potentially get severely injured; or worse! And so, with this warning of possible death still ringing in my ears, I donned the equipment that I would be wearing to protect myself.

Over my working uniform I wore my overalls. Over these I wore a thick, fireproof, hooded suit, called a "fearnought suit." This was extremely heavy, beige in colour, and was my protective layer from the heat and flames. They were often referred to as "teddy-bear-suits" due to their cuddly appearance. Over my head and hands I wore an anti-flash hood and gloves (designed to prevent flash-burns from explosions); and on my feet I wore thick, steel-toed wellington boots. To finish off this ensemble I had a heavy helmet to protect my head from falling objects, and thick gloves to protect my hands. Even before any fires had been lit, on a summer's day, I was already feeling like I was being baked alive in an oven! Dehydration was going to be a major issue...

As we would be entering into burning compartments we needed to wear, and be familiar with, full-face breathing apparatus (BASCA). As the name suggested, the mask covered your face, supplying a constant flow of air from a tank carried on your back. It was heavy and cumbersome, but was essential for survival in a fire situation. It was similar to a diver's breathing equipment except that the tank was inverted and supplied air constantly, whereas the diver's air was supplied on-demand by sucking it through a regulator.

We began by learning simple entry techniques. We worked in 3 or 4 man teams. The first two would direct the heavy hoses (one hose acting as a water-wall spray to protect us from the heat. The second hose acting as a jet, directed through the water-wall to attack the source of the fire). Behind them stood operator three who used a Thermal Imaging Camera (TIC) to locate the seat of the fire, and to direct the hoses at it. Operator 4 was to the rear, heaving the hoses through doorways and hatches, preventing any tangles or blockages. And other members of the team were stood at a distance monitoring air consumption and preparing replacement fire fighting teams, as required.

The time had come for my first taste of fire fighting. I was operating the jet-hose. I stood facing a large smoke-blackened metal box the size of a room. The front swing-door was open to reveal a large, well-established fire within. Thick acrid clouds of noxious black smoke billowed out of the door, spiralling away into the sky; and beyond this, I could see the whole interior of the compartment glowing orange from the flames and heat. In a crouched position, I edged nervously towards the fire, the spray operator at my side. The controller stood behind us and had a firm grip of our shoulders, pushing us forwards. Suddenly, my hose gave a massive jolt under my arm as the high-pressure water was applied. The protective water-wall was established and my visibility dropped to zero! All I could see was the water dripping off my face-mask; I could not even see the fire, let alone fight it! Now I understood the importance of the controller who could locate the fire with his thermal imaging camera.

I slowly moved forwards, entering the room. Despite the protection from the water-wall, the heat was tremendous. Sweat was pouring off every inch of my body. Through the water, I could make out the glow of the fire; it seemed to fill the whole of the far wall of the room. Still I advanced towards it. My jet was aimed directly ahead, and when the controller wanted me to alter direction, he would tap my shoulder indicating where he wanted me to aim. Eventually, I reached the source of the blaze. I blasted it with my jet, and then kicked it to pieces, dispersing the oil-soaked wooden beams to ensure it was extinguished fully. Water pressure was reduced, and the hose went limp in my hands. We all exited the compartment for a debrief. At this point I had my first glimpse of how big the fire had been. The metal walls were still glowing red from the heat, and the smell of burnt wood and oil was intoxicating. But I was chuffed that I had fought, and won, the battle against the fire. However, this was merely the first of many fires I would tackle; each one progressively bigger and more difficult to fight. But I now had confidence in the equipment, and in my abilities. I felt invincible.

Entering a compartment from above whilst fighting a fire within it was a whole different problem. Heat tends to rise, so climbing down a ladder to get into a room that was ablaze on the floor, walls, and ceiling, meant passing through various heat layers. We were warned that the heat was the main hazard if we were not careful, NOT the flames. So this was going to be our next obstacle to overcome.

As before, we operated in 4-man teams. The spray-hose was lowered through the hatch, bouncing against the ladder on its descent into the inferno below. Its purpose was to reduce some of the dangerously high temperatures inside. The hose operator then climbed down to the foot of the ladder and established a water-wall to protect the rest of the team as they descended. I was next. As I climbed down each rung of the ladder, I passed through the heat layers; I was thankful for the clothing I wore as it deflected the majority of the heat, but at the top of the ladder the heat was unbearable despite this! We later heard that someone doing the same exercise had not fitted his anti-flash hood correctly, and when climbing down the ladder, the heat had penetrated around his face and head, causing his ears to blister and burst!

At the bottom, I fired my jet towards the fire's base; however locating its source was difficult as the whole compartment was burning. Literally, the floor, walls and ceiling were aflame, with waves of fire surging towards me at head-height. Added to this, the instructors threw ladles of oil in our direction; the heat so great that they instantly ignited, creating fire-balls flying through the air towards us. I fought the fire to the best of my ability, acutely aware that I had limited time due to the air that I was guzzling at a rapid rate of knots. But gradually the fires got smaller until they finally extinguished. The room was awash with water, blackened from the smoke, and roasting from the retained heat within the metal walls; but once again, the techniques we were learning had proven effective.

The climax of the fire school training was a simulation of a full-ship fire. Everyone was involved, forming a rotating team of fire fighting units to replace one-another as their air ran out. The gigantic three-storey ovens that we had seen during basic-training were to be our playground, so we mustered on the top-deck in our teams. Initially the fires were small, self-contained affairs; easily extinguished. But as we progressed, one fire led into the next until we were continually fighting fires. We utilised all of the techniques we had learnt, including hatch entries; only this time, as we won the battle against one fire, the instructors would relight it, or start fires behind us in areas that we had already passed through. The exercise continued for hours, as it would in reality, and we swapped teams regularly as our air ran-out. We would return to the top-deck, grab some much needed fluids, change air-tanks for a full cylinder, then prepare to go back into the fray as other teams ran low on air. And so it continued; each of us getting progressively more and more exhausted...

Finally the exercise was terminated; we had won. I had learnt valuable techniques that, hopefully, I would never have to use; and experienced the most frightening of situations. In later years, whilst working in Belize as a diving instructor, I was shipwrecked after the dive-boat caught fire and sank. I am sure that the training I had here was instrumental in ensuring that we stayed calm and survived this ordeal.

My Sea Safety Course was now complete. For days afterwards, I walked about with soot coming out of my ears and nose, and black eye-liner around my eyes where the smoke had penetrated. Despite all of the protective equipment, the smoke had managed to get inside everything, entering my lungs, noses, ears and eyes!

I was now ready to start my year at sea, and my learning-curve was about to increase rapidly. But I was buoyed by the confidence gained from my pre-deployment training, and excited at what I was about to encounter afloat...

CHAPTER 9

HMS Scylla

HMS Scylla (pronounced Cilla) was a broad-beam Leander Class frigate. She was built at Devonport Dockyard at a cost of £6.6 million, and commissioned into the Royal Navy in 1970, being given the pennant number F71. She was named after a monster from Greek mythology that lived in a cave near the Straits of Messina between Sicily and Italy, capturing passing sailors. Her sister, Charybdis, also became the name of a Leander Class frigate. HMS Scylla was 113.4m long, 13.1m wide, and weighed 2500 tonnes. She was home to 260 men, and could travel at a speed of up to 27 knots powered by her steam-turbine engines.

There were many Leander Class frigates, and although essentially built to the same design, each behaved differently and had its own character depending on how it was fitted-out. Some had 4.5 inch guns mounted on the front, or Ikara missile systems, which tended to weigh-down the bows. Others had towed-array sonar which tended to twist the keel causing the ship to corkscrew through the sea (very uncomfortable if you suffered from sea-sickness). Scylla was one of the faster, more stable ships, being fitted with exocet and seawolf missile systems. Despite being a relatively old ship, she had been re-fitted in the mid 80's with some of the most modern weapon, radar, and sonar systems of the time.

In the 1970's, Scylla was involved in The Cod Wars against Iceland. This was a series of confrontations over the fishing rights of British and Icelandic fleets, resulting in a 200 mile exclusion zone around Iceland's shore. In the 1980's, Scylla was deployed to the Caribbean as the West Indies Guard Ship, and then to the Persian Gulf as part of the Armilla Patrol. However, she missed being deployed to the Falklands Conflict due to being in refit at the time.

I was lucky enough to join HMS Scylla on July 6th 1988. I arrived at Portsmouth Dockyard in my little metro car, loaded to the gunwales with kit. Portsmouth was Scylla's home port, the base that I would return to following every period at sea. The MOD police officer on the dockyard gate directed me through the maze of berths, dry-docks, and jetties to where Scylla was moored. I parked the car and strode up the gangway, part-way along the ship's length; keen and excited, if a little nervous. Before stepping aboard, I came to attention, faced aft, and saluted the flag (even though I could not see it from this position). I had been told that this was the procedure before boarding any Royal Navy ship. The Officer of the Day said,

"You must be new then? You don't need to salute unless you're in uniform."

"Of course," I said, feeling rather embarrassed. Not the best first-impression to give!

After showing my ID and draft orders, the Leading Hand of my messdeck was summoned to collect me. I was escorted into the belly of the ship, and taken to 3Ea messdeck, home of "The Greenies" (as all weapon engineers were called). This was to be my home for the next year.

Two-Deck was the "main-drag," the major passageway that ran the full length of the ship. Off of it were all of the ship's departments, showers, toilets (heads), galley, and control room. It was littered with pipework and hatches, damage-control and fire-fighting equipment. It was a hive of activity, constantly bustling at all times of day and night. Beneath it were the various messdecks and living quarters of each department; plus the engine rooms, and the weapons magazines. Above it was the upper-deck, hanger, and flight-deck; and above this were the bridge, the mast, and upper-deck magazines. For the first week, the ship's layout remained a mystery to me; as small as it was, when everything looked the same, it became a confusing labyrinth of interconnecting compartments and ladders. The low deckheads (ceilings) and hatches were a nightmare; I lost count of the number of times I forgot to duck, hitting my head; or tripped-over pipes or hatch combings. The first couple of days I spent completing a "Joining Chitty." This was a form to be signed-off by the head of each section on the ship, and involved me visiting every compartment, thus helping me to get my bearings as soon as possible.

On descending the ladder into my messdeck, there were two main areas. To my right was the sleeping area. It consisted of blocks of three bunks, one above the other. Each was about 2.5m long with a space the length of my arm between one bed and the one above. This was cordoned-off with a home-made curtain to offer a little privacy. Once inside these bunks, it felt as if you were lying in a coffin, unable to move, turn or stretch-out. It was cosy, or claustrophobic, depending on your inclination. On the opposite wall, across a 1.5m gap, were three small lockers to keep your uniform in (one per bunk); any excess civilian clothing had to be stowed away anywhere you could find a space. Each series of three bunks was known as a "gulch," and in this section there were about 18 bunks. The higher your seniority, the further back your bunk was located as it afforded less noise and fewer disturbances.

To my left was the small living area. It was about 8m in length, tapering to a point at the bow end, and about 4m wide. Along the right (starboard) edge were a series of cushioned seats covering storage boxes. At the rear wider end, were the TV and video player, as well as the beer fridges. And along the left (port) side of the room were 4 more bunks which folded-down into additional seating. Being the newest person, and a "Tiff," I was allocated one of these fold-away bunks! The problem with these beds was that there were watch-keepers in the mess square at all times of day and night, and they would have the TV on while you were trying to sleep. Also, if ever there was a mess party, you had no chance of getting any sleep because if you tried, you would be pelted with beer cans and boots! On a positive note, it did mean that you were the center of everything that happened in the mess; the center of all parties, the center of all meetings, and it ensured you were always up early for work. Not to worry though, it would not be forever; as soon as I got promotion to Leading Hand, I would get a bunk in the "gulches" and someone else would be relegated to the mess square area. As they say, "That's life in a blue suit..."

Life below decks worked on a hierarchy system where the Leading Hand of the messdeck was God, and discipline was enforced with physical punishments. This was a time where corporal punishment at school was still commonplace, and health-and-safety was in its infancy. If anyone answered back to the Leading Hand they were taken into the "gulches" and given a beating; senior rates and officers accepted this as the norm. In a military environment there was no place for "discussing" orders; if you were told to do something, you jumped at it as your life, and those around you, could depend on your prompt action. Living in very confined quarters with your shipmates for months on end often resulted in arguments, but these could not be allowed to fester or grudges to be held. So it was normal for these to be resolved by means of a boxing match arranged away from prying eyes in the hanger. And the one offence that would *never* be tolerated aboard ship was theft! Trust was everything, you needed to trust your mates, and they you; so on the one occasion that a thief was discovered, it was dealt with by means of a suitable punishment (namely a hatch was dropped on their hands) before they were discharged from the navy.

But things change. By today's standards these actions would be unacceptable; even by the time I became a senior rate, these things were being discouraged. But the rot had set in! As a Petty Officer, I was seeing ratings come out of basic-training with no discipline; they would argue and refuse to follow simple orders! It was clear that their problems originated way before joining the navy, when they were at school. The knock-on effect of schools abolishing punishments and slackening discipline procedures was having a drastic effect on people's attitudes in the workplace. Having lived through the harsh, physical regime of discipline I can honestly say that it was a good system; it worked, and it produced the right sort of attitude that you needed to live and fight aboard a warship.

Life aboard HMS Scylla worked on routines. There were routines for when alongside in port, and there were routines for when at sea. There were routines for operating in a cold climate, and routines for working in a tropical environment. There were routines for normal day-to-day conditions, and there were routines for battle or emergency situations. The Royal Navy ran on routines! When in Portsmouth, unless I was duty, I generally worked a 9 to 5 day, and was free to go ashore in the evening. When at sea, I worked a shift system which varied depending on the requirements of the department, and whether I was rostered to be fire party.

Cleanliness in the ship was paramount, so each messdeck was allocated an area that they were responsible for. Our areas were the forward heads and showers, and the canteen flat (the section on Two-Deck directly above our messdeck). In addition to this we had our messdeck itself, plus each of the department offices and equipment. Inspections occurred daily by the Officer of the Day; and overnight, duty personnel would be polishing the decks ensuring a gleaming finish at all times (not dissimilar to Nelson's day). Cleaning was THE main duty we performed on the ship! It took up the majority of our time, both alongside and at sea. But it was not as simple as it sounds. For example, polishing the canteen flat; this was the major part of Two-Deck where everyone passed through. It housed the NAAFI shop, so there were always people buying sweets and goodies, loitering in our area. It also housed one of the coffee dispensers, and so had a constant stream of users at all times of day and night; along with subsequent spillages onto our polished decks! As a consequence, trying to partition-off sections of the floor to lay polish without someone stepping on it, or spilling something on it, was a thankless task. The one good point was that this section also housed the Midshipmen's quarters; trainee officers. They were treated as even lower than "Tiffs," and were onboard to experience *all* aspects of life at sea. So we often conned them into polishing our decks for us; as "good experience" for when they became full officers in the future. The showers and heads were constantly in use, so again, it was difficult to shut them for cleaning; but needs must. At sea, this could be a horrible task. The heads were flushed with sea-water, so they constantly stank! But in rough weather, the water pressure varied as the ship pounded the waves. This often caused a phenomenon known as "Blow-Back!" When this happened, the contents of the toilet exploded violently upwards, all over the walls of the cubical and the floor. And when it happened, it tended to explode in sequence; one toilet followed by the next in line, and so on. God help you if you happened to be on the toilet at the time as there would be no warning until a last minute gurgling sound; then, "BOOM!" A very messy experience; equally messy for those of us who then had to clean it up afterwards!

  Duties aboard Scylla for junior ratings were simple; I would be rostered onto a Fire Party team every few days. This lasted for 24 hours until relieved by the next duty team. I would muster first thing in the morning to be allocated my task within the fire party. This could be "initial-attack" where you fought the fire as a first response with extinguishers, or "fire-fighting-team" where you wore fearnought suits, breathing apparatus, and fought the fire with hoses (as per training at HMS Raleigh). I would then be on standby all day and night in case a fire was reported. I would continue with my normal work during this period, listening for a call-to-action on the PA system; and there would be at least one fire exercise called per day. During the night period I would be employed as part of the cleaning team for our department, but I would also conduct fire-rounds of all weapon engineering departments and equipment once every hour. There was a set route to follow covering every area from the depths of the ship to the top of the mast, and I could not take short-cuts, or omit any of the checks because I was required to initial a fire-rounds form located in each compartment. When not cleaning, we tended to base ourselves in the computer room which was central, and conduct the fire-rounds out of there. This meant that we had very little sleep when on duty; however, we worked in teams of two, so often one person would do two sets of rounds consecutively, allowing the other to catch a quick nap. I became an expert at sleeping anywhere. No matter how noisy it was, whether it was too light, or too rough; I could sleep wherever I happened to be. My personal claim-to-fame was the ability to sleep sitting on a backless stool, slumped forward; my legs wrapped around the legs of the stool to stop me falling off!

When off-duty, out of working hours, we were free to do as we wanted. Alongside, this normally meant going ashore; but at sea, you had access to music, TV and videos in the messdeck living area. TV was a bit hit-and-miss depending on how close to shore you were and what was available locally. It was usually rubbish, so we tended to watch videos more. The mess had its own video collection, but each ship also had a selection of films supplied by the BFBS (British Forces Broadcasting Service). These were collected from their offices prior to a sea deployment, and broadcast over the ship's internal TV system. The problem was that they were limited in number so we watched them again and again and again... On long sea trips, they became so repetitive that you could recite the film word-for-word. On one occasion we saw the film "Beetlejuice" so many times that the ship had a minor mutiny and it was duly dispatched overboard in a ceremonial ditching! On the other hand, films like "Top Gun" became firm favourites and we recited excerpts, and songs from it on a regular basis whilst travelling in the USA in the forthcoming months (usually drunk in a bar somewhere). Whenever Scylla came across another British ship, there was great excitement when we swapped our films with theirs, simply because it relieved the monotony of watching the same things repeatedly!

The crew of Scylla also had other ways of amusing themselves at sea. Apart from the BFBS radio which could be accessed 24 hours a day, volunteers ran an internal radio and TV station. This was a bit like hospital-radio, but with a navy bias; playing music, interspaced with news of forthcoming events, or details of what was on offer at our next port of call. Amateurish it may have been, but it kept us sane on those long weeks at sea.

They say that the army runs on its stomach; well, the Royal Navy can be said to sail on its belly. The biggest morale boost on ship was the food (or "scran" as it was called); everybody's best friends were the cooks (regardless of which department you came from). The food was tremendous. No matter how limited the supplies, there was always a good selection available. The chefs created miracles in their tiny galley area; producing meals to a professional standard despite everything that the sea and weather could throw at them. Apart from the three regular meals of breakfast, lunch, and dinner; they provided snacks at 4 O'clock and midnight every day; and the smell of baking bread was lovely to wake-up to as it permeated throughout the entire ship most mornings.

Food was served and eaten in the dining hall; a series of long communal tables fixed to the floor, with a raised edge on all four sides. The food was supplied on a platter, with indents for the main meal, pudding, and snack. One of the first lessons learnt was that in rough weather, NEVER sit at the end of the table. The platters had a tendency to slide as the ship rolled, throwing their contents over the person at the head of the table. Another lesson learnt very quickly was to eat fast, one handed (the other hand pinning the platter to the table-top). And when your pudding spilled custard all over your main meal of curry, you learnt not to bat-an-eye-lid; simply shovel it all into your mouth. It all ended up in the same place, after all.

Drinking tea and coffee in rough weather was an art learnt quickly too. I soon gained my sea-legs, and was able to walk the length of Two-Deck holding an open-topped mug of fluid without spilling a drop, despite the ship rolling side to side, and dropping like a stone as it battered its way through mountainous seas. Everyone was issued a green, plastic mug at HMS Raleigh; the majority did not make it as far as a ship. But those that did were like gold-dust; they *must* be preserved at all cost. Because of this, nobody ever got to use your mug; it was yours and yours alone. To put people off taking yours, you generally did not wash it; EVER! You might swill it around now and then, but by not washing it, you created a brown crusty layer of grime on the inside, which was enough to put most people off. Yes, it was probably very unhealthy and full of bacteria, but it helped strengthen the immune system (or so we told ourselves). Either way, it worked because I kept my original mug intact for 7 years.

My first actual trip to sea was a few days after I joined HMS Scylla. The plan was to sail up the English Channel for 5 days doing a few exercises and machinery checks. We would also have the honour of hosting a visiting class of school children onboard for a couple of days, experiencing life afloat. Being one of the newer people onboard, I was given the onerous task of escorting them around, showing them life aboard ship; and keeping them out of trouble. Bearing in mind that I had only just joined the ship myself, it was a case of the-blind-leading-the-blind!

As luck would have it, the weather was very rough during this period. The ship was thrown around like a rider on a rodeo horse. The sea battered the ship's hull, making her rear-up the side of huge waves before plummeting down the other side, our stomachs in freefall as we held on for dear life. The school pupils loved it; the excitement and fun, but as for me, I suffered badly from sea-sickness! Before I joined the navy, it had crossed my mind as to whether I would be sea-sick; I had not experienced it before so I did not know what to expect. But from day-one at sea, I had a churning in my stomach, a feeling of queasiness. My head was pounding, and things were looking ominous.

"God, Andy, have you seen yourself? You look green, mate," said one of my colleagues.

I rushed to the nearest mirror to take a look, but they were wrong.

"Nah, I'm more sort of grey than green. Wonder if this is the colour you go when you die? I certainly feel like I'm about to..." I said, feeling the bile rising in my throat.

Then I was sick; great I thought, at least that is out the way now. But that was just the start! Over the next three days, I was constantly sick; a brown paper bin-bag became my constant companion. After a while, there was nothing to be sick with; it became a dry wretch! And that was the worst part, as it strained my chest and belly. I quickly learned to eat; it did not matter what, but being sick was much better when you actually had food in your stomach to throw-up. I also learned to spend as much time as I could on the upper-deck where you could see the horizon. Unfortunately this was a double-edged-sword! Yes, it made me feel better, but I had to take the kids with me. They were running from one side of the flight-deck to the other as the ship rolled; I was convinced I would lose one over the side at some point!

On day-four I awoke as if in another world entirely. I felt fine! There was no sense of sickness, no sore head, no red eyes, and no grey skin. Had I dreamt it all? What was going on; it was still rough, surely I ought to feel sea-sick still? But no, that was it; my body had become accustomed to it. From that day to this, despite spending years at sea in all extremes of weather, I have never had any more sea-sickness. I was cured...

Following this first week at sea, I had weekend leave so I jumped on a train heading to London, to visit my parents. As I alighted at Rayners Lane Station and started walking down the hill towards my house, I could have sworn that the pavement was moving to the rhythm of the sea! To anyone watching, it must have been hilarious as I overcompensated for the perceived movement of the ground, raising my knees high and lurching from side to side as if drunk. I had a soak in the bath shortly after arriving, and when lying in the water, my mind told me that the bath water was swaying side to side; the nauseous feeling returned briefly, but it was merely the continued movement of the fluid in my inner-ear fooling my brain. I soon became accustomed to this phenomenon. Whenever a ship returns from sea, it is amusing to go to the nearest pub and watch as the off-duty sailors lean against the bar drinking their pints of beer, swaying side to side in synch with each other. It affects everyone...

The social life aboard HMS Scylla was very important; it was a bonding process, and our mess was like a family. We went everywhere together, lived together, and socialised together. There was always banter; banter between weapons sections, banter between ship's departments, and banter between different ship's companies; not to mention, banter between the Navy, Army, Marines, and Air-Force. On many levels there existed rivalry and competition, but on the whole, it was good-natured and fun. What it did do was nurture a feeling of belonging; I was a member of 3Ea mess first, then I was a weapons engineer, then I was a member of HMS Scylla's ship's company, and finally I was a member of the Royal Navy. I belonged...

As part of the bonding process, humour was essential. In fact, it was essential to survive life-at-sea full stop, confined in close quarters with 260 other men. Nicknames were very common, but not always politically correct to modern standards. Navy humour could be cruel! Some nicknames were self explanatory and applied to everyone of the same surname. For example "Nobby" Clarke, "Buck" Taylor, "Bungey" Williams; others were a play on someone's name or character, such as Ramsbottom becoming "Sheep's Arse," Adcock becoming "Strap-On," and Badcock becoming "Syph" or "Syphilis." The surname Graves became "Digger" (dig-a-grave), Wood became "Balsa" (as he was not the cleverest person), and some nicknames defied explanation; one lad was called "Striker," but nobody knew why! In my case, I became known as "Professor" due to my academic qualifications; I got-off quite lightly, it could have been so much more offensive, I'm sure.

In Portsmouth, socialising revolved around pub-crawls. Every member was invited (other than duty personnel), and *expected* to attend. The route would start at the first pub outside the dockyard gate, literally a stone's throw away, and would then progress through the center of town until ultimately you staggered into "The Mucky Duck" pub (actually called The White Swan). From here, there were two options; return to ship, or climb into a taxi. Those who chose the latter had no need to tell the driver where to go (usually they were too drunk to do so anyway) as they would whisk you away to "Joanna's" (aka "Jo's," or "Jo Spanners"), a nightclub in Southsea. To say this place was rough would be an understatement! It stank of spilt alcohol; you stuck to the residue left beneath your shoes; and it had a tree growing out of the middle of the dance floor! But it was cheap. It was probably 90% navy personnel, 10% local "ladies," and the bouncers were Royal Marines moonlighting in their spare time. Not the most salubrious of places!

Returning to ship in a drunken state was a normal part of ship's life. So long as you could clamber up the gangway, come to attention, and slur your name and number at the Officer of the Day, you would be allowed onboard. It was amazing to see people suddenly become momentarily sober at the top of the gangway. One even tried to ride a bike up the gangway, doing a somersault as the front wheel hit the first step; the gangway staff in hysterics as he still managed to declare his name and number.

My worst "mishap" when returning drunk onboard occurred whilst trying to climb through a kidney-hatch onto a ladder, to get to my messdeck. The hatch had been used for refuelling earlier in the day, and some spillage had occurred. As I climbed through the hatch, which was the width of my shoulders, and had a deep metal ridge on the underside; I slipped on the fuel spill. My legs shot forwards and up, ramming my shin into the metal lip of the hatch! In my drunken condition, I felt nothing, so I continued to bed, staying dressed as I was. Next morning, I awoke with a thumping head, but my legs felt strange; sticky and wet! On inspecting the damage, I found a gaping hole in my jeans, blood everywhere, and a hole in my leg with the bone exposed, still seeping blood. A few stitches later, and I was fine again, regaling the rest of the mess with stories of my exploits. The scar left behind is what is commonly referred to by navy personnel as "hatch-rash" and is a badge-of-honour worn with pride by all long serving seamen.

Onboard, socialising took the form of messdeck parties. The Royal Navy did not operate a dry-ships policy like some countries did. Instead, you are allowed up to two tins of beer/cider per person per day. Obviously for a party, this was pretty tame, so we tended to accumulate our daily allowance, building-up a stockpile of crates of beer in preparation for the big day. If you got on the good-side of the Canteen Manager ("CanMan," who was a civilian who ran the NAAFI shop on the ship), you could quite easily supplement the alcoholic reserves with additional crates. And by inviting selected guests, usually department officers or senior rates, it was customary that they supply a few extra crates as a thank-you. Another custom that all messdecks enforced was that if you invited a guest into the mess, party or not, they would be given a crate of beer EACH. They were then prevented from leaving until they had finished their allowance. In reality, this was just an excuse to start an unplanned party.

Drinking at sea was left to individual discretion. The rules were there; but rules were there to be broken. On the whole, people were sensible about how much they drank. A warship could be a very dangerous place if you over-indulged. Parties and special occasions aside, most people stuck to the 2-tin-rule, or simply did not drink except for these occasions. But there were always exceptions; a few had definite drink problems!

On Scylla, people generally fell into one of two categories; those who over-indulged, and those who turned to fitness instead. The ship's officers obviously promoted the latter, as did I. Every ship had a physical training instructor (PTI) aboard, and we were no exception. At sea, he would organise daily circuit-training sessions, or running around the upper-deck (avoiding all the obstacles, pipes, hoses, and other hazards that litter the outer passageways). Despite the cramped areas, these gym sessions were great fun, but hard work. Try doing press-ups pushing against the rise and fall of the ship's deck! It is like doing press-ups with someone sat on your back! Not easy... Our PTI was a character. He was a family-friend of The Kray Brothers; London gangsters of the 50's and 60's. I remember him once receiving a letter from either Reggie or Ronnie which he showed around; the writing was like that of a child, but you could tell that our PTI was held in great esteem by the brothers... Clearly someone to keep on the right-side of.

CHAPTER 10

The Sea Journal

Although I was part of the ship's company on HMS Scylla, I was primarily an Artificer Apprentice under-training, and the purpose of my year at sea was to gain practical experience of all aspects of weapon engineering to further my education, and to help me decide which area to specialise in when I returned to HMS Collingwood. To achieve this, I had a strict schedule to follow which placed me on each of the weapons sections for about a month at a time. There were other apprentices onboard, and we worked in rotation, moving from section to section. On special occasions such as live-firings of the weapon systems, or when extra personnel were required for a particular job, we would be amalgamated to form an extra unit.

  Before joining, I had been issued a "Sea Journal," or "Task Book;" a blue clip-file filled with page upon page of tasks to complete, research, or observe whilst working on each section. At first glance, it looked daunting, but I had a year to complete it, and it would provide a means to alleviate the boredom on night-shifts as a watch-keeper. Obviously, the sooner I could complete it, the more spare-time I would have. The added advantage was that if I finished it early, I might get promoted to Leading Hand sooner than expected. A "win, win" situation, so I attacked it with gusto.

HMS Scylla had two missile systems that I worked on. She was fitted with four MM38 Exocet missiles which were mounted in self-contained launch tubes, fitted side-by-side on the bows of the ship. Because they were self-contained units, they were often referred to as, "fire-and-forget" missiles. After initial targeting from the ship's weapon radars, each missile had its own onboard guidance system to home-in on its target. As such, there was very little to do on this section. I helped maintain the integrity of each missile launcher, and ensured all testing and targeting systems were operational; but other than that, they looked after themselves. The Exocet was a French-built missile, 5.21m long, weighing 735kg, designed as an anti-ship weapon. It carried a conventional high-explosive warhead, and was powered by a single-stage rocket motor that took it to a speed of Mach 0.9, skimming the surface of the sea at a height of about 100m. Its range was between 4 and 42 km from the launch platform. Unfortunately, due to the excessive cost of these missiles, I did not have the opportunity to witness a launch of one during the year I was onboard.

The second missile section that I worked on was the Sea Wolf department. Each missile was 1.9m long, weighing 82kg, and was contained in a sealed canister housed in the deep magazine onboard. We carried 30 of these missiles under normal conditions, and when launched, they achieved a speed of Mach 3 before detonating their high-explosive warhead on contact, or in proximity to their target. They were designed to target incoming missiles or aircraft, and were a last line of defence to protect the ship. The missiles were fired from a sextuple GWS25 launcher mounted on the bows just ahead of the Exocet system. This consisted of six tubes arranged in pairs, three deep. Each tube had opening front and rear doors, and the missile was loaded manually (one of my tasks on this section). Once launched, each missile was targeted by a radar system (967/968); the ship's computer calculating speed, range, and direction-to-target, and updating the missile in-flight. However, as a secondary control, the missiles could be operated manually by using CCTV and a joystick. This was great fun, very similar to a computer game, only with deadly consequences. When in Portsmouth Dockyard, to test the system, we often used this CCTV mode to lock-on to vehicles travelling along the M27 motorway. Had the motorists known, I am sure they would have been unimpressed to have seen our radar and launchers following their progress at excessive speed across the horizon. Little did they know that no missiles were actually loaded!

There was a live-firing of the Sea Wolf system during one of the many war exercises that Scylla took part in. For days prior to the launch I had been involved in the testing, simulation, and preparation of the missile system. Because a live-shoot is very expensive, you generally only get to conduct it once a year, so there had to be no mistakes; all eyes would be on us. Each of the launch tubes had to be manually greased, so we selected the smallest engineer, Ralf, to crawl inside and slop the thick gelatinous substance on all surfaces that we could not reach ourselves from either end. Our overalls covered head-to-foot in this grease; we successfully completed the task, and awaited the launch day.

The morning arrived and I dressed in my anti-flash hood and gloves, overalls, and helmet. The weather was predicted to be ideal for the launch, so I helped load the launcher with two missiles; carefully removing them from their protective canisters, inspecting their delicate controls and fins for damage, and when satisfied, sliding them gently into the tubes and connecting their control leads. The term, "using-kid-gloves," seemed very apt; it was a delicate, slow process.

Having withdrawn to a safe location, the missile team waited. Everyone was excited, bubbling with anticipation.

"Hey, Ralf, what's the routine if one of the missiles misfires?" I asked.

"Didn't they tell you? You're the one who's gotta do it...!"

"What? What have I gotta do?"

"Well, when they give the order, you gotta go to the launcher, open the back door, and give the missile a poke with that metal rod over there!"

"Are you taking the piss? What if it goes off, I'll be right behind the rocket motor. I'll be fried!"

"Exactly. Why do ya think the Tiff gets to do that vital job?"

We waited and waited... Eventually I spotted a minute black dot in the sky; it was the target, an unmanned drone aircraft. Moments later, there was a deafening "Woooooosh" sound followed seconds later by another; a salvo of two missiles was on its way. Looking towards the launcher, all I could see was a cloud of white swirling smoke; and emerging from the far side were two vapour trails arcing into the sky towards the dot. The drone was obliterated, but it was an anticlimax; I had expected a loud bang, or a blinding flash, but instead, it simply vanished! Any explosions may have occurred, but my ears were still ringing from the launch, despite wearing protective ear-defenders. The firing had been a success; we were chuffed. But now the real work began! The missiles' jet engines had devastated the upper-deck paintwork behind the launcher. Everything needed to be chipped-off, prepared, and re-painted. Not to mention the fact that the launcher now needed a full overhaul, including re-greasing, in preparation for the next launch (whenever that may be). Hours of graft were about to begin...

The Minor Weapons section on HMS Scylla covered a number of areas within the weapons department. Its main weapons were the two Oerlikon 20mm cannons; one fitted to the rear of the flight-deck, the other fitted on the upper superstructure, starboard side. These were known as "Gambos" and were an anti-aircraft gun which fitted inside a manually operated housing, capable of rotating and elevating freely. The operator would be strapped into the shoulder supports in a standing position; by using their body-weight, they could look through the sights, and direct the weapon at incoming targets, firing in a semi-automatic mode. It was an old system (dating back to before WW2), but it was effective against close-range targets. It was capable of firing belt-fed 20mm by 128mm projectiles at a rate of approximately 900 rounds per minute.

As an apprentice, I followed routine maintenance schedules which, in this case, meant stripping, cleaning, and re-assembling these weapons on a regular basis. This was a heavy, dirty job requiring at least two people simply because of the size of the components. Once done, all exposed areas and the inside of the barrel had to be greased heavily to protect the surfaces from salt-water corrosion which would occur if the guns were left in their mountings at sea. However, prior to any firings, this grease had to be removed in preparation. It became apparent that this was an essential job because an incident on another ship had resulted in a breech explosion where the grease had not been fully removed; it vaporised as the weapon was fired, causing the breech to explode and injure the operator! We had a number of live-shoots during my time on Scylla, so by the time I departed, I had become quite an expert at this procedure.

The Minor Weapons section also maintained the magazines aboard ship; both deep within the belly of the ship, and ready-use ones on the upper-deck. It was responsible for the safe storage of all number of bombs, missiles, and explosives; both those that were used by Scylla's own weapon systems, and those used by the Lynx attack-helicopter (which was run by the Fleet Air Arm; a totally separate branch of the Royal Navy, who used our ships purely as a platform from which to deploy). Apart from checking that all contents were secured safely, we were responsible for all of the fire alarm systems, and fire fighting equipment within these magazines. As part of the planned maintenance routines, I had to physically test each part of the alarm system, ensuring that it operated correctly, and activated the sprinkler system to drench any magazine fires should they happen. Because this became routine, I was always forgetting to give advance warning that I was about to enter the deep magazine to conduct these tests. Due to the nature of the contents, these magazines were always locked, but within them, we housed a contingent of Royal Marines; their purpose to protect access to the compartment. Quite often, I would get halfway down the ladder to find a marine with a 9mm pistol aimed at my head; a cheeky grin on his face. They got used to me doing this, and despite the protocols of gaining advance notice of entry, they knew I was coming as they had CCTV coverage of the outside of the access hatch.

The final weapon system that Scylla carried was a triple-barrelled torpedo launch system called STWS-1. There were two launchers; mounted just forward of the flight-deck on the port and starboard walkways. These were capable of firing either Mk46 or Stingray torpedoes in an anti-ship role. As with the Exocet missile, this was a "fire-and-forget" system, as once launched by compressed-air, each torpedo had its own onboard tracking and targeting equipment. And, as with the Exocet system, apart from regular maintenance, it did not require a lot of work on our part.

In order to protect Scylla from potential missile attacks, we carried a defence system that deployed millions of pieces of aluminium foil into the air, called "chaff." The system was called SRBOC and Seagnat. Incoming missiles often used radar as a targeting device, but to radar, these clouds of foil appeared to be an alternate target. This confused the missile, causing it to either lose contact with the original target, or divert to attack the cloud; either way, the ship survived. Yet again, regular maintenance was conducted on this equipment to maintain its effectiveness. There was one live-firing of the system which I had been especially looking forward to seeing. On the day, I helped to load each of the multiple launch tubes with the canisters containing the chaff; the electronics were tested, and the equipment prepared. As apprentices, we had been given permission to be on the upper-deck to witness the firing. Suitably protected with clothing and equipment, we huddled in anticipation. Having never seen chaff operate before, I assumed there would be a big explosion followed by dense clouds of foil; similar to the images you see of "ticker-tape" parades in America. How wrong I was! Yes, the sound of the launch was loud, but visually, I was very disappointed. The aluminium strips were so fine that from a distance, they were virtually invisible. To radar it may have looked like an impenetrable wall of metal, but to me, it was a major anticlimax. I just had to trust that any incoming missile would find it too tempting a target to turn down...

As well as the weapon systems themselves, the weapon department also included electronic sections that I worked on. These covered the multitude of weapon and navigational radar systems that the ship was fitted with, the sonar detection and countermeasures equipment, the computer mainframe, and the ship's gyro (the Heart-of-the-Ship which was linked into all electronic sections providing stability and location data). The majority of my time on these departments was routine; fault-finding with electronic testing devices, tweaking radar and sonar displays in the control room; and trying to understand the myriad of complex operating manuals and circuit diagrams that was required as part of my Sea Journal.

I did have the opportunity to help fit a satellite communications system called SCOT just prior to our deployment to the USA, where I was used as labour to fit the nuts-and-bolts of the equipment together, while the senior rates with the technical knowledge concentrated on the electronic side of things. But on these sections, manual work was a rarity; the majority of it was technical or academic.

The electronic departments did not fill me with enthusiasm. Yes, they were more technical, requiring academic knowledge and aptitude; and according to my results at HMS Collingwood, I *should* have been better suited to this area of weapon engineering. But to me, they left me feeling uninspired; I much preferred getting my hands dirty, playing with guns and explosives, and the like. From my time aboard HMS Scylla, my future path within the weapons engineering world had been set; I was determined to head into the weapons maintenance side of things, as opposed to the electronic control side. It was what I enjoyed, and what I felt comfortable with.

But before then, I had the small matter of completing my Sea Journal. Aside from the areas already covered, I also had to spend time in the ships armoury (which I loved); and had to learn about other aspects of the ship such as the engine rooms, and seamanship departments. After all, I was being trained to be a sailor first, an engineer second. As such, I also had duties associated with the running of the ship; action-stations, store-ship, and roles assisting the seamen when entering or leaving port. I worked hard, completing the Task-Book in well under the year that I had been given. The quality of the work I produced was such that I was recommended for 7 days early advancement to Leading Hand, which occurred towards the end of my time on Scylla. Job done...

CHAPTER 11

Norway bound

Exercise "Teamwork."

This was the name given to a major training exercise that HMS Scylla was involved in during October 1988. It was scheduled each year, to be conducted in, and around the waters of Norway; and would involve the cooperation of a number of NATO land, sea and air resources from different countries. For the purposes of the simulation, there would be two forces; Blue versus Red (red being the enemy). We would be deployed in the seas around Norway, protecting the fleet of ships that were landing Royal Marines on the mainland to attack enemy forces; and we would be at sea for a number of weeks.

As I sailed out of Portsmouth harbour, I knew this was going to be a hard deployment. The exercise was not due to start for another week, during which time we would need to transit to the area. But during this passage we would not be sat twiddling-our-thumbs; we would be practicing day and night to ensure that we were battle-ready.

As the ship progressed steadily northwards the air got colder, the skies looked more leaden, and the seas got bigger! HMS Scylla was a relatively small ship, and in waves as large as we were encountering, she was thrown around like a rag-doll; pitching and yawing, climbing and falling. But still we prepared. Each of the weapon sections ensured that they were fully functional, ready to spring into action at a moment's notice. All weapons were loaded, as if in a real war. The crews were honed to perfection; practice, practice, practice... Slowly, the ship's company became a single, highly efficient, highly motivated unit; we were determined to be the best, and to show the other NATO forces how efficient we could be. By the time we arrived in Norwegian waters, we were ready; if a little battered from the conditions on the way up.

But the bad weather on the journey to Norway did have one advantage; when not otherwise occupied, we were encouraged to stay in our messdeck for safety while the ship was being thrown around. To us, this seemed to be the perfect excuse for a "rough-weather-party," and so beer was purchased and the party began. Due to the weapon engineers' messdeck being in the bows of the ship, whenever we rode a wave, the deck rose sharply at an angle close to 40 degrees, before plummeting into the trough behind. Everyone was left in a state of free-fall; and so a new drinking game was invented! Each of us would take turns to sit on a freestanding chair in the pointed-end of the living quarters, closest to the bows. As the ship rose, climbing a wave, we would hold-on tight, concentrating on the timing. As she fell sharply away, we would launch ourselves into the air, effectively weightless in free-fall conditions, and try to do as many somersaults as possible before we came crashing down to earth against the metal deck beneath us. The more we drank, the funnier the game seemed; however, the next day, the catalogue of injuries bore witness to the stupidity we had shown! Luckily, we mostly acquired minor bruises and bumps, but had we gained any broken bones, the Royal Navy would have been none too pleased at our self-inflicted traumas.

The rough weather also brought news of more serious problems aboard our American counterparts' ships. Scylla had rendezvoused with other members of the fleet a day earlier, taking up position on the edge of the flotilla heading north. From this location, I had a good view of the other ships, and how they were coping with the still raging storm. An American destroyer was battling its way through very heavy seas, and I could clearly see gigantic waves breaking over its bows, reaching over the top of its mast. Nobody should have been on the upper-deck in those conditions, but it appears one US sailor was working on the bows, suitably tied to the deck with a metal safety-line. The force of the wave was such that it lifted the man, snapping his safety cable, and threw him the entire length of the ship before dumping him in the broiling sea behind! He was never seen again!

As the storm slowly abated, I saw that we had been joined by a US aircraft-carrier. Compared to us, it was massive, dwarfing us into insignificance. I was highly impressed by its appearance; however, this sense of awe was not to last too long. Faced with a window of opportunity as the clouds broke, the Americans decided to launch some of their jet aircraft to support the landings on the Norwegian shores. As I watched, a jet was positioned on the steam-catapult ready for launch. There was a plume of white smoke, followed by a roar as the jet's afterburners engaged, forcing it towards the end of the ship. I had expected it to lift and soar into the sky, but instead it dipped and plopped into the sea ahead of the ship!

"Oh!" I thought. "That shouldn't have happened should it?"

To compound the problem, the US command then ordered a second aircraft to launch shortly afterwards. It too, dived straight into the ocean! Clearly there was a problem with the catapult, but I hate to think how many millions of dollars were wasted establishing this fact. This showed the difference between our navy and that of the Americans; we would test and prepare beforehand to ensure such incidents did not occur, the US fleet try something, it fails, so they try again, before attempting to repair it! A costly way to do business...

As a break from the constant pounding of the seas, HMS Scylla moved into the shelter of the fjords. And it was VERY sheltered. On three sides we were surrounded by cliffs, and beyond them, towering mountain ranges. There was no sign of life, simply dense green pine-forests; and at a point midway up the cliffs there was a distinct line above which the mountains were covered in a thick layer of snow. Yet, at sea-level, we were so protected from the elements that it was comfortable to stand on the upper-deck wearing only shirtsleeves. Alongside us were a number of other ships, including the British amphibious-landing ship, HMS Intrepid, loaded with Royal Marines awaiting the order to assault the shoreline. This was our rallying point; the area that we would prepare for the final push, the final attack on the land forces. We readied our weapons and equipment. Our Lynx helicopter conducted sorties, deploying anti-submarine sensors, and we closed up at Action-Stations.

Action-Stations were where each crew member was deployed when in a battle situation. Some were engaged in fire fighting, others manning the weapons; but my action-station was in the control room, manning the *incident board*. I was dressed in overalls, anti-flash, and carrying my respirator and life jacket. My job was to listen to reports on the radio network regarding damage, fire, and flood to our ship; and to mark them accurately on the incident board so that the Captain had a clear view of what was happening at any location, and could deploy troops, as they were needed, to fight these situations. Although cramped, in a dark, claustrophobic room, sweating in the re-circulated heat, and surrounded by officers shouting over each other in a state of utter chaos; my job was fun and exciting. I had the best, overall view of what was happening on our ship, as well as being able to see and hear the bigger picture; how the battle was progressing. It was a very exciting and adrenaline-pumping job, and my role was vital in ensuring accurate communications throughout the ship.

Over the course of the next day, our ship was constantly attacked and bombed by enemy forces. We received severe (simulated) damage throughout the ship, and the crew fought valiantly to extinguish all fires and control all floods. The gun-crews fought off wave after wave of attacking aircraft, but judging by their condition when the exercise was over; I guess they lost that particular battle! Each returned from the gun-mounts covered head to foot in white powder. It seems the attackers thought it would be funny to bomb our crews with flour-bombs! But they were lucky compared to others. I heard stories that some ships had observers positioned up the masts; the attacking aircraft swooping so low that their afterburners burnt the eyebrows off these men!

Finally the battle was over, but the exercise continued into the last phase. We reverted to Defence-Watches, which involved working alternating shifts of 8 hours. On one such shift, I was on the upper-deck doing my magazine temperature checks in the midst of night. As I looked around, I could just make out the crests of the mountains surrounding us, before the utter blackness of the night sky took over. Above, was a galaxy of twinkling silver stars. But to the rear, something did not feel right!? Everything appeared completely dark, not a star to be seen except for one solitary beacon directly above us. As my brain processed this information, our ship emitted a loud piercing blast on its fog-horn; they had noticed what was behind us moments before me. It was not the blackness of night approaching us; it was a blacked-out aircraft-carrier, over four times our size, bearing down on our ship. Had they seen us? Did they expect us to move out of their way? We may never know. But they made a hasty exit from the fjord once they realised their mistake...!!

For the last part of Exercise Teamwork, Scylla left the safety of the fjords, heading into open water again. It was still rough, but not anywhere near as bad as before, and there was a distinct icy chill to the wind. We steamed north across the Arctic Circle.

Everyone had heard of The-Crossing-of-the-Line-Ceremony when you passed over the equator, but most of us had no idea that there existed a similar thing for crossing the Arctic Circle. So it was with some surprise that I received an invitation to attend a "Blue-Nose-Ceremony" to be held in the hanger. What was it all about? What would happen? I had no idea.

On arrival in the enclosed hanger, I was lined-up with all the other newbie's, the more experienced ship's company watching on. One of the senior rates appeared, dressed as Neptune, trident in hand, followed by his helpers who carried a container of foul-smelling pellets. Neptune proceeded to give a speech welcoming everyone to his realm in the arctic. He then faced each of us, one at a time. As my turn arrived, the helpers held my arms to the side to prevent any struggling, as Neptune painted a blue smudge of colour on my nose. He then held my nostrils together, forcing me to open my mouth, as he placed a dark blue "pellet" on my tongue. As to what it contained, I have no idea; but it was the most revolting smelling, disgusting tasting substance I have ever experienced. It clearly had chilly and curry powder in it judging from the heat generated, but much, much more besides. To loud cheers of encouragement, I was made to swallow the pellet, downing copious amounts of beer to wash away the residue. I had now been initiated into the Order of the Blue Nose, and was later given a certificate to prove it.

Having been at sea for weeks by now, Scylla was running low on fuel; we needed to pop into a garage and top-up. At sea, this is done by means of a RAS (replenishment at sea). We met-up with an RFA (royal fleet auxiliary) ship; a fuel tanker. The process was to steam into the wind side-by-side at a set speed and distance. A line would be passed from us to them, across which a fuel pipe would be hauled, connecting to our intake via an umbilical. Fuel could then be passed whilst on the move. We had done this many times before, but on this occasion we were to do it at night, in choppy conditions!

My role was part of the "tackles" team. When the fuel pipe was in position it would be secured by ropes that would run down the upper-deck walkways. Our team would pull on these ropes creating a tension to keep the hose securely in position. It was similar to playing "Tug-o-war" with a ship! I dressed for the cold in foul-weather gear, and took the strain as the hose was positioned. Fuel started to flow. Stood on the walkway, I had the sea to my right, one meter across a wire railing; and as we steamed ahead, waves sprayed me out of the darkness beyond. The way the hose was configured, it hung in a number of U-shaped drops from the cable between both ships. Suddenly, without warning, the rope that I was hauling on lurched forwards through my hands, wrenched from my grip. My natural instinct was to grip harder to stop it, but there was no way I could compete with the speed and weight it was exerting. Instead, the rope flew through my hands, stripping the skin from my palms, and soaking the open wounds with spilled diesel fuel! At this point, I could feel nothing as my hands were frozen-solid from the icy air; but later, as I thawed-out below decks, the damage and pain became apparent! In our daily briefing by the Captain later that day, we were informed that it was believed to be a whale surfacing between the two ships who had inadvertently hit the drooping hose with its tail before escaping to the depths below. It was a shame that I had been unable to see this due to the darkness, but it was some consolation for the pain that I now found myself in.

As HMS Scylla continued to patrol above the Arctic Circle, a request was made over the ship's intercom; they were looking for a volunteer to train as a "Splash-Target-Pilot." As a weapon engineer, I knew that a splash-target was a device towed behind the ship at a distance creating a large plume of water which could be targeted by aircraft to practice their shooting and bombing runs; there was no "pilot" required, as if you were on it, you would die. It seemed obvious to me; clearly there was a joke being played on someone. Surely nobody was gullible enough to apply for the position? Over the next few days, the offer was improved upon with promises of extra pay, danger-money, and extra leave. Eventually, a junior seaman applied, and was accepted. I was sworn to secrecy, but I wanted to play along with the joke anyway.

This chap was issued with a diver's wetsuit and mask. He was given two table-tennis bats (one red, the other blue) so he could communicate with left and right signals from the splash-target. He was given a fluorescent-yellow bib with a target marked on the back, and issued a pair of flippers so he could move the splash-target from side to side by dipping his feet in the water. Everything was set; he awaited the day of his first sea trial...

The big day arrived, and the seaman was called to the hanger. He got dressed with all of his *special* equipment, and sat astride the splash-target which was laid-out on the hanger floor. He had a practice, signalling left and right with his bats. From his actions, he had no idea it was a wind-up. As he was preoccupied with his "training," the hanger door was slowly raised. Behind it, stood the whole ship's company trying desperately not to giggle. Eventually, the temptation became too great and everyone burst-out in fits of laughter. Shouts of, "Numpty," were heard above the din. It suddenly dawned on the lad that he had been set-up. He grabbed his head and slumped down in a sign of defeat; but later, he saw the funny side, and for the rest of the deployment he was forever known as, "Splash."

Exercise Teamwork finally came to an end and we prepared to sail south, back to Portsmouth. But, no sooner had we set off, than a message was received stating that there was a suspected drug-smuggling ship heading away from Europe towards UK waters. The Coast Guard had chased it, but it was making-off from them; could we chase after them and assist? Too right! We were a good 12 hours away, but at full speed we might be able to help, so off we set.

It was a fast, bumpy ride south at that speed. We passed within sight of the Piper Alpha oil-rig which had exploded a few weeks earlier, and was still ablaze on the horizon. The plan was to use one of our gun-crews to fire across the bows of the drug-smuggler to get it to stop. The gun-crew was ecstatic; this would be the first chance they had to fire at someone in anger. So began the drawing-of-straws to see who would be the lucky two to shoot at them. Once settled, they loaded their gun and prepared for action. Unfortunately, almost within sight of the target ship, we were ordered to back-off; the drug ship would enter Southampton of its own accord! We were SO disappointed. Little did we know that the following month, Scylla would actually be moored alongside this very same ship in France?

As we were virtually back at our home port, we slipped into Portsmouth Dockyard with very little pomp or ceremony. Norway was over. It had been eventful and fun, but now it was back to normal daily routine...

One bit of news that awaited me when we arrived back in Portsmouth was that my parents had moved house whilst I was away! They had sent me a letter (which did not arrive until our return) saying that they had moved to a place called Watton.

"Great," I thought, "Where is Watton anyway?"

It turned out that Watton was in central Norfolk. I had not known my parents were even thinking of moving, let alone moving out of London to the middle of nowhere! Were they trying to tell me something by waiting until I was at sea before moving? Probably not; but now I would need to make my way up to Norfolk for my weekend leave following the Norway deployment...

CHAPTER 12

Standing Naval Force Atlantic

The Standing Naval Force Atlantic, designated STANAVFORLANT (or SNFL for short) was a NATO task-force which was set-up in 1968 to protect sea lanes across the Atlantic. It developed into a reactionary force that could be deployed anywhere in this region when required, and consisted of between 6 and 8 ships from a number of countries which were assigned to the force for a 6 month period (ships from the USA, Canada, Germany, and The Netherlands were permanent members, joined by ships from the UK, France, Norway, Spain, and other areas of Europe on a temporary basis). In practice, the flotilla conducted many training exercises whilst at sea, cooperating with each of the NATO naval commands; and when alongside, it was responsible for developing good relations with each of the country's visited by providing public Open Days to promote its ships and equipment, and by hosting social events for the visiting dignitaries.

In November 1988, HMS Scylla was assigned as a member of SNFL for 6 months. Having left Portsmouth

Dockyard, she set sail to rendezvous with the rest of the fleet in the North Sea where we would conduct some initial training exercises with them. This was our first encounter with the other members of the force, and being very competitive, and very proud of our reputation, we were determined to give a good first-impression of ourselves, as we had done in Norway. We were still sizing each other up; deciding what each ship was capable of, but we were at the peak of our performance during these first tentative encounters.

The training successfully completed, it was decided to have a pre-Christmas celebration before our first foreign visit as a NATO task-force. A "Christmas Sail-Past" was considered the most appropriate course of action; a formal display of seamanship, saluting each vessel as it passed along the line. It would also act as a *welcome* to us upon joining the flotilla. The day dawned overcast and choppy, but the crew was bubbling with anticipation. Scylla had been "dressed-overall," meaning that small pennant-flags had been hung from the bows, to the top of the mast, and back down to the stern, as a form of decoration. All flags were flying proudly; and messages of Christmas goodwill had been positioned around the ship for everyone to see. Everybody not involved in sailing the ship was given leave to stand on the upper-deck to witness the spectacle about to unfold. We had been ordered to be on best behaviour; to cheer and shout festive messages. However, the other members of the fleet had not been given such instructions and they had other ideas! As the sail-past began, we saw a battle erupt between the passing ship and each of the ships that it overtook. The crews fired water-cannons at each other, streamers and ticker-tape flew through the air, and attempts were made to destroy each ship's decoration efforts. Clearly a challenge had been set; we needed to act fast in order to defend our honour. Our officers relayed a message that we could "fight back," within reason; and so we did...

As each ship passed us, we launched our attack, unleashing high-pressure fire hoses, throwing potatoes at their crews, and detonating smoke canisters. The other ships responded by upping their attacks, pelting us with various types of vegetables; in one case, even throwing FULL tins of food at us! Clouds of flour and paint-powder were fired at them; their response being to do the same in return. Our once pristine ships were now swathed in water, covered in congealed flour and paint; and our decorations ruined! But everybody regarded this as a much more suitable "lower-deck-welcome" to the fleet, and everyone (even the command) was happy.

And so, it was on this positive note that the SNFL fleet sailed for Brest in France. This was to be our first foreign visit, and on the run-up to Christmas, we were all looking forward to it.

Whenever entering or leaving port, my duty was to operate the forward communications. Standing on the bows of the ship, ahead of the exocet launchers, I facilitated communications from the bridge to the seamen who moored the ship. It meant that I had the best view as we arrived in a new port, or left an old one.

Brest was situated in Brittany, northwest France, and in WW2 it was home to a Nazi submarine base. As HMS Scylla approached on a dank, drab morning in December 1988, I could clearly see these concrete monstrosities lining the far side of the harbour; a heavy bomb-proof slab overhanging their entrances, each pen gated and closed to the world. We moored at the far end of a sweeping arc of a jetty, which led directly in front of these cavernous submarine sheds, before heading up a slight incline, through the dockyard gates, and into the town of Brest. We were here for a couple of days, working during normal hours, and free to go ashore in the evenings. Duties were arranged such that each of us would work one day, and get the other day as time-off; my day off being the second day.

Prior to my joining HMS Scylla, certain tabloid newspapers in the UK had nicknamed her, "The Drug Ship" after she had visited Amsterdam and members of the crew had allegedly been caught with drugs! There was NO evidence supporting these allegations, and the truth of the matter was that a certain reporter had engineered the story to please his editor. However, not wanting the story to die-a-death, on our arrival, a few local youths had been stirred into action to cause trouble with members of our crew on the first day of shore-leave. Coincidentally, this same reporter was present and seen to be inciting the locals to fight! We were being provoked into conflict so that the newspaper could re-ignite its front-page story, and damage our reputation. Those involved were quick to spot the ploy, and aside from a few minor skirmishes, all trouble was avoided. The tabloid reporter left very disappointed, with no story to print on this occasion...! But from then on, the whole ship's company became very wary whenever we entered a new port; always on the lookout for reporters trying to entice us into causing trouble.

Whilst in France there were no open-days scheduled, however, we did meet members of the other ships' crews, and visited for a look around their ships. According to mess protocol, when they visited our messdeck, they were duly given a crate of beer *each*. This worked the same when we visited their ships. We soon learnt that a visit to the Canadian ship was the best because their beer was much stronger than anything we could get. Likewise, there were streams of Americans wanting to visit our ship because they were not allowed to drink at sea, and they loved the fact that we could. From our point of view, we were happy with this as it was a cheap round; the Americans were usually paralytic after 2 or 3 cans of beer! But ultimately these inter-ship social events were a chance to build bonds with the other navies, and a chance to swap items of clothing and equipment. Quite often, the friendships we made carried over ashore whenever we were visiting another foreign port.

Whilst alongside, it was deemed a good opportunity to clean all of the electronic sensors and equipment at the top of the mast; and me being the apprentice on the section, had the honour of doing it! The items that needed cleaning were located at the top of the mast, at the end of the yardarms which stuck-out horizontally, about 6m from the mast center. I climbed up the ladder inside the mast, then halfway up, I transferred to an external ladder in order to reach the tiny platform from which the yardarms were situated. At this height, the views of Brest and the other ships were amazing, but on arrival at the platform, I was met by an extraordinary sight. My section Petty Officer and Leading Hand were stood side by side, their backs against the mast structure, with a look of utter terror on each of their faces. The mast was swaying gently at this height, which was fine by me, but the other two obviously suffered from vertigo.

"HiYa, guys. You both OK?" I asked.

In a shaky voice, the PO said,

"Yeah, we're fine. We'll just stay here as your safety numbers; just in case... You need to connect your harness and shin along the yardarm to give those sensors a bit of a scrub."

"No worries, Boss, I'm on it."

They were speaking in short staccato bursts, trying hard to control their breathing and suppress their fear, which did not inspire confidence in me. Regardless, I donned my safety-harness, connected it to the securing points on the platform, and sat astride the thin tubular yardarm, edging my way out over the void beneath. Cleaning the equipment was easy, so I returned to the platform, noting that the other two had not moved a muscle. It was only later that it occurred to me that they were my safety-numbers; if I fell, I would be dangling 2m beneath the yardarm, over 20m above the deck, until they came to my rescue. In the state they were in, that would be a long time hanging; they would need rescuing before I did!

On the second evening, I got my chance to go ashore with some of my mess. We were aware of the trouble the previous night so were determined to avoid any conflict this time. But on arriving in the town-center, the place was dead; not a person to be seen! We located a couple of bars, having a few drinks in each, but there were no local people around at all. Was it a bank holiday? Or had they all decided to avoid trouble by staying at home? Regardless of this, we set-off exploring the area. We found a burger-van selling what I took to be horse-meat, and then continued our search for the elusive night-life. It was nearly Christmas and everywhere had Christmas trees; either real pine trees covered in decorations, or plastic ones. Another new drinking game was invented... As we roamed the town, on spotting a suitable tree, one of us would run towards it at full speed, leap into the air, and see how high up we could get as we grabbed the branches in a great bear-hug. Anyone who has ever handled a Christmas tree will know that the leaves, or "needles," are aptly named; we returned to the ship cut-to-ribbons along our forearms and faces!!

Brest was the first place I encountered the challenge of obtaining, "Gizzits!" Whether this was purely a Scylla challenge, or whether it was more widespread, I do not know; but it involved obtaining items from a foreign port to display as trophies within the messdeck. Nobody knew who set the targets, nor why, but the whole ship was on the lookout for them; it was extra "brownie-points" if our department could get to them before the other messdecks did. In Brest, our targets were a French sailor's "bobble-hat," and the French Submarine Service's Plaque mounted above the submarine pens. The hat was relatively easy to obtain; drunken French sailors returning to ship within the dockyard often dropped or lost their hats. The plaque was a challenge beyond our capabilities though! It was probably 2m square, and mounted high on a wall, within a high-security naval base. Nobody achieved this target, but the ship was awash with naval bobble-hats by the time we left port after two days.

From the moment Scylla arrived in Brest until the time she docked at our next port (in this case, Portsmouth);

the whole crew were on extra pay known as Foreign-Port-Allowance. This was a subsidy paid to us to account for the extra cost-of-living when visiting a foreign port; and its value varied from country to country. By tradition, you were also paid the same rate at sea upon leaving port until you arrived elsewhere, and were then paid the new rate for that location. During the next 6 months, we were to remain on this allowance almost constantly. It was a nice bonus for us on the build-up to Christmas.

Over Christmas, all ships returned to their home ports, reuniting after the festive period to continue our SNFL deployment across the Atlantic. We returned to Portsmouth about a week before Christmas, and the majority of the crew went on leave immediately; but not me! I was selected to remain onboard as part of a skeleton-crew to cover Christmas-duties. Tiff's often got *selected* for quality tasks such as this!

Working over Christmas involved operating a shift system with the few others remaining onboard, to cover fire-party duties and weapon engineering checks. It was pretty relaxed, working one day on, one day off. And when not working, it was party-time. The 2-tins-of-beer rule was suspended, and everyone tried to make the best of a difficult situation. In 3Ea mess, our mess, there seemed to be a constant party going on. We decorated the ship with a Christmas tree on the bridge roof (as did neighbouring ships), and our living area was decorated by linking ring-pulls from beer cans to make decorative chains; the rule being that whoever added the final ring-pull causing the chain to touch the deck, had to buy the next crate. By the time the rest of the crew returned, our mess was covered ceiling to floor in these looped, hanging chains; I hate to think how much we drank, but I would guess we must have been drunk most of that Christmas period!

On the morning of Christmas Day it was time for a touch of "SpecOps" as we covertly attempted to board the ship next to ours, and claim their Christmas tree as our own. With the tree almost within sight, just at the last moment, one of their crew spotted us, raising the alarm. We made a hasty retreat, hotly pursued by their crew, shouting and jeering. As we got back aboard Scylla, the neighbours began climbing our gangway, only to be beaten back as we directed our fire hoses at them. They thought it was all over, but later that day we made a second attempt, this time armed with fire extinguishers! We grabbed their tree and made-off with them chasing us; but just before we left, we blasted them with foam from our extinguishers. We had won; challenge completed.

Naval tradition dictates that on Christmas Day the ship's officers serve the junior ratings with their dinner. And so it was that I sat down to a full Christmas Dinner with all the trimmings, cooked by a team of two chefs, and served by the three duty junior-officers. In return, we invited the officers for an evening social in our messdeck. They were a bit unsure, especially the on-duty officer, but they all attended and were given the customary crate of beer each! The on-duty officer said he could not drink as he was in-charge of the ship, but customs are customs, and it did not take long for his resolve to falter. Come midnight, he staggered around the ship in a vain attempt to conduct a set of fire-rounds, completely drunk, and with his epaulettes and cap held hostage in our mess, awaiting his return. Needless to say, a good time was had by all...

Once Christmas and New Year was over, the crew returned, and things went back to the usual dockside routines in preparation for our imminent return to SNFL duties. We conducted a major store-ship where the whole crew loaded the ship with everything that we would need for the next 5 months in terms of food and equipment. Human chains were formed, and crates of drink, and sacks of food, thrown from person to person; all under the watchful eye of the "CanMan." It was known that if a crate of beer or soft drink had damage to it, then the four corner tins were written-off as scrap; it is amazing how often a crate was "accidentally" dropped resulting in free drinks for the crew loading it!

Of an evening, I could be found frequenting the bars and clubs of Pompeii (Portsmouth), along with the rest of my mess, in a last vain attempt to socialise before setting sail for the next 5 months. As a result, drunkenness was common most days. It was during this period that I became the owner of a rare accolade?! On one particular night I was out socialising as usual. The night was coming to an end, and we were returning to the ship in dribs and drabs. I had staggered through the dockyard gate, and was making my way towards our berth on the far side of the establishment. Suddenly I had an urgent need to urinate! There were no toilets available so I looked for a suitable wall or passageway to hide in. In my confused state, I was stood near the black metal fencing that separates HMS Victory (Nelson's flagship) from the road leading into the dockyard. It was dark, nobody was around, and I was desperate; so I did what I needed to do. Midway through, two bright headlights slowly approached around the arcing perimeter road, stopping, with me in the center of their beam. It was a patrol of MOD police. They duly arrested me, taking me to their offices, before returning me to the ship with a slap on the wrist. I thought that was the end to it, but no...

Next day, I was summoned before the Captain at a formal disciplinary "Captain's Table."

"Heasman, quick march. Left, right, left, right...HALT. Salute. Stand at ease." The Master-at-Arms (ship's police) commanded me.

"You are charged with urinating on a national monument! How do you plead?" the Captain said. HMS Victory was regarded as a national monument in navy law.

"Guilty, Sir." I replied.

"Do you have anything to add?"

"Yes Sir. I am sorry for what I did, but I was desperate. Oh, and I didn't actually piss on Victory, Sir, it was only on the fence around her."

Although this was a serious charge, and despite this being a formal situation, I could see the Captain and The-Master-at-Arms trying desperately not to laugh. More than once their voices cracked as they suppressed a giggle.

"I have noted your comments, Heasman, but regardless of that, I find the charge proven. I sentence you to 7 days removal of leave entitlement commencing immediately." The Captain decreed.

We were sailing next day for at least a week at sea, so this was purely a *token* punishment. However, aboard ship, being charged for "urinating on a national monument" was regarded as a badge of honour, one that very few people can claim to have got; I had become famous, or infamous, in my little world...

CHAPTER 13

Heading west

At the start of January 1989 we departed from Portsmouth Dockyard, not to return until May. Of course, we would not be at sea the whole time; there would be numerous foreign visits, and lots of adventures to come. And so, mid-channel, we rendezvoused with the rest of our SNFL flotilla and set a course west, into the Atlantic Ocean.

    The initial week was regarded as a work-up week; lots of cleaning to get the ship back to the high standard that it deserved, lots of training exercises to get the crew back in the right frame of mind following the Christmas break, and lots of anticipation of where we were going to visit in the coming months. It was early in the year, so the weather was not particularly good, but the further west we travelled, the calmer and warmer it became. News arrived that our first port of call would be a brief pit-stop at the Azores Islands. We would only be there slightly longer than a day, but it was promised that each of us could have a few hours ashore as a break from the ship's sea routines.

The Azores consists of 9 volcanic islands; an autonomous region of Portugal situated about 1643km west of Lisbon. We were heading for Ponta Delgada on the island of São Miguel. As Scylla slowly crept towards the port through a light sea-mist, I had my first view of the islands. They were clearly volcanic, with lush green vegetation covering a number of volcanic peaks in the distance. They had been described as Europe's answer to Hawaii; and with their shear drop-offs and tropical looking plant-life, I can see why. As we edged closer, the town could be seen spread across the lowlands, surrounding an enclosed harbour with a long protective sea-wall made of concrete. We moored midway along this sea-wall on the inner, enclosed side, along with the rest of the fleet.

On arrival, the ship's divers set to work visually inspecting the hull under the waterline. This was one section of the crew who would not be getting any shore-leave. These divers were always the first deployed at each port, in order to protect against potential threats from hostile forces. It was not until after we had left the Azores that they were told that local fishermen had spotted a number of huge Great White Sharks swimming just outside the harbour wall a few days before! Was it a lucky escape? Or an opportunity missed to interact with these beasts?

That afternoon, some of our mess went ashore. There was not a lot to do, and not a lot of time to do it in as we were under a curfew; but we headed into town to explore. If I had not known better, I could have been in any number of typical Mediterranean towns; low whitewashed buildings, piazzas, and narrow winding cobbled streets. It was very picturesque, but rather sleepy. We found a little tavern for a drink or two, and then moved on to see what else we could find. Suddenly, from behind me, I heard a shout of,

"RUN. Run, they're after us!"

On turning, I saw a few of our mess, and a couple of stokers (marine engineers) running down the hill, struggling to stay upright on the slippery cobbled incline. Chasing them were 4 local men, shouting at them in Portuguese, one waving a large knife or machete! I had no idea why they were running, but I was not going to hang-around waiting to find out, so we joined the others and ran as if our life depended on it (which it may well have done). We split up, going in different directions, eventually regrouping at the ship later that evening, still none the wiser as to what had happened.

Next morning, on entering our mess square, sat pride-of-place at the head of the room was a 1m high, wooden plaque, with the words, "Cafe" and an intricate design hand-painted on it. Where had this come from? It became apparent that somebody had stolen it from a cafe around the corner from where I had been, but they had not just taken it; it had been bolted to the wall, and they had levered it off, complete with a few bricks, and run off with it as a "Gizzit!" Now the chase through the streets made sense; our group had been mistaken as part of the group that had taken it.

As we were due to return to this port on the way back from our deployment, it was considered a conciliatory act for said item to be anonymously returned before we set sail that morning. So this was done with minimal fuss, and we set off for the long slog across the Atlantic...

The next couple of weeks seemed to drag. I was kept busy most days with exercises and mini-wars amongst our NATO colleagues, but out of working hours, there was a lot of spare time to kill. I used this productively, tackling my Task-Book, participating in the daily circuit-training sessions held on the flight-deck, running around the outer walkways, and generally just relaxing. I spent a lot of time sitting in a quiet location, away from the crowds and hubbub, just staring at the horizon, watching the waves, and thinking. I saw weather fronts closing on the ship from miles away; the lines of black clouds sparking into life as forks of lightning shot towards the sea's surface. I saw the most glorious sunsets and sunrises, and galaxies of stars in the night sky. I saw albatrosses gliding effortlessly on the thermals. I saw schools of flying-fish bouncing and gliding from wave-crest to wave-crest. I saw whales breaching, leaping out of the water; and I saw dolphins riding the bow-wave ahead of our ship. The ocean was full of life, full of things to keep you interested, and to help while away the time; you only had to look. Unfortunately too many crew members had no interest and resorted to drinking, or sitting bored in the mess. I found that I needed time away from my shipmates, time to think and consider where I was and what I was doing. And time to look, to see the world around me; to experience the many places I was going to visit. So I made a decision that at each port I docked, I would not just go to the nearest bar and get drunk (I could do that anywhere), but instead, I would make time to see the sights, experience the country; and to try to have a run in each and every country I visited (safety and time permitting). My plan was made...

Our next stop was St Croix in the US Virgin Islands. Scylla was not going to dock, simply anchoring-off the shoreline for respite following our Atlantic crossing. By now the Caribbean sun was beating down on us, so the weapons department had an additional task to complete; all of the upper-deck magazines had thick hemp matting tied to their tops, and we had to soak them in cool water *every* hour to keep the internal temperature at a safe level. We did not want any explosions, did we? It was a good excuse for a bit of sunbathing though, so nobody complained.

Whilst here, the Captain ordered, "Hands-to-Bathe." Every non-duty crew member had the opportunity to relax, and have a swim for a couple of hours. There were cheers and cries of excitement as people leapt from the ship's side into the azure sea below; scrambling back aboard up the cargo nets that were hung from the deck. Had they looked up, they would have noticed the four armed guards stood on the ship's superstructure; "Shark-Watch," they were there to protect us from any potential shark attacks!

Later that day, the crew became even more excited as a stream of Second World War landing-craft came alongside, and we climbed aboard to be taken to a secluded beach for a force "Banyan." This was a navy beach party, and we spent the afternoon soaking in the sea, and reuniting friendships as we played volleyball against the other ships in the flotilla.

But, all too soon, the fun was over and we returned to our respective ships. We pulled up the anchor and continued our voyage, patrolling around the US and British Virgin Islands before heading for the island of Puerto Rico.

Puerto Rico was a much larger Caribbean island, to the east of the Dominican Republic, and we were scheduled to stay here for a week. We moored at "Roosevelt Roads." This would be my first experience of an American navy base, and I had heard that they were like a home-away-from-home to the Americans. It would be our first opportunity to receive mail from home too (although, as it turned out, there was NO mail! The closer we came to the USA, the longer the mail took to reach us!).

As our ship approached the base, from my vantage point on the bows, I could see docks filled with huge US warships, as far as the eye could see. Beyond, laid the base itself. It was open-plan, low-rise and modern. I could have been forgiven for thinking that it was not a base at all, it looked how I would imagine an American town to look; complete with its own accommodation, schools, social centres, bars, and sports facilities. There were the obligatory fast-food outlets; burgers, chicken, pizzas, tacos, anything you could think of. It had its own drive-in cinema, and a couple of baseball fields. It even had its own military air base; the lifeline linking the US personnel back to the mainland. And everywhere that I looked I would see American cars and pick-up trucks, as if plucked from the US, and deposited here in the Caribbean. But the overriding impression that I got from this base was its overwhelming magnitude! It was absolutely huge; I had been told it was 15 miles from the east gate to the west!

We were given rules for our visit: During working hours, if we went into the base we were to wear normal working-uniform with berets. Out of working hours, when not duty, we were free to have shore-leave as if back home. However, it was regarded as "dangerous" for naval personnel to venture off base alone, or in small groups, and so was discouraged. Also, there were a couple of salubrious strip-clubs situated just outside the main gates which were out-of-bounds to us. Of course, as soon as we were told there were areas that we were not permitted to go to, so plans began to be made to find a way of getting there.

A few of us headed onto the base to look for the PX (postal exchange). This was supposed to be similar to a supermarket, but on entering, it was more of a department store, selling everything from snacks to sofas. As I walked down the aisles, it seemed the American personnel stood to one side and stared at me. What had I done wrong? Something seemed amiss! I assumed that they were shocked to see the state of my uniform; faded and patched as it was, but on asking some of our US colleagues, the real reason was that they assumed I was Special-Forces because I wore a beret. Apparently in the US military, *only* Special Forces wear berets! I had now achieved a celebrity status, and who was I to put them right? I played along with the myth. But it would not have surprised me if they had been staring at my uniform because my working-rig was absolutely disgusting. Whether it was the material it was made from, or the fire-retardant coating it was given, within a few weeks at sea it began to rot; losing its colour, and gaining holes on the shirt collar and the saddle area of the trousers. As navy tradition dictates, we repaired our own kit, and were allowed up to two layers of patches before replacing them. The Chinese Laundry onboard ship did not help. The chemicals used seemed to accelerate the rotting process; but there were no other options. Every British ship carried a contingent of civilian Chinese laundry personnel (supposedly from one single family in Hong Kong), and on Scylla they doubled as cobblers and tailors too. Ours also did a nice line in pickled chillies, and occasionally Chinese takeaways.

There were numerous bars and clubs on the base, and we were encouraged to frequent them, mingling with our US counterparts. They were dotted all over the base, usually involving a long walk in the pitch darkness, being buzzed by giant fruit bats. At first I had assumed they were vampire bats after our blood, not that I knew any better; but once I became accustomed to their behaviour I would often see them hanging inverted from tree branches in the dusky twilight. We were invited to various social events arranged by the Americans; one being that year's "Superbowl" final. I had no idea of the rules, but it was entertaining watching the Americans becoming so animated over a mere game of football. I did enjoy their tradition of eating chilli-con-carne throughout the game though. We also noticed that the local personnel ordered beer by the pitcher, sharing it amongst their mates. This looked a good idea, so we followed suit. However the beer was "Bud," which to our taste was watered-down, so we soon slipped into the habit of ordering a pitcher *per person*. You should have seen the faces of the Americans as we downed pitcher after pitcher; you could almost read their minds thinking, "How can they drink so much without collapsing?" Remember though, the US did not drink at sea, whereas we had lots of practice... One evening ended as we walked back to the ships chatting with some Americans. The guy I was talking to seemed, to all intents and purposes, to be of a similar rank and educational level as me (he was in civilian clothing at the time). As we went our separate ways, he invited us for a visit next day.

"Who should we ask for?" I said.

"Oh, just get them to call Lieutenant Commander such and such!"

It turned out this down-to-earth person, equivalent to us, was actually the skipper of the ship! I was stunned. But it did indicate the difference in structure between our two navies.

On another day, Striker, Lemon (Curd), and I decided to try and go off-base to see the "real" Puerto Rico. We had been told it was dangerous, but we went anyway. Outside of the gates, we flagged-down a passing pick-up truck and, through broken English, managed to get a lift to a beach a few miles away. A great day was had, experiencing the tropical lifestyle, swimming, and relaxing under the swaying palm trees. The journey back in the rapidly darkening skies was not so relaxed! I had flashbacks of our Captain's words warning of the dangers we potentially faced. We tried hitch-hiking back to base, but then thought, "What if we get picked-up by someone who kidnaps us, or worse?" But needs must, and it was the only way we were ever going to get back to the main gate. Luckily, the vehicle that stopped was driven by a female civilian member of the base's staff, and she not only took us to the gate, but drove us to the ship's gangway. Relieved, and finally safely onboard, we were to think twice before ignoring advice again...!

As darkness fell, we approached the partially lit car park situated near the US staff living quarters. Before us lay a multitude of vehicles of all types and sizes, but the one thing they had in common was the number plate to the front and rear. Crouched forward, and moving slowly, I crept from the bonnet of one vehicle to the next, pinning myself as flat as possible to the bodywork to avoid detection by the roaming security staff.

"Psst, Striker, to your left, over there; do you see it?" I whispered.

"Yeah, see it."

"Shhh. Patrol to your right. Steady, don't move."

The patrol passed by without spotting us. We crept towards the elusive Florida number plate with the space-shuttle pictured on it, which I had seen moments earlier. Equipped with our flathead screwdrivers, we carefully undid the two retaining screws and removed it; slipping it under a jacket, and exiting as stealthily as we had arrived. Mission accomplished.

In reality, this was just the first of the number plate missions that we were to embark on. The "Gizzit" challenge had been set; gain a Florida number plate for the messdeck. However, each vehicle had different number plates depicting scenes from each of the 50 US states, so getting one seemed pretty tame; surely it would be better to try and get *lots* of different ones? Over the course of the next few nights, the whole ship's company embarked on their covert missions, and as a consequence, hundreds of number plates went missing! The US authorities were perplexed, and arranged extra mobile security patrols purely to counter this threat; but they never caught any of us, and so remained confused, and somewhat angry.

Things came to a point when an unknown seaman from our ship shinned-up a flagpole directly outside the sheriff's office one night, and removed a large brass eagle! The Americans were not impressed; our Captains were summoned, and the return of all stolen items was demanded.

The following day, our flotilla set sail, a day earlier than planned. Had we been deported? We were not sure. But from then on, it was made abundantly clear that the "Gizzit" challenges were to stop- FOR GOOD!!

CHAPTER 14

Mainland USA

During our transit through the politically sensitive waters around Cuba, the SNFL flotilla was invited to participate in exercises with the US fleet, as a show-of-force. We met up with the USS Iowa, and her attendant ships for a sail-past. The USS Iowa was a battleship dating back to 1942. It was absolutely massive, being over 270m long and 33m wide. It was armed with nine 16-inch guns capable of firing shells, each weighing the same as a small car, over a distance of more than 20 miles; not to mention numerous secondary guns and missile systems. Its armour was so thick that at one point an exocet missile had been fired at it, and it *bounced off*; the dent still being visible on the bridge-wing!

On the 20th January, USS Iowa gave a demonstration of her firepower by conducting a "broadside" firing of her 3 main turrets. During this, she set a world record by firing one of her shells 23.4 miles. I witnessed the broadside from our upper-deck, and it was impressive; but our helicopter was filming it from above. The footage was amazing as you saw the ship cruising along, its wake in a straight line behind. The turrets fired, smoke erupted from the barrels, and pressure-waves could be seen on the surface of the sea; the ship seemed to shift sideways through the water, her wake jumping 10m to the left! From all accounts, the entire crew suffered from whiplash injuries as a result of this sharp movement! It certainly put our measly armament into perspective..!

By the start of February '89, Scylla had passed through the Gulf of Mexico, and had arrived at Mobile, Alabama, in the USA. We had arrived in time for the Mardis Gras celebrations, dating back to 1703, and pre-dating its more famous neighbour, New Orleans, about 100 miles to the west. To add to the excitement, ours was the first British ship to visit this port in many a decade.

It had been decreed that all crew members would wear their number 2 uniform for the first couple of days ashore, to coincide with the Mardis Gras parades. To us, this was great; we looked smart, and the locals loved our navy, our accents, and our uniforms. So much so that within the first two days, over 60% of the crew had either lost, swapped, or given-away their caps! The ship placed an emergency request to the Admiralty in the UK to have more flown out to us. I am sure that the merits of the original order were debated long after we departed this city!!

For two nights, I wandered around the downtown streets of Mobile with the rest of my mess, soaking-up the atmosphere, forced shoulder to shoulder with the thronging crowds. It seemed the entire city had turned-out for the parades, the finale of the week-long celebrations. From the far end of the street I heard the beating pulse of the drums approaching, increasing in volume to a deafening crescendo as they passed me by. As with New Orleans, there were waves of brass jazz-bands, each playing a different tune; and between them were massive, highly decorated floats depicting scenes from years gone by. Many were based on the Mystic-Societies-of-Mobile, but this was lost on me; they were simply big, bright, multicoloured, and adorned with people dressed in impressive, sparkly costumes or formal masked-ball attire. Some of the revellers rode horses, whilst others carried flaming torches, adding to the spectacle. As was customary, as each float passed-by, we were pelted with gifts from above; bright plastic necklaces, gold doubloon coins, wrapped sweets, and moon-pies (chocolate-coated biscuits with marshmallow fillings), to name but a few.

It seemed that the parade went on forever, but as it neared the end, I followed the stragglers, along with the whole of Mobile, to a large plaza; and there, the sky erupted into a multitude of exploding colours and noise, as fireworks were detonated to light-up the night sky as a backdrop behind the stunning vista of downtown skyscrapers. The climax of the "Fat-Tuesday" celebrations had begun...

During the daytime in Mobile, we hosted ship open-days, welcoming the friendly people of Alabama aboard as a thank-you for the hospitality they had shown us. And in the evenings, I upheld my promise to run in each port I visited, exploring the residential areas of the city. Away from the modern business area of downtown, Mobile was a very beautiful city. Wide, tree-lined streets opened out into wooded parks and recreation areas. Houses were big, weather-boarded affairs, with wrap-round, spacious verandas, complete with rocking chairs and swing seats; the well manicured lawns enclosed in white picket-fencing. The moist, warm atmosphere of the southern states smothered everything; and the fading sunlight bathed all that it touched in a mellow, ochre tint. It was like stepping into a scene from, "Gone with the Wind."

With the local inhabitants being so amenable, our "adopt-a-sailor" scheme went from strength to strength. Before our arrival, volunteers were asked to sign-up to be shown around the city by some of the residents; they were to "adopt" us for a day or two. It was pure luck who adopted who, but in my case, I was shown the sights by a midwife and her friend. It was a great way of seeing the lesser-known areas that only the locals would be aware of. One member of our crew thought he had drawn the short-straw when he was collected from the ship by a woman in her 80's in a big, expensive looking car! But he had the last laugh; when we arrived back in the UK, she was waiting on the jetty for him. She bought him a car, and in years to come, he left the navy and moved over to Mobile to live a life of luxury at her expense. He must have made quite an impression on her...

All too soon, our time in Mobile was at an end, and we reluctantly set sail around the coast of Florida. There was a distinct dampening of spirits on leaving this city, but we soon cheered-up at the thought of our next stop in Fort Lauderdale. Unfortunately, this was a very short visit; just long enough to have another open-day, and to entertain the high-and-mighty of Florida's elite aboard our ship. I saw enough to know that I would like to return later in the month when I had a period of leave during our next visit in South Carolina.

Heading up the eastern seaboard of the USA, we continued our exercises with the SNFL fleet. It was nearing the midpoint of our deployment, and so a bit of leave was needed. The plan: to dock at the naval base in Charleston, South Carolina for a month, during which time, each half of the ship would have two weeks leave to travel and explore. We began making plans, everyone wanting to go to a different part of the States. Four of us decided that we would like to return to Florida, so I made arrangements to hire a car and head back down south.

On arrival in Charleston, I was rostered to work aboard ship for the first two weeks, with leave during the second two. We were moored in America's 3rd largest naval base and repair dockyard. It had responsibility for providing dock, and dry-dock facilities, to maintain the US Atlantic Fleet. It was also home to both the US and UK ballistic missile submarine fleets. Day-to-day life was similar to that back in Portsmouth; routine never falters. But soon enough our leave period arrived, so we readied our plans, and finalised our arrangements.

Collecting our blue rental Buick car, "Cyst," "Routie," Brian, and I embarked on our road-trip, following Interstate 95 and Highway 1 down the east coast of the USA. I was the only driver, but it was not a chore as the roads were big, wide, and empty; plus we had cruise-control, so I could relax and concentrate on the steering. Unfortunately, this resulted in a minor altercation with the Georgia Police Department!

We had just crossed the border into the state of Georgia, cruising along the 4-lane highway at 70mph on cruise-control, when, from behind a roadside billboard, a patrol car emerged; sirens singing and lights flashing. It was like a scene from a movie. I pulled over and exited the car to find a police officer pulling a gun on me, screaming,

"Stay in the car or I'll shoot," in his southern drawl.

It emerged that my theory that speed limits were the same as in the UK was wrong; I had been speeding, and was duly fined. The fact that we had a Union Jack draped across the boot of the car may also have drawn his attention in an otherwise empty freeway!

At a more sedate speed, we continued our journey south, stopping in motels in Jacksonville Beach, Daytona Beach, and finally Orlando. Our trip coincided with the American college students' Spring Break, and unbeknown to us, they flocked to the beaches of Florida to celebrate. As we cruised along the sandy beach in Daytona, our flag on the boot drew many an admiring look from the merrymakers. We mingled with the crowds as MTV broadcast live from the beach parties; and watched awestruck as a world renowned girl-group (whose name eludes me) filmed part of their next music video.

Ultimately we reached our goal; the realm of Disney. We spent a number of days acting like big kids, running around Disneyworld, Epcot, and SeaWorld. Minnie Mouse blew kisses to us, we rode the Runaway Train, and we entered the Magical Kingdom. We had a pint in the British pub in the British Zone at Epcot, and we were splashed by the killer whales at SeaWorld. We ventured out to a zoo to see alligators leaping 2m clear of the water to snatch a dead chicken from the mouth of their handler, and we took time to explore the nightlife that Orlando had to offer its tourist visitors.

All too soon, our two weeks of holiday were nearing their end, the ship was under sailing-orders, and we made our return journey back to Charleston. I had had a truly magical time; memories were made that will stick with me forever. But now it was time to return to the real world...

Within hours of returning the car, we were slowly bidding farewell to America, departing Charleston in the company of the rest of SNFL, and heading north for pastures new.

As HMS Scylla progressed steadily northwards into the cold climate of the Iceberg Zone, the tropical warmth we had coveted slipped into distant memory. The dangers we were exposed to were brought into perspective when in March, we stopped mid-ocean to lay a wreath at the last known location of the RMS Titanic; resting peacefully nearly 2.4 miles beneath us. From now on, our radars were on the lookout for "bergs," and we prepared to chip ice from the upper-deck to prevent the added weight tipping us over!

Ahead of us lay a visit to Canada, and in the intervening sea passage, a request was made for volunteers to go ashore to help the "Mounties" hunt polar bears. Was this another joke like the splash-target-pilot incident? I thought so. But it did not stop a number of the crew from putting themselves forward; enticed by the prospect of extra pay and the opportunity to work with the renowned Canadian Mounted Police. Over the next few days, these volunteers were trained. They had shooting practice, firing at rubbish bags jettisoned from the flight-deck. They were issued arctic clothing, and locked in the deep-freezers to become acclimatised. They were given briefings of how to enter the Chinook helicopter when it landed on the flight-deck to collect them (even though the Chinook was probably 3 times bigger than our flight-deck!), and how to exit by abseiling down a rope from its belly. Despite all of this, none of them realised they were being set-up.

A pipe was made, saying that all volunteers should report to the hanger immediately; the mission had been brought forward and the Chinook was inbound! In a frenzy, they mustered, donned their arctic jackets and white ski-masks, readied their rifles, and prepared themselves. They were lined-up as the Captain congratulated each of them; shaking each individual's hand. They waited... Slowly, the hanger door was raised, and there stood the entire ship's company to greet them. It dawned on them what had happened; some laughing at their stupidity, others crying at the loss of potential pay. But above it all, the raucous laughter of the rest of us could be heard.

"Not again...!" they cried.

CHAPTER 15

The Return Leg

By April '89 all thoughts had turned to our impending return to Portsmouth. The SNFL deployment had been a success, and great fun; but the best adventures were over, and everyone wanted to get home. However, there were still three more visits left; not to mention a long and arduous return crossing of the Atlantic.

On entering the modern city of Halifax in Nova Scotia, Canada, I knew that this was going to be a cold few days alongside. Reports that outside of the city-limits, roads were blocked with over 2m of snow did little to enthuse me (even though inside the city it was virtually snow-free); this was like nothing I had experienced so far.

The main purpose of this visit, as with other locations, was to put-on a show for the local dignitaries, and to hold another open-day. However, certain factions ashore had decided to protest against our arrival, believing our ship was carrying nuclear weapons. The main protests consisted of CND banners and large crowds, held outside the main dockyard gates; but previously, similar protests had resulted in small groups of activists getting aboard the ships, creating chaos. Our command was determined that this should not happen to us, and so additional security was organised. We were armed with pickaxe-handles and cable-ties, and advised to *invite* the activists into the hanger area before detaining them or using the weapons. That way, any prying eyes, or cameras, would be oblivious to our actions! As it turned out, no attempt to board us was made, and all protesters were contained outside the port. The open-day could go ahead as planned...

Halifax was a city of contrasts. On one hand, the downtown area was clean, modern, and every office-block seemed to have been crafted out of pure glass. On the other hand, there were areas that looked like they had been transported back to the 1800's with white shutter-board buildings, wooden lighthouses, and pastel-coloured warehouses reminiscent of the former whaling industry on which the city was founded. Sat atop Citadel Hill, to the rear of downtown was the star-shaped Fort George, the fourth fort to be built at this site, dating back to 1856. Constructed to defend the city and the navy dockyard from attack, it originally housed rank upon rank of cannons that looked out over the domed tower of the Halifax Town Clock (built in 1803), protecting the eastern slope of the hill and the city beneath it.

In an attempt to sample some Canadian culture, some of us decided to watch Canada's national sport, Ice Hockey. I had never seen a live game before (only on TV) so I was excited as I entered the Halifax Metro Center to watch the Halifax Citadels play a league game. The noise was tremendous following every "play," when music was broadcast and the crowd cheered wildly. Whenever the referees made a debatable decision, the crowd surged towards the protective perspex hoardings surrounding the ice-rink, and pummelled on them with such force that I thought they would shatter under the battering; it was a very supporter-proactive sport. And when one player used their stick to hook an opponent across the throat, both teams, plus all the reserves, congregated on the ice, gloves, sticks and helmets flying through the air, as they proceeded to have a mass brawl; fists flying everywhere! Unlike UK soccer, nobody was booked; it was accepted as part of the game...

After a highly entertaining, and rather exhausting match, we were invited to go for a few drinks with some fellow supporters. As we had suspected, Halifax proved to be a very hospitable place; and as the name "Nova Scotia" suggests, very similar to Scotland (except with North American accents).

Canada had proven to be a surprisingly good visit, but all too soon the SNFL flotilla had to set its course to the east, sailing across the Atlantic on the final leg of the deployment. The journey itself was long and uneventful, with a brief return visit to The Azores Islands; Yes, they did actually let us back in after the antics of our outbound visit!

On the First of May '89 I was once again summoned in front of our Captain! Only this time it was NOT to receive punishment, it was to be promoted to Leading Hand. My Sea Journal was complete, fully signed-off, and of such quality that I was to be promoted a week early.

On returning to the messdeck, there were many pats-on-the-back and congratulations from the others. There was also quite a bit of *banter* about how Tiffs get accelerated promotion; but it was all in good humour. I was upgraded to a new bunk in the "gulches," meaning someone else had the opportunity to experience sleeping in the mess square; and arrangements were made for a celebratory party that evening. But, life goes on, and we were still at sea. We had one more visit to conduct before our return home; and my draft orders had just been received, meaning I would shortly be leaving HMS Scylla for good! A sad thought...

Our final visit as part of the SNFL fleet was to Lisbon, in Portugal. The flotilla moored beneath the "Ponte 25 de Abril" suspension bridge; at the time, the largest suspension bridge in Europe. To one side stood the impressive Moorish Castle of São Jorge, complete with castellated curtain-walls and square turrets; to the other, the Belem Tower and the Padrão dos Descobrimentos (Monument of the Discoveries). These became the main landmarks on my daily runs up-and-down the waterfront of Lisbon, in the warm spring sunshine.

During our time-off, we decided to do the tourist thing, and jumped on a train to the resorts of Cascais and Estoril, a few miles up the coast. These offered white sandy beaches, friendly bars and cafes on the promenade, and a chance to top-up the tan and relax in the sun before our return to dreary Portsmouth. We were enjoying ourselves so much that we decided to give the return train-trip a miss, and walk back along the coast-road instead! Whether it was too much sun, or over exuberance, but somebody underestimated the distance we needed to cover! At first, the walk was fun; following the road that hugged the cliff-tops, affording dramatic views of the rocks and sea beneath. But after a few hours of walking, and still no sign of the huge city, I began to think we must have taken a wrong turn; but how could we, we were following the coast? We just had to continue and trust to luck!

Eventually, exhausted and dehydrated, we all staggered back up the gangway, and flopped into our bunks; we were back, just in time to get ready to sail again.

Once back at sea, we conducted some final exercises with the flotilla as we transited The Bay of Biscay in good conditions, then said our final farewells as we departed up the English Channel for Portsmouth. We had a thorough clean of the ship, internally and externally, so that she was in pristine condition for our families to visit on our return; and we prepared for the ceremonial arrival in our home port.

The Captain decided to conduct a Procedure-Alpha return to Portsmouth. As we rounded the Outer-Spit-Buoy, the crew of Scylla (resplendent in their best uniforms and newly-acquired caps), stood to attention, equally spaced around the upper-deck of the ship. I could see the crowds waiting on the dockyard walls, waving and cheering our return. No sooner had the gangway been positioned, than the crew poured ashore to meet family and friends; inviting them back aboard for a brief tour before heading home on some well-earned leave.

My parents were waiting to greet me too. The only slight difference to everyone else was that I was leaving the ship *for good*. I removed my kit, loaded the car; and following a few good-byes, headed-off for some RnR before commencing my Leading Hand Leadership Course at HMS Raleigh.

As to the fate of HMS Scylla: Well, she remained in service until the cut-backs during the "Options-for-Change" policy in 1993. At this point, she was decommissioned and left to rot in the dockyard. However, this was not the end of her story. She was sold, and cleaned-up and finally sunk in a dramatic explosion in 2004, to become an artificial reef and a popular dive-site just outside Plymouth Harbour.

She sits in 25m of water, and over the years, has become encrusted with soft corals, and is home to a wide variety of sea life and fish species. As a diving instructor of about 2000 dives, HMS Scylla has found her way onto my "Bucket-List" of dives to complete, so watch this space...

It is fitting that such a much loved ship should continue to have a valued role (albeit a different role to that originally envisaged), and not to be relegated to the scrap-heaps of some distant shore to be broken-up, or left to decay, as so many other ships have been condemned to before her.

CHAPTER 16

HMS Collingwood – Application School

Before returning to Collingwood to continue my apprenticeship, I was posted to HMS Raleigh for two weeks to complete my Leading Hands Leadership Course (LHLC). The course took newly-appointed Leading Hands from all branches of the Royal Navy, and gave them a little basic leadership training. To be honest, it was not very different to my initial training; lots of fitness, lots of assault courses, and lots of problem-solving exercises; all with an emphasis on leadership-and-control. I completed the assault course and squad runs, but this time, to make it harder, we would carry a lead-filled telegraph pole between us; one of our number having been appointed leader for the exercise. I completed the same trek around Bodmin Moor as I had done in basic-training, but this time in reverse, and in a time of 12 hours instead of two days; leaders having been selected to take charge of different aspects of the preparation and execution. But the major disappointment with this course was that it did not give any input as to the day-to-day duties of a Leading

Hand. I guess that would be left to learning from experience once employed in a specific role in the fleet.

The course complete and another box ticked, I moved on to the final part of my apprenticeship training back in Fareham, Hampshire.

I am sure every Artificer returning to HMS Collingwood felt the same; a mixture of happiness at being back with friends that they had originally joined-up with, dread of the technical knowledge they would have to acquire, and disappointment at being confined to a shore-base after having spent the last year afloat. To me, as I walked through those oh-so-familiar gates, I had an overwhelming feeling of being back home; a warm feeling of familiarity. Nothing much had changed in the intervening year; everything looked just as I had left it. The only difference was me; I was now a Leading Hand, I had experienced life at sea, and travelled the world. I was confident, but I had forgotten that I was still under-training, with an apprenticeship to complete!

I had chosen to specialise in the weapon-systems and ordnance side of weapon engineering, and as such, I had been allocated the "Weapon-Data-and-Ordnance" (WDO) program of courses whilst at Application School. Others had chosen to follow the radar and sonar path, and so would follow a different route to myself. However, application training worked by completing a series of individual modules, some of which overlapped with the other program, so we would often bump into one-another to compare notes. The big difference between our previous training in Technical School, and that which we now faced, was that previously we were acquiring the foundation of technical and academic knowledge that we needed for the apprenticeship; now we would be applying this to actual weapon systems and equipment, as we would do on ship. This was a much more practical course; less classroom, more hands-on on simulated, or actual weapon systems. Over the next 14 months, I would be employed on mock-ups of 4.5-inch gun turrets, loading them by hand; or missile system simulators, operating them, or changing components within them. I learnt the complexities of planned-maintenance-schedules, and got to study detailed system manuals. It was a sharp learning-curve, but thoroughly enjoyable because I could see how it would benefit me on my next sea draft.

Life at Collingwood was much more relaxed than my previous visit. I was treated as a Leading Hand, given respect for having sea experience, and was no longer required to march everywhere, or wear gaiters. The new Tiffs and WEMs looked up to us. I still had to do rostered duties on the base Fire Party and at the Main Gate, but now, I was in-charge of the people doing these duties; I told them what to do, and was responsible for their training.

But, although I worked hard, I also played hard. I was very much into my running by now, so I took every opportunity to further my training, improve my fitness, and compete in local road-races at weekends. I saw a notice at the gym looking for people interested in starting boxing training. I had never done this before, which was ideal as it was described as, "novice boxing," so I signed-up immediately. I did have one proviso; I wanted to do the training for the fitness benefits, but I had no intention of doing any competitions. The PTI's said this would be fine, so all was set...

I embarked on a three-times-a-day training program. I was up before breakfast for a squad run around the base. Lunchtime was spent doing weight training or circuits in the gym, followed each evening by more circuit-training and actual boxing training; sparing, punch-bags, and speed-balls. It was extremely intense, but I enjoyed it. As all boxing is based around weight categories, I was weighed before and after each session. I was surprised to find that in a one hour training period, I could easily lose 10 pounds in sweat! Of course, this was instantly put back-on in the evening as we all rehydrated in the bar!!

Towards the end of the season, the Chief PTI came up to me and said,

"Oh, by the way, I've put you down for the light-heavy fights in the Collingwood Boxing Championships!"

"What? I was only meant to be doing the training. I don't want to do a competition." I replied.

"Well, we're short of people in that category; we need 4 to make up the numbers," he said. "Besides, it's only a demonstration bout or two; you won't really be fighting as such."

My fate was sealed; I could not really pull out now.

The first night of the competition arrived. I was in the changing rooms getting ready. The noise of the crowd was deafening even from here. Two bantamweight boxers were fighting before me, and judging by the noise, it was a right ding-dong battle. Suddenly there was a huge roar as one knocked the other unconscious; the two of them being carried back behind the scenes with blood covering both of their bodies! If I was nervous before, I was petrified now! My name was called, and I was taken into the ring to face my destiny. I tried not to make eye-contact with my opponent, choosing to look at the judges instead. This was a mistake as their pristine white dress-uniforms were spattered in blood droplets from the bout before! The bell was rung, and I stepped forward to face my attacker. After a few sharp jabs, we settled into the attack/defend dance. The punches did not hurt as we were wearing padded head-guards as all amateur boxers were required to do. Unfortunately this was to be my undoing! Without warning, my head flew to the right as a swinging punch was landed from my blind-spot; hidden from view by the head-guard. I span and fell to my knees. By the time I was upright again, the fight was over; I had not even lasted one 3-minute round! But I had gained a black-eye for my troubles. It emerged that my opponent should not have even been fighting as it was "novice" boxing, and he had fought at county-level before joining-up! Just my luck...

The next evening I was due to fight another opponent, this one actually being a *novice*. To my credit, I lasted the full three rounds, only loosing on points. I was duly awarded a lovely gold trophy which took pride-of-place at the bar as I drowned my sorrows, and washed-away the pain, sharing a pint or two with those I had fought. Outside of the ring, we were still mates. That was the end of my boxing career. The training was amazing, the fighting not so. But I enjoyed it, and the skills I learnt were to come in pretty handy in later years whilst working in the police force in Lincolnshire...

In early 1990, I had the opportunity to participate in another fitness-based activity. Each year, HMS Collingwood hosted a Field-Gun Competition where all Royal Navy shore-bases fielded a team to compete against one-another for the Brickwoods Trophy. The competition dated back to the Boar War in 1899 when navy gunners helped to relieve the siege at Ladysmith by transporting their field-guns over difficult terrain. This evolved into a competition between naval commands, to be held annually at The Royal Tournament in London, where the teams had to run, disassemble, reassemble, and transport their guns over a chasm; these were the *professional* teams. The Brickwoods competition was merely a flat 170m run against each other, but still required the 8cwt gun-and-limber to be dragged at high speed, disassembled, reassembled, and fired a number of times. It was renowned for its injuries; people often got run-over, legs and arms broken, and fingers cut-off by the gun breech! But still the competition for the few places to represent your base was fiercely fought for. I was to become one of those hopefuls...

The competition was not until 23rd June 1990, but selection and training began months earlier. As with the boxing, training was conducted three times a day, with the morning session being run in the dark, icy conditions of early spring. This in itself was enough for quite a few to withdraw; the thought of leaving a warm comfy bed too daunting. Due to the dangers, we wore traditional field-gunner's uniform of rugby shirt, brown hessian three-quarter-length trousers, gaiters, and steel-toed boots. The boots made the lengthy training runs and outdoors circuits extremely hard and uncomfortable; blisters being the order of the day. The field-guns were extremely heavy (one wheel alone weighing about 80kg), so weight-training was needed; but not just free weights, we also trained with telegraph poles as our buddies! We would run as teams carrying them above our heads. We would do sit-ups and push-ups with them laid across our chests or backs. They became our constant companions. Although stamina was needed, so was sprinting ability; and so we began doing grid-sprints, explosive runs over short distance at maximum speed. Once we moved onto operating with the guns themselves, we began to appreciate the dangers we were exposed to. One lad slipped during the drag-stage of a run, and the gun thundered over his legs, snapping them like twigs!

In my case, I endured months of this high-level training, loving every minute of it. Then, one cold damp morning, whilst doing the dreaded grid-sprints, I felt, and could virtually *hear* my thigh muscles rip as I fell to the ground in agony...! I had torn the two parts of the quadriceps muscle in my right leg that forms a point above the knee! On crutches, heavily bandaged, and popping pain-killers on a regular basis, my Field-Gun career was over for this year! Watching the competition on the 23rd June was just as painful as the injury itself. I would have loved to compete, but this was a physical impossibility. Even so, I supported the rest of my team as if I was still running; and despite a valiant effort by all concerned, our team was unable to win this year, losing-out to HMS Sultan, the marine engineering base.

As a member of Application School, I was one of the more experienced personnel at Collingwood. As a result, I joined a specialist unit known as Delta-Force. Our purpose: to protect the nearby armament-depot at Gosport from potential terrorist attack. To be fair, most of us did not even know this depot, or Delta-Force existed. After our initial training, we would only operate on a callout basis depending on the current threat level. I began my training, which involved becoming more proficient with rifles and machine-guns than I was already; spending hours firing live rounds on the ranges. Having completed this, I effectively forgot I was part of the force; I was never called for, and I had not even been to the armament-depot to see what I was protecting!

Then, unexpectedly, whilst on weekend leave in Norfolk, I received a phone-call. The threat level had risen to its highest level, and I was required back on base IMMEDIATELY...! There followed a mad panic as I tried to explain my sudden departure, and I shot down the motorway; in two minds as to whether I was allowed to speed under the circumstances.

On arrival, I was met by the rest of our team, arriving in dribs-and-drabs, each equally confused by what was happening. We eventually came to the conclusion that it must be a mobilisation exercise to test our readiness; how wrong we were! Once everyone was there, we were given a briefing. Intelligence had been received that a named IRA terrorist had been seen in Fareham, and that threats had been made against our base specifically. The threat level was at a maximum, and we were shown photos of the suspect. We were immediately issued with sub-machine guns (SMG) with live rounds (in those days, live rounds were virtually never issued!), and reminded of the rules-of-engagement (In simple terms, you could NOT shoot unless shot at first!). Wearing camouflage jackets, we set-off in two-man patrols around the perimeter fence, our only means of contact, a dated radio system that only worked in certain areas; most of the base being a black-spot. We operated a shift system so that we could patrol 24 hours-a-day, but by day-two, we figured the threat had passed, so we relaxed a little; chatting and joking whilst patrolling the fence.

It was a hazy day, and I was patrolling with another Tiff, along the northern perimeter of the base. We were wading through waist-high grass in an open area of wasteland, the mesh-wire fence with its barbed-wire top, glinting in the light about 20m ahead of us. Through the fence, I could see a neatly manicured grass area leading onto a residential road that arced away from us towards town. Through the misty sunlight shining directly into my eyes, I noticed a cyclist coming towards us on this road. At first, I thought nothing of it, but as he got nearer, he cycled off the road, onto the grassy area, taking a direct route towards us. He was in no rush, pedalling slowly but purposefully in our direction. We stopped and looked closer. I turned to my colleague, who looked at me, and both of us read each other's thoughts; could this be our terrorist? It certainly looked like him. The closer he got, the more I was convinced. I tried my radio, but to no avail, I was in a black-spot! Still he came towards us. I could see a sly grin on his face. What was he planning? Would he lob a bomb over the fence? Did he have a gun on him? The adrenalin was pumping now. What should we do?

We both dropped to our knees, aiming our SMG's at him. I knocked my safety-catch off, and prepared to open fire (if I saw a threat first). At the last moment, the cyclist laughed, spun his bike to the right, and returned to the road, pedalling away. I breathed a sigh of relief. He had been that close to getting shot...! We were both shaking with nerves and excitement.

As I reported the incident, I debated the whys-and-wherefores; I came to the conclusion that, yes, it was him. Probably he had been testing our reactions or preparedness; maybe in preparation to attack another time! Had we deterred a genuine terrorist attack? Who knows; but in our minds we had, and we were keen to tell everyone else on base all about our close-call.

By the summer of 1990, my apprenticeship had reached its conclusion. I was now confirmed in the rank of Leading Weapon Engineering Artificer, and had received my first long-service-and-good-conduct-badge (a single gold stripe worn on the left sleeve of my best uniform, beneath the Leading Hand insignia). I had opted for "Ordnance-and-Control" as my final specialisation, which was granted; and I now had the official title of LWEA (OC). On conclusion of the course, I was presented with a BTEC OND and HNC in engineering, as well as City-and-Guilds certificates in electronics, and fitting-and-turning. These were internationally recognised qualifications which, if needed, would serve me well in "civvie-street" at a later date. The time had come to apply for my next draft. As before, I had a limited selection of available ships to choose from. I asked around to find out their itineraries, and then selected what I thought to be the best one for me.

A few weeks later, I received my next draft order. I was to be posted to ARE Helston for 9 or 10 months, before joining the aircraft-carrier, HMS Invincible. At this time, the first Gulf War had just started (August 1990), and HMS Invincible was being deployed to the Eastern Mediterranean as part of the UK task-force. I knew the Petty Officer I was to replace was a family man, and was coming to the end of his posting; the last thing he would want would be to go to war. I, on the other hand, was single, and eager to go. So we arranged to do a swap-draft so that I could join Invincible early for this deployment. Despite all party's being willing, the powers-that-be decided not to allow it; and so I would be posted to ARE Helston initially, before joining Invincible in June 1991 (depending how the war went).

My next question was,
"Where, and what, is ARE Helston?"

I knew Helston (the town) was at the top of The Lizard, in Cornwall, but I had no idea what ARE stood for. It turned-out that it meant "Admiralty Research Establishment," but I was still none-the-wiser as to my role once I got there. Occasionally, a rare and obscure drafting is given that few people know about; this was one of them.

And so it was, that at the start of September 1990, I departed HMS Collingwood (unbeknown to me, for the last time), and drove into deepest, darkest Cornwall in search of ARE Helston...

CHAPTER 17

ARE Helston

Admiralty Research Establishment (ARE) Helston had a grand title, but could not live up to this image, consisting of a team of 4 people based in a spare hanger on a navy airfield! But despite this image problem, the work conducted there was varied and vital. At times secretive, it was a little-known and undervalued unit whose role was essential to the safety of ships and crews involved in the First Gulf War, and to submariners at all times.

ARE Helston was an independent unit based at RNAS Culdrose (Royal Naval Air Station), a few miles outside of Helston in Cornwall. Also known as HMS Seahawk, Culdrose was a sprawling airbase, built in 1947, and situated either side of the A3083 road from Helston to the Lizard Peninsular. It consisted of 3 runways and numerous hangers to the east of this road, and accommodation and admin-blocks to the west. The base was home to 771 squadron (Air-Sea-Rescue) and numerous other Fleet Air Arm squadrons who operated from carriers and ships of the fleet. It was one of the largest helicopter bases in Europe, and also housed all of the associated engineering, and ground-support units needed to run a base of this size.

On arrival, I was allocated my own private room; a big step-up from the shared accommodation I had experienced so far in the navy. I located my unit, who operated from a hanger at the furthest edge of the airbase, way beyond the reach of the longest runway. It consisted of "The Boss," (a Chief Petty Officer of many years service), a Petty Officer (who was the technical-expert), and "Robbie," a fellow Leading Hand, but of the seamanship branch. Although based on Culdrose, our unit was totally independent of it. We did not take part in their duty rosters, or have any connection to them other than somewhere to live, eat, sleep, and operate from. As such, there was a distinct feeling of "them-and-us." It was a pretty lonely place, both because of its secluded location, and because we were treated as *outsiders* by the rest of the base. The consolation was that I was only here for 9 or 10 months, and that I would be working away from the base for the majority of the time.

The role that ARE Helston performed was three-fold. Firstly, as the name suggests, it was responsible for conducting research and trials into weapon-related systems. Secondly, it maintained and operated the ONLY Royal Navy submarine-rescue ROV (remotely operated vehicle); a sort of unmanned, submersible robot tethered to the surface by an umbilical cable. And thirdly, it ran the "mine warfare and torpedo ranges" off the coast of Falmouth. It was clearly going to be a very busy, but varied, and exciting few months...

When you think of a research establishment, you think of big budgets and Hi-Tec facilities and equipment. Our unit was the exact opposite; we operated on a shoestring with no funds allocated specifically for research purposes. Our facilities consisted of a borrowed hanger and a few shelves of spare-parts, salvaged from who-knows-where! Our task during the period I was there was to design, build, and test a precision mine-laying device for use in the mine warfare ranges off Falmouth.

Mines were not the floating pineapples of WW2; they were highly intelligent electronic devices that could detect a ship passing overhead from its noise or pressure signature. They could be programmed to detonate when a specific profile was detected, or to sit silently and wait until a set number of ships had passed before exploding. They were very clever, but they were also very big and weighed at least half a tonne. Therefore, the device we built needed to be sturdy and robust enough to take this weight, as well as the battering it would receive onboard ship. From an operational point-of-view, our team needed to be able to lay such a mine (loaded with electronic sensors) accurately on a specific alignment and bearing, at a specific depth; and have a quick-release mechanism to set it free from the crane that would lower it.

After some trial-and-error, we developed a device that should, in theory, be capable of achieving all of these criteria. The main working motor was salvaged from an electric screwdriver. It was enclosed in a sealed, hardened-steel tube connected to the surface by metal hawsers (for handling) and watertight electrical cables. On the working end of the tube, an underwater camera was mounted, borrowed from the Scorpio ROV that we also operated; and beneath this was a compass and depth gauge liberated from the diver's department. The whole contraption was then connected to the mine itself via a rotating lock that allowed a fast release once positioned, or in the event of an emergency. It looked a very Heath-Robinson affair, but would it stand up to the rigours of life-at-sea?

The only way to know for sure was a sea-trial... From Falmouth Harbour, we boarded an RFA converted-tugboat. Already aboard was a gigantic metal cylinder; the dummy-mine. Our device looked even more flimsy when compared to the bulk of the mine it was to lay! Undeterred, we headed-off to the south of Falmouth, and anchored in the middle of the testing ranges. As is the way with these shallow-draught boats, the moment the anchor was dropped; it bobbed-around like a cork, creating a very unstable platform to launch the mine from. But having connected all the components together, the side-mounted crane took the strain and lifted the colossal mine, attached by our experimental device, into the air. It swung from side-to-side as the swell rocked the boat; clattering against the gunwales with a thunderous clunk of metal on metal! But still our device survived. Relieved, we began lowering it over the side, and it soon disappeared from view beneath the murky brown water. By watching the onboard CCTV monitor, I could see the compass and depth gauge. Once the seabed came into view on the screen, I was able to rotate the mine on its cable to align it with the bearing that had been chosen. Thus far we had achieved the criteria of laying the mine accurately at a known depth and bearing; it all depended on whether the screwdriver motor was man-enough to release the mine safely... I crossed my fingers and pressed the control. Breathing a huge sigh of relief, the mine stayed in position, released safely, and the crane returned its hook aboard ship. Job done. Our device had worked, and achieved all aspects of the brief. All that was needed now were further sea-trials, and a budget to get it manufactured professionally (assuming it passed the Admiralty inspection and was deemed valuable enough to fund).

Imagine a submarine trapped underwater, unable to surface, the crew slowly suffocating as their air runs out! What do you do? Who do you call? If it was a Royal Navy submarine, the first people to call would be us at ARE Helston. Another of our roles was to maintain and operate the navy's ONLY submarine-rescue vehicle named "Scorpio."

SCORPIO stood for "submersible craft for ocean repair, position, inspection and observation." It was an ROV (remotely operated vehicle); 2.75m long, 1.8m high, 1.8m wide and weighing 1400kg. It was effectively an unmanned mini-submarine that could dive to a maximum depth of

914m. It was equipped with two manipulator-arms which could have a variety of cutting or gripping devices fitted to them. Its eyes were the three cameras and six extremely bright halogen lamps fitted to its fluorescent-yellow body; and it had two sonar systems that could locate submerged objects in the murky depths at the bottom of the sea. With a forward speed of 4 knots, it was operated from the surface-control-room (located inside a shipping container), and attached via an umbilical fed from a deck-mounted winch.

Scorpio was housed inside our unit's hanger at Culdrose. It was here that all maintenance work was carried out to ensure it was available to be deployed in an emergency at any time. However, when operational, we worked from a civilian converted-dredger ship that was based in Largs, Scotland. To ensure that we were ready to go at a moment's notice, we trained regularly, flying up to Scotland (on expenses), and practicing the launch, control, and recovery of the ROV in the Firth of Clyde. The main pilot was the Chief, the trouble-shooter was the Petty Officer, and Robbie and I were the deckhands and winch-operators responsible for the launch and recovery operations. We were a close-knit team. Yes, I did get to occasionally fly the ROV, steering the impellors via a joystick, and controlling the cutting arms; but this was a highly skilled job requiring years of practice, so most of the time the responsibility fell to the Chief.

In a live situation, the primary role of our team was to locate the submarine. Once done, we could use the ROV's arms to carry air canisters to it to re-supply the air onboard. We could also inspect the submarine for damage, and repair anything within our capabilities; or assist in the escape of the crew from the escape-hatches. However, the incidents of submarine-rescue are few and far between, so when not training, the Royal Navy hired our team out to oil companies and telecoms companies like BT, so that we could assist with their underwater pipeline inspections. For us, it was added practice at operating the Scorpio, but the advantage was that we got to work aboard civilian ships where money was no object; the living conditions being like luxury compared to what we normally endured in the navy. We also got to work with their modern ROV's which were like "flying-eyes," and with their *manned* mini-submarine. This was a white 20m submarine with a semi-spherical glass dome window to the front, and a smaller one to the top. It too had manipulator-arms, cameras and lights; but because it was manned, it had an open "Moon-Pool" in the center of the cargo area to connect to submarine hatches, or allow divers to enter and exit. If you watch the film, "The Hunt for Red October," you will have a good idea of the shape and capabilities of their mini-sub.

I was lucky enough to be offered a trip in this mini-sub whilst in Scotland. Having clambered aboard through the top hatch, my first impression was how claustrophobically cramped it was inside. I sat next to the moon-pool, from where I could see clearly out the front dome window, and below into the inky blackness. Swaying on the crane before being lowered to the surface of the sea was an experience; but watching the bubbling sea-water slowly rise up the dome window until we were fully submerged was so exciting. As we dropped beneath the waves, I could see fish swimming-by outside, and I could not stop myself from dipping my hand into the icy water in the moon-pool. Even though I know the physics involved, it still amazes me to this day that I could sit beneath the sea with an open door to the ocean next to me, and the mini-sub did not flood...! It was truly amazing.

22nd November 1990.

The Antares was a 15m wooden fishing trawler weighing 34 tons. She had been at sea a number of days fishing in the Firth of Clyde, returning daily to off-load her catch at the port of Largs. On this particular day, the crew of 4 were working hard, deploying their trawl-nets in the Bute Sound, as they had done hundreds, if not thousands, of times before. It was just a normal day. But things were about to change dramatically! Suddenly, the trawler was stopped in its tracks. The ropes disappearing beneath the choppy waters went taught as a massive weight started dragging the nets downwards; the winches screaming in protest. Had they caught a rock on the sea-bed? Two crew members went to investigate on the boat-deck, while a third manned the wheelhouse. Before anyone could react, the Antares began to be pulled backwards; the waves crashing over the stern. Within seconds, the rear of the boat was flooded; she began to list, and then turned-turtle! She was dragged down beneath the surface; her crew never to see the light of day again. It had taken a matter of seconds to disappear!

At the same time, the Trafalgar-class nuclear submarine, HMS Trenchant, was leaving Faslane naval-base, transiting up the deep-water channel in the Firth of Clyde, beginning a "Perishers" course for its trainee officers. Due to the hectic conditions and stressful situation, no-one onboard noticed the tiny blip on the sonar indicating the trawler. Moments later, external scraping noises were heard as something (later identified as the trawler's nets) was pulled the length of the boat. It was another 8 hours before this incident was reported to the authorities!

As soon as the Royal Navy heard of the incident, and realised the Antares was missing, our unit at ARE Helston was scrambled and flown immediately to Largs to assist in the search for the missing trawler. Luckily, the Scorpio and its support equipment were already aboard the dredger awaiting our arrival. We set sail immediately.

At the last known location, we anchored, and deployed Scorpio. It was dark, cold, and choppy, as it had been when the Antares went down. I manned the winch, feeding out the umbilical as Scorpio descended slowly into the depths; its lights visible from the surface, like an alien-craft flying through space. The rest of the team operated the controls from the container unit; the Chief as the pilot, while the other two acted as *eyes* scanning the camera monitors for signs of wreckage. Not knowing exactly where the Antares was located, a systematic search-pattern was established, and sonar activated. It was now a matter of time. We waited...

Relatively quickly, we located the blip on the sonar indicating the trawler. She was sat upright on the sea-bed, her nets floating around her, enveloping her in a protective cloud. Visibility at this depth was not good. Through the cameras, I could only see about 3m ahead, and this view was full of silt from the sea bottom. The next stage was to locate the crew. Again, a search-pattern was established. Over the next few hours, Robbie and I rotated working on the winch, with scanning the monitors. Using the sonar, we located the two crew members who had been on the deck at the time. I had assumed that dead people floated (as depicted on TV), but these two were face-down, spread-eagled on the sandy sea floor. It seems that they were like sponges, absorbing the water, and sinking! As there was a strong bottom current, we did not want to lose these bodies, so using the manipulator-arms, the Chief pinned each one to the sea-bed using heavy metal bars, and attached a transponder so we could locate them easier. Only another two crew members to find...

It seemed likely that these two were inside the boat, but getting close enough would not be easy due to the nets; if Scorpio got tangled in them, she too would become part of the wreck! I helped to fit cutters to her arms, and re-launched Scorpio to try and cut-away some of the netting. As work progressed, we were able to get near to the wheelhouse. It was a wooden structure with small square, wood-framed windows to the front. As I looked through the cameras, the screen focused on the framework of the windows; something was swaying, blurred, behind the glass.

"Chief, did you see that? Something moved across the screen, left to right. Bit blurred though," I said.

Adjusting the focus, and straining my eyes through the silt, I gradually began to get a better view of the moving object. The current momentarily stopped, and the object steadied and came into focus.

"Shit... Bloody hell, it's one of the crew...!"

In front of me, I saw the face of the skipper, bloated and white, his eyes unseeing but open, staring into the abyss! I physically stepped back as the shocking image went out of focus again, stunned by what I had just seen. Having recovered my composure, we resumed the search for number four until it became too dangerous to continue.

All of this had happened within the first day, but our team remained on-site for a week searching for the missing person. On local news, we saw images of the grieving families who had not been told that some of the bodies had been located. The press were everywhere; helicopters flying overhead filming our activities. From our humble position, it seemed that the MOD was milking the situation. Clearly, the Royal Navy had sunk the trawler, so now, as far as the press could see; it was doing its best to recover the crew (even though we had already located them days before!).

Eventually, the bloated, decaying bodies were brought ashore by saturation-divers. We were allowed to return to base; praised for our efforts by the powers-that-be. Had lessons been learnt? Well, following the incident, distinct areas were set-up for fishing, well away from submarine transit zones. Trawlers were banned from welding their winches to the deck, fixing them with quick-release bolts instead. And the trainee captain of the submarine was court-martialled!

This was the closest our unit came to a live "rescue" situation; but years later, in 2000, our Scorpio was deployed to assist in the rescue of a stranded Russian nuclear submarine (K141 – Kursk), trapped in the Barents Sea, at a depth of 110m. Unfortunately, due to the Russians initially refusing help, and not reporting the incident immediately (and quite a bit of political wrangling), our team were unable to rescue them; many Russian sailors dying as a result!

The third role that our unit at ARE Helston performed was the running of the "Mine Warfare and Torpedo Ranges," located south of Falmouth Harbour. Our primary task was to train the Minesweeper crews before they deployed out to Iraq in the First Gulf War.

It had been found that the Iraqi's were using a new type of plastic mine which our minesweepers were having trouble detecting. Special Forces (SAS or SBS) had "acquired" one of these mines which was transported back to the UK amid high security; only to be loaded on the back of a lorry with a tarpaulin thrown over it, and driven through the center of town to be delivered to us! Having fitted it with detection sensors, it was laid in the mine warfare ranges for the minesweepers to calibrate their equipment on before heading to the Gulf.

But this was just one aspect of running the ranges. Robbie and I were constantly involved in one type of trial or another; always at sea, operating from a high-powered, twin-engine, bright orange, 8m RIB (rigid inflatable boat). This was housed in our hanger, but launched from Falmouth, so getting it there involved towing it through the narrow winding streets of the town, and under a couple of very tight, low bridges! As a result, I was required to pass my MT Drivers Permit, for which I was tested at towing and reversing trailers until I was suitable proficient.

Much of the time, Robbie and I were needed to marshal the ranges; keeping unwanted civilian vessels clear of the dangerous areas. Other times we were utilised to set-up bombing targets; or in recovery-work. This meant that once prepared, we had a bit of free-time to use the boat for wave-riding, surfing the crest of a ridge of waves. It certainly improved our boat-handling skills.

But the majority of the time we were busy. When the SAS or trainee pilots needed to practice their parachuting into the ocean, we were there, chasing the parachutists as they gently drifted with the wind; collecting them, and their equipment, as they plopped into the water. When the Harrier pilots wanted to practice their bombing manoeuvres with dummy nuclear bombs, we were there, inflating the giant orange "blob" they used as a target (and rapidly exiting the area in our RIB when they mistakenly targeted our orange boat instead of their orange target; both being the same colour and size!!). However, the bulk of our time on the ranges was spent working on torpedo helicopter-release-mechanism trials.

The Fleet Air Arm was trialling a new type of release device to drop torpedoes into the sea. As we bobbed on the sea's surface in all weathers, we would watch the approaching Lynx or Sea King helicopter drop its dummy load; a small parachute being deployed to reduce its speed on contact with the water. Being a practice torpedo, it would be inert in the sea; designed to float either neutrally, or nose/tail upwards (depending on the requirements of the trial). My job: to locate the torpedo amid the peaks and troughs of the sea. Then to rescue the silk parachute (which I was told was more valuable than the torpedo); and finally to grapple the torpedo in a bear-hug, holding it securely against the side of the RIB as we slowly towed it towards an RFA tugboat that could winch it aboard safely. In itself, this job did not sound too difficult, but imagine the torpedo; 2.6m of cold, slippery, wet metal. It floated out-of-sync with our boat's movements, meaning I had to hang half-in, half-out of the boat, soaked in icy salt-water. As we began to tow it to the tugboat, a bow-wave was created, soaking me even further; and by the time we reached the tug, my hands are so cold that I had no feeling left to connect the torpedo to the lifting equipment. Not so easy after all...!

In addition to recovering these torpedoes, I also had to lay them in the ranges so that a civilian helicopter (run by Castle Air) could use experimental torpedo-recovery-nets to collect them. The idea was that the helicopter would hover over the torpedo, lower its net device entrapping the floating weapon, and then activate a closing switch before lifting it clear of the water. Sounded simple enough in theory...

As I watched from a safe distance, the trapping phase went perfectly, but as the lift began, I could see that the torpedo was not secure, and was slipping, causing the helicopter to go off-balance! The pilot was unable to release it, but at the same time, unable to take it into the air in case it fell and injured someone on shore. There was only one option; WE would have to try and release the torpedo manually! Robbie steered the RIB directly at the hanging net, fighting against the downdraught from the helicopter blades that pushed us away. I was sat in the bows of the boat taking the brunt of the hurricane-force winds that were blasted off the sea's surface, spraying me in a never-ending flood of blinding water. As we got directly beneath the helicopter, I fought against the pressure of the wind from above, and tried to untangle the torpedo as best I could. I could not see much of what I was doing, blinded by the spray. So, at the top of my voice, I screamed to Robbie,

"BACK AWAY. I CAN'T SEE WHAT I'M DOING...!"

He could not hear me over the noise of the helicopter, so I tried to get the message across by sign language. Finally, he understood and attempted to back-off to get a clearer view. Unbeknown to us, the pilot decided at the same moment to try another lift. As he did so, the bows of our RIB started to rise! We were now trapped in the net too! If he continued, it would not just be the torpedo dangling beneath him...! Luckily, with the sudden increase in weight, he realised what was happening, and lowered us back into the sea with an almighty thump!

"ROBBIE, WE'RE TANGLED IN THE NET. I'M GONNA TRY AND GET US FREE," I yelled. But Robbie still could not hear me.

Still blinded, and with no other options available, I leant forward, grabbed anything that felt like rope, and started hacking at it with my sea-knife. Regardless of the expense of this experimental equipment, our only choice was to cut our way out; so that was what I did. We had escaped, at the expense of the net device; but saving the cost of a new helicopter, and without loss of life. It was a good result, in my opinion.

At the beginning of December 1990, I was summoned to The Captain's Table at Culdrose; I was promoted to Acting Petty Officer. A Petty Officer was a non-commissioned officer, equivalent to a sergeant in the other armed forces. All of my reports and training was going well, with favourable recommendations from all of my superiors. This did mean something of a culture-shock though! I changed cabins as I was now a Senior Rate; but it did not mean a bigger room, just one in a different building. The main difference was moving into the Senior Rates Mess at Culdrose. This was a joint mess for Chiefs and Petty Officers, and seemed very *formal* compared to what I had been used to. Meals were eaten in the Dining Hall which was laid-out with tablecloths and serviettes. Food was served by navy stewards (waiters)! It was nothing like I had experienced before; it was a bit of a novelty. Was this how things were going to be aboard ship as a senior rate? I had no idea, but somehow, I doubted it. I had better enjoy the privilege while I could...

Although living quarters differed as a Senior Rate, day-to-day working conditions stayed the same. We were a small unit with defined roles, and that had not changed with rank. So for my remaining couple of months at Helston, things continued as before. The only changes were a couple of two-day courses that I attended at Raleigh and Collingwood prior to my next deployment on HMS Invincible.

After the New Year break, I received a new draft order; the joining of HMS Invincible was confirmed; no change there. But I had an additional posting; I was being sent to HMS Royal Arthur for the whole of February 1991 for a Petty Officers Leadership Course (POLC 2053)...

CHAPTER 18

HMS Royal Arthur

HMS Royal Arthur: The name spread fear in our hearts, its reputation going before it. Was it just a myth, or was it to be dreaded as much as the stories suggested? The Royal Navy was awash with tales of those who had attended Royal Arthur for Leadership Training; tales of the "beastings," of the harsh physical regime, and of the extreme expeditions. But it also told of the camaraderie, the team-spirit; and those that survived regaled you with stories of their exploits, each being more outlandish than the one before. Each of us who passed through the gates of Royal Arthur did so with a mixed sense of foreboding and excitement. It was not for the faint-hearted, nor those who were ill-prepared!

HMS Royal Arthur was a shore establishment located in the remote countryside near Corsham in Wiltshire. Originally located at what is now "Butlins" in Skegness, the name was given to an already existing base in Corsham in 1947. From then, until 1992, it was the Royal Navy's Leadership Training School for junior and senior ratings. It consisted of 36 single-storey, concrete buildings, spread over a site of about a square kilometre. It had its own gym, church, offices, and pool. Accommodation for the staff and trainees was basic to say the least, consisting of long, narrow concrete dormitories with corrugated metal roofs. Surrounding the main base were many winding, narrow country lanes that I would get to know intimately over the coming weeks as I ran around them as part of a squad; and further-afield were the infamous obstacle course and cliff-and-chasm sites!

POLC 2053, my class, consisted of a mixture of Chiefs, Petty Officers, and Leading Hands from all branches of the navy. We began as complete strangers with varying amounts of experience, varying ages, and varying expectations; but all with the same sense of purpose, namely, to get as much out of this course as we could. We were to leave in a few weeks time, a whole lot fitter, and a lot more confident in our own abilities, and physically and mentally prepared for our roles as senior rates in the navy.

Almost from day-one, the fitness training began. Those of us with any sense had been preparing for this in the preceding weeks, running, and training in the gym. Inevitably though, there were a few within the group who were weaker than the rest when it came to fitness. We began with the compulsory fitness-tests to gauge our current standard. These consisted of a mile-and-a-half run in a set time (thankfully, I had spent hours running around the runways and roads of Culdrose), followed by various gym tests; push-ups, squats, sit-ups, burpies etc. We even got to attempt the new incoming fitness-test; the "Bleep Test." Fitness was to be a major part of my time at Royal Arthur; every day I would be running, or working-out in the gym. I would tackle the obstacle course, or assault course; often carrying a telegraph-pole or sandbag with me. And I would be re-tested at regular intervals to see how I was improving, if at all, over my time here. Some of the gym sessions were so intense that members of our squad were physically sick after, or even during the class! For them, the myth of the "beastings" became true.

But, on the whole, the fitness training was not half as bad as I had expected.

The main purpose of our time here was to develop leadership; some had it naturally, others had to learn it. Everything we did had an emphasis on command-and-control. When we had drill sessions, we were nominated to instruct the class, roaring-out orders at the top of our voices. When we went on squad runs, we were nominated to take charge, calling out the pace, or helping those that struggled. Even when off-duty, we had nominated roles, such as Social Secretary, or Class President. Leadership was everywhere...

As with the Leading Hand Leadership Course at HMS Raleigh, there was NOT a lot of formal input on the role of a Petty Officer. However, there was a lot of classroom training. To begin with, it came in the form of an ice-breaker; one, two, or three minute snap-talks on random subjects, with no time to prepare. Subjects as obscure as "The-Inside-of-an-Egg," or "Doctor-Who's Scarf" were not uncommon; the weirder and funnier, the better. The purpose was to put each of us under pressure, and to gain experience of talking in-front of others; a task that we would all need to master as senior rates. These developed over time into preparing and giving 20-minute lectures on subjects of our choosing; and ultimately giving briefings on tasks or expeditions that we were to tackle later in the course.

We also had problem-solving exercises to complete, with a nominated leader controlling the team and giving their plan of how to achieve the objective. Now-a-days, in industry, people pay lots of money for this "team-building" training, but it originated from its military beginnings. I was given tasks such as getting my team and a barrel from point-A to point-B using planks and ropes, without touching the ground! When placed in-charge of a group with a task such as this, I learnt very quickly to think on my feet. I also learnt good styles of communicating; shouting orders did not always work to best effect; sometimes, a gentle approach worked better. These tasks, in particular, were a great help to me in later years, as part of the selection process for the Police Force was to do exactly this. I started with a good advantage over others.

Royal Arthur had two notorious challenges for which records were kept, dating back many years. They had huge, prominently displayed, notice-boards which proudly showed everyone the top-ten best performances. These challenges were the Obstacle Course, and the Cliff-and-Chasm...! Both of which I was to tackle many times during my stay here. Initially, both were taken as a series of obstacles to be overcome individually. Then they were combined one-after-another, and finally you would tackle them as a RACE, trying to defeat the current record. Both were extremely hard work!

The Obstacle Course was an army-style assault course, with high walls to climb, tunnels to wriggle through, nets to traverse, and leopard-crawls to slide across; all connected by lots of running through mud and water. When tackled as a team, with individuals having specific tasks within the group, a fast time could be achieved. Knowing that we could have a shot at the title in our last week, we trained hard, volunteering to practice in our spare time to give us the best chance of success.

The Cliff-and-Chasm, on the other hand, was a challenge specific to Royal Arthur. Nowhere else in the navy would you come across anything similar; it was unique to here. It was also notorious; everyone in the Royal Navy knew of it. The course that it was run over consisted of an undulating area of steep climbs and deep valleys, crumbling sandy slopes, and muddy inclines. It was reportedly built on the waste-piles excavated when they constructed an underground nuclear bunker in the area (not that we knew anything about that). The race started in the camp. The team had to get a concrete-filled barrel, a 2m telegraph-pole, numerous ropes and pulleys, and a wooden hand-cart around the course as fast as possible. Each team member was allocated a specific task; mine being the telegraph-pole-handler as I was the fastest, and could run ahead with it; hence my nickname, "The Whippet!"

As the whistle was blown for the start, all equipment was thrown into the cart, which everyone took hold of and sprinted downhill, out of the main-gate, and along a path. At a certain point, the route turned left, cross-country; but we needed to collect the cart from further along the path on our way back. Having off-loaded the kit, I sprinted with the hand-cart to the end of the path, before sprinting back again, picking-up my pole, and chasing after the rest of the team ahead of me. My field-gun training from Collingwood was making a big difference. By the time I had caught up, we were at the cliff. The first runner had climbed up the steep, crumbling precipice, taking a rope with him. Having attached the top, we all clambered up the near vertical cliff-face, me still carrying my pole. A bit more running through the tree-lined top, and we came to the chasm; a deep U-shaped valley rising up the opposite side, level with us. Here we rigged a leopard-crawl rope, and a pulley-system to transport all of the heavy items across, before getting ourselves over too. Once this was done, we picked-up all remaining equipment and sprinted over the rough terrain for what seemed like miles, before eventually coming back onto the path where I had left the cart. Everything was thrown into it, and we gave one last maximum effort as we sprinted back uphill to the finish-line in the center of the camp. We were exhausted, but clearly the leadership training was coming to the fore in this race.

We experimented with different techniques and methods of tackling each obstacle, over the coming weeks; settling on what we considered the best solution to the problem. In the final week, having practiced endlessly, we attempted the race record...! Everything went smoothly, and we were rewarded with a top-ten placing. We were chuffed...

Not everything at Royal Arthur was designed to test you; there was a social side too. It was a time to de-stress and relax between bouts of intense training, and a time to nurture

team spirit. Many an evening would be spent in the Naafi Bar, or going into Corsham to "The Carpenter's Arms" or "Flaming Joes." But there was always a proviso which was summed-up in the camp's unofficial motto,
"Hoot with the owl – but only if you can soar with the eagle next day."

In other words, enjoy your time-off, but God help you if you let it affect your performance throughout the course. It was your responsibility to know your own limits and stay within them; "self-discipline," another form of leadership training...

The only other opportunity our class had to get away from the base environment was during the two planned expeditions. One was conducted on Salisbury Plain, the other in The Black Mountains of Wales; both were infamous for their brutality!

The first that we encountered was Salisbury Plain. It was a two-day Exped involving setting-up a camp, a 20-hour overnight navigation trek, and various problem-solving exercises. Each of us was allocated a task within the team; be that navigating, fire lighting, team leader, or numerous other things. The equipment was distributed amongst us, and we were deposited in the most remote and desolate area of Salisbury Plain, with a map and compass, and instructions of various waypoints that we had to check-in at. As luck would have it, this was the coldest time of the year, with the normally muddy and rutted tracks frozen solid in sub-zero temperatures. The bitter wind was blowing across the vast flatness of the plains, cutting straight through our navy-issued winter-wear. But despite this, we attacked the challenge full of energy and enthusiasm. However, this feeling soon wore-off as we traipsed from one marker to the next. The cold bore into our very souls, eating away at our commitment to the task; draining our energy, and making us question what we were doing here! As darkness fell, the lack of visibility added to our sense of isolation, further attacking our resolve. In the distance, we could see the lights of the army fighting some unknown battle over the horizon, occasionally hearing the sharp report from a rifle being fired, or feeling the rumble of an explosion through our boots. But to all intents and purposes, we were alone out there...

As the overnight temperature hit minus 20 degrees and tiredness took effect, we resorted to continuing in "zombie-mode;" walking in single-file, shuffling along, heads bowed towards the earth. Our eyes fixed on the compass bearing, our minds slipped into neutral. We plodded along, unaware of time, simply wanting the exercise to finish. It was so cold that our breath, creating clouds of white puffy mist, condensed on the rucksack of the person ahead, forming ice-stalactites hanging from their back! Our exposed faces, feet and hands, went through the pain-barrier as the flesh began to freeze, until they became completely numb; oblivious to the external conditions. And still we marched on...

Eventually, through my cold-induced stupor, I spotted a light up ahead. Dawn was breaking, and we neared the final point on our maps. As we approached, the light morphed into a roaring bonfire a good 2m high; the instructors had been busy overnight too. We huddled around it, much too close for safety, but desperate for some warmth. Yet, even at this distance, the heat could not penetrate my frozen exterior. It took some considerable time before I began to thaw-out, slowly coming back to life, as a butterfly emerges from its cocoon.

Considering the extreme conditions, I thought, "Surely the instructors will call an end to the exped and rush us back to base." But NO, revitalised by hot tea and a "rat-pack" breakfast, we then spent the rest of the day *playing* at getting barrels across streams on ropes, or up trees, or under bridges! The leadership training was never-ending; or so it seemed to me at that point.

With this experience still fresh in my mind, and the weather conditions having deteriorated over the intervening days, I prepared myself for my next expedition to Wales. If I had thought that Salisbury Plain was tough, by all accounts, Wales would be twice as bad! I readied my kit, psyched myself up, and planned my route. We were to tackle the notorious "Horseshoe-Walk" which encompassed a number of the major peaks in this range of mountains. The plan was to be away for 3 days, camping overnight. However, much to my disappointment, just as we were on the verge of loading our kit onto the transport, the senior trainer informed us that the expedition was cancelled! Half of us wanted to cheer; not being exposed to extreme temperatures, or the pain and discomfort. But the other half of us felt disappointed at having to miss the climax of our course after having reached the peak of our fitness and preparedness. The reason for the cancellation was given as the extreme weather conditions; it was simply too dangerous to go ahead! Two members of the Gurkha Regiment had been training in the area, and had died due to exposure the day before!

And so, by the end of February '91, POLC 2053 had reached its end. Our class went their separate ways, dispersing to the fleet to continue their careers. Each carried a printed report of their progress during the course, and areas of distinction or further-action were highlighted for their commanding officers to address.

As for me, my report stated that I had performed well throughout the course, and that nothing specific needed addressing. A good result, I thought. On turning over the single A4 page, I noticed a small, innocuous box with a tick in it. Next to the box were the words,

"Recommended to return as an instructor - Yes / No."

My box had been ticked "Yes." I had been recommended as an instructor of leadership! This was something that *never* happened. It was very rare to get this on your report. In fact, I had never met anyone who had received this; especially not someone, like myself, who had only been a senior rate for a matter of weeks before taking this course. I was stunned, but impressed (as was my commanding officer when they received a copy of this report). Unfortunately, despite it being a highly prized award, it was not something that got added to your official navy records; nor was it a guarantee that if you applied for a posting as an instructor, that it would be granted. None-the-less, it was an honour to receive, and something that I will always be proud of achieving.

CHAPTER 19

HMS Invincible – A/POWEA (OC)

11th June 1991.

At the start of June '91, I joined the crew of HMS Invincible as the Petty Officer in-charge of "The Minor Weapons" section. This was to be my biggest challenge yet; the ship was massive, internally it was a maze, and there were hundreds of crew, way more than I had experienced aboard HMS Scylla. To top it all, I was to run one of the biggest, most varied sections on the ship; and it was my first draft in-charge of my own team of mechanics. No pressure then...!

HMS Invincible, pennant number RO5, was one of the Royal Navy's light aircraft-carriers. Commissioned on 11th July 1980, having been built at Barrow-in-Furness, she was 210m long, 36m wide, and weighed about 20000 tons. Powered by 4 Rolls Royce gas-turbine engines, she had a maximum speed of 28 knots (although she cruised at 18 knots normally). Her crew consisted of around 1100 personnel (male and female), 740 of them being ship's company, while the remainder were air-crew. There was also a contingent of Royal Marines, and quite often the RM Band onboard too. Invincible had a 7-degree ski-jump on her flight-deck, allowing the FA/2 Sea Harrier jets to operate. She also carried a number of Sea King helicopters for anti-submarine-warfare and early-warning purposes. To protect herself, she was fitted with 3 Goalkeeper CIWS guns capable of shooting down incoming missiles, 2 Oerlikon GAM-BO1 guns, and the Sea Dart Missile system. She carried enough supplies to support 1400 people for up to 6 months at sea; and she was designated as the Royal Navy's FLAGSHIP.

As I drove towards Invincible on that first summer's day, the early morning sun was obscured behind her superstructure, her immense bulk magnified by the high-tide, causing her to float way above the jetty. I approached the foot of the gangway, angled upwards at 40 degrees, to face a wall of grey metal. Climbing this steep incline only got me as far as the boat-deck entrance; the flight-deck being another two decks higher, and the "island" towering many further levels above that. Once within the complex labyrinth at the core of the ship, my head began to spin. Unlike on Scylla, where everything ran off of a straight passageway on two-deck; on Invincible, the "main-drag" of two-deck was a loop surrounding the vast open space of the hanger in the belly of the ship. There were 6 or more decks beneath this level and two above, not to mention a further 4 or 5 decks within the "island" sat upon the flight-deck. There appeared to be no direct route from one place to another; I was definitely going to need a map! Getting lost was going to be the norm over the coming few weeks... And so it proved. Despite completing my joining-routine, visiting all of the main departments and sections, the only true way to get my bearings was by walking the decks, hour-after-hour, staring at my map, knocking on doors, and finding out the quickest route from one place to another. Slowly, I learnt my way around.

Having come from the relative luxury of Culdrose, I was a bit disappointed to find that my sleeping quarters were nearly identical to those on Scylla; rank did not have its privileges at sea after all! I was allocated one of three bunks in a "gulch" within the Chief's and Petty Officers Mess. Small, cramped, and claustrophobic, there was nothing to distinguish them from junior rates bunks. However, our living quarters were a big step-up. We had a comfortable sitting area, TV room, separate dining hall, and our own bar (Yes, a proper bar, with draught-beer, spirits, the lot). It was similar to the Wardroom where the officers lived; the only difference being that they had stewards to look after them, whereas we did not.

Most routines aboard Invincible were similar to those on Scylla. Breakfast, lunch, and dinner were served at set times. Snacks were served at 4 O'clock, as were watch-keepers snacks at midnight. As a senior rate, though, I was required to change into mess-uniform, or evening-rig, every time I entered the mess, dining-hall, or after 5pm each day. This soon became a pain, especially during the day when in the middle of an engineering job, wearing overalls, and covered in oil and grease. If I wanted any food, I would need to get showered, changed, eat, and then change back again into dirty kit afterwards!

One major difference, compared to Scylla, was that Invincible now had Wrens onboard ship. From the end of 1990, Wrens were allowed to serve on ships-of-the-fleet. Wrens were the Women's Royal Naval Service. The first ship to accept them was HMS Brilliant, and HMS Invincible followed shortly afterwards. With them, came a whole host of rules and regulations; the main one being that there was to be no fraternising onboard ship. It was an enforceable, *No-Touching-Rule*. What you did ashore, however, was a different matter. Obviously, with men and women cooped-up in a ship for weeks or months at a time, these rules were going to be broken; especially if it was allowed ashore, then *not* allowed once back aboard! On the whole, the ratings kept to the rules; the only offenders who were caught and punished were officers, but I guess they have to set the example and so need to be seen to be punished. The Wrens had their own accommodation complex where men were not allowed after 10pm; and vice versa. The main rule that affected me as a senior rate was that all Wrens should be treated as *equals* to their male counterparts; how this was interpreted was a different matter. Some older senior rates were very much *against* the introduction of Wrens-at-sea. As a consequence, they went out of their way to make it hard for them. They thought that if a male can lift heavy items, then so should a Wren; and when they were not physically able to do the task, they used it as evidence against them! From my point-of-view, it was down to what jobs you, as a senior rate, allocated people. I had male sailors who were weaker than their female counterparts, so I gave everyone jobs suited to their abilities. Wrens may not be physically as strong as most men, but they could do other things better than their male colleagues; it was just a matter of those in-charge accepting this, and using everyone to their strengths. I never had any problems with the Wrens working on my section; it was down to the attitude you engaged with them. We were all part of the same team, and having bad-feeling amongst us would help no one...

My section on HMS Invincible had the not-so-grand title of, "The Minor Weapons Section." This was a bit of a misnomer, because there was nothing "minor" about the amount and variety of equipment I was responsible for. Once I had completed my handover period from my predecessor, I had to *personally* sign for all of the equipment, ammunition, and associated paraphernalia, amounting to millions of pounds! How they expected me to pay for anything that I lost or damaged, I have no idea.

I, and my team, was responsible for maintaining the deep weapons magazines (and their contents – missiles, explosives, bombs), all smoke-detectors and fire-fighting equipment housed within these magazines, plus all of the upper-deck ready-use magazines. We were responsible for the two ancient weapons-lifts that ran the full height of the ship from the deep magazines to the hanger. We ran the ship's armoury, and maintained all of the small-arms weapons (of which there was a multitude of different types). We maintained, and operated the two Oerlikon GAM-BO1 anti-aircraft guns; as well as the numerous Seagnat and SRBOC chaff rocket-launchers. We operated the three WW1 saluting-guns, used for ceremonial gun-salutes to Royals and dignitaries; and we operated and maintained the ship's degaussing equipment, which was used as a countermeasure against mines attacking us from below. As you can see, there was a lot more to this section than what first meets the eye. But in addition to this, we also had to assist on other sections when they needed us, so we got to help on the Sea Dart and Goalkeeper sections too. It was a team effort...

To cope with all of this equipment, the Minor Weapons Section consisted of me, my second-in-command, LWEM "Nobby" Clarke, and about 4 mechanics at any one time. The mechanics changed regularly as they rotated between all of the weapons sections for training purposes. Occasionally, I would also be joined by midshipmen, training to be officers, and trainee Tiffs, both of which came to learn how the section operated, and to gain knowledge of the systems we worked with.

As a new Petty Officer, I was soon to realise that there was more to running a section than simply looking after the equipment. Yes, I had to conduct planned-maintenance of everything within my department (ranging from daily, weekly, and monthly checks; to six monthly or yearly tasks), as well as dealing with unplanned repairs, as-and-when they occurred. However, the admin side of the role meant keeping records of EVERYTHING; from records of maintenance, to records of spare-parts, to records and reports on all members of staff. I had to develop my psychic-powers so that I could predict which piece of machinery was going to breakdown, and when; and arrange for the spare-parts to be flown ahead of the ship to the next port-of-call, anywhere in the world! I was also responsible for the operation of all of the equipment within the section, meaning getting the crews trained properly. And, of course, training itself was a role I had to perform; training of the mechanics on my section, training of my Leading Hand in the more technical aspects of the kit, training of Tiffs and Midshipmen, and in the initial few months, training of myself. Those first few months were the steepest learning-curve I have ever experienced! I spent hours poring over the technical-manuals housed inside my office, learning everything that I could about every aspect of every piece of equipment I was responsible for. It seemed never-ending, but the hope was that in the event of a breakdown, the solution could be found inside my brain, and brought to the fore.

The other aspect of being a senior rate that was never fully covered during any leadership courses was that I was now responsible for the welfare of all of those employed on my section. As we developed into a close-knit family, I took on the role of the "Sea-Daddy;" the mechanics being the *naughty* children. And a lot of the time they did act just like naughty children! I had to learn very quickly how to deal with things that I had no experience of; it made me grow-up very fast! One of my team had something of a drink problem. Most of the time it was under-control, but occasionally he would turn-up for work stinking of alcohol, red-eyed, and fit for nothing. Another person was going through domestic problems with his girlfriend, which escalated during the months he spent away from home. Yet another came from a split family, and had problems in relation to that. For me, as a mid-twenties Petty Officer, with little or no experience in these matters, it seemed daunting! I had to find solutions to help, or contain these situations until they could be resolved by those concerned. I effectively became the section's social-worker! I did not know it at the time, but this was to become an invaluable experience, because when I joined the police in later years, dealing with other people's problems was to become my bread-and-butter.

Within the section, I tried to make things as relaxed and comfortable as possible. If I had happy workers, hopefully they would perform well, and the section would run smoothly. We had an office, doubling as a workshop, located in a boat-bay on the port side of the ship. It was open to the elements, with lovely views of the ocean on a good day. Overhanging the sea, it offered views of dolphins frolicking in the pressure waves, or flying-fish hopping from wave to wave. The downside was that it was directly beneath the flight-deck, immediately under the area that the Harrier jets landed; so during flight operations, the noise was unbearable. Each of us was issued a set of ear-defenders; mine never being more than an arm's-length away from me at any time (more often than not, they were clamped to my head like eyes on a bug, or hanging out of my overalls pocket). To make things more homely, I got my team to run a tea-boat so we always had supplies of tea and coffee without resorting to the long trek down to the galley each time. I ran a roster allowing every member of my sea-family an afternoon-off per week; running in rotation. And my door was always open should any of them have personal problems, or needed extra tuition on any aspect of their training or naval life. I think the lads and lasses appreciated this atmosphere as they would often be seen relaxing on our boat-deck on their down periods...

As well as sectional responsibilities, I also had ship responsibilities. A lot of my equipment and weapons were located on the upper-deck, or on the "island." They may have been well maintained and operational, but they were also exposed to the salt and bad weather. This had the effect of peeling-off paint and creating rust. As we were the navy's Flagship, Invincible had to be immaculate at all times; she had to always look her best. As a consequence, my section spent a lot of time chipping-off old, damaged paint, and re-painting everything a lovely shade of battleship grey. As with the Forth Road Bridge, this was a never-ending task; one we grew to hate! But it was a necessary evil.

Being a fighting warship, Action-Stations was another ship activity that I had a specific role in. My station was in the Admiral's Bridge (which was a secondary bridge located beneath the ship's main bridge). From here, I helped run a damage-control and fire-fighting center. As a weapons engineering senior rate, my task was to attend any reports of damage or fire in, or around, any weapons mountings or upper-deck magazines. Other weapons senior rates were distributed around the ship in similar roles at other locations; the theory being that if one center was destroyed in the battle, others would be able to function unaffected.

This was similar to my regular duty-rosters onboard ship. I was rostered to be "Duty Weapons Senior Rate" every few weeks. When on-duty, for 24 hours, I would be responsible for ensuring whole ship safety in the event of a fire, with emphasis on ensuring the magazines did not go "Bang!" This duty was completed according to the roster, both at sea, and alongside. However, in my second year on Invincible, I took on a new duty roster. For this period, I joined the "Duty Regulating Petty Officer" list. A Regulating Petty Officer is effectively the ship's police. The Regulating Branch were full-time ship's police, led by The-Master-at-Arms (in our case, The MAA was a female Chief Petty Officer). Alongside in a foreign port, Petty Officers from other branches took over their duties for 24 hours at a time to give them a break. It involved conducting the evening rounds of the ship with the Officer of the Day, as well as dealing with any discipline issues that arose during the duty period. Primarily, it involved manning the gangway and dealing with drunken sailors returning onboard from a night ashore, confiscating alcohol from them, and organising shore-patrols to look-out for the safety of our crew when in a foreign port. It was quite a challenging, fun, and interesting duty; totally different from my day-to-day responsibilities. I was given a lot of trust, and even given the key to the MAA's safe where

I had access to a slush-fund of foreign cash with which to bribe local police officers to release our drunken crew in the event that they should get arrested!! Not that that ever happened...! Again, this may have been sowing the seed in my mind for a future career as a police officer; at the very least, it was experience in a similar role, which may have had an influence on the selection-board years later.

Having joined HMS Invincible in June '91, we remained in Portsmouth Dockyard for a few weeks. During this time my predecessor gave me a thorough handover on all aspects of my new section. He passed on a few tips regarding the temperamental weapons-lifts which, by all accounts, were on their last-legs! He went through the planned maintenance schedules for everything, pointing-out which jobs were still outstanding or had not been completed on time; offering a few operational excuses. And, all too soon, he was off to his next ship, and I was left with the weight of the section on my shoulders! And VERY heavy it was too...!

A short while later, it became apparent that these "delayed" jobs had actually been cherry-picked because of their complexity or difficulty! I would imagine that as my predecessor neared the end of his posting, he entered his run-down-period (RDP) and opted to leave these jobs for the new-boy to deal with. Either way, I got stuck-in, in an attempt to get the section up-to-date before our first sea trips.

I did not have long, because we set sail a number of times over the next couple of months; mainly on three or four day trips into the channel to get systems operational in readiness for our next big deployment. This was to start with a return trip up north to Norway...

CHAPTER 20

European Deployment

August 1991 arrived, and HMS Invincible left Portsmouth at the start of a European deployment. But instead of heading east, as expected, she went west, along the south coast of England! Had plans changed? I had no idea, until the Captain announced over the PA system that we were going to Portland for a mini-work-up! The thought of Portland in Dorset spread fear throughout the navy; it was where you went to conduct a BOST or COST before a major deployment; a week of full-time battle preparation. It was intensive and stressful for all involved; where the "wreckers" from Portland came aboard your ship and simulated battle-damage whilst you were fighting-off air and missile attacks from other vessels. It was as close to *real* war conditions as you could get without having to cause actual damage to your ship.

The good news was that we were only going to endure these conditions for a couple of days in order to prepare us for the yearly war exercises to be conducted off Norway over the next month. For two days, we were bombed, flooded, and had fires flaring-up at the most inconvenient times and locations, as we fought-off potential missile attacks from aircraft and ships around us. We lived in defence-watches or action-stations; and we were constantly on the alert for submarine attacks. This was my first opportunity to see Invincible as a fighting warship, and the first chance to see my team in-action, making sure our section was fully battle-ready throughout the training period.

At the end of the work-up, de-briefs were given at all levels. Overall, the ship had been successfully prepared for the war in Norway; yes, there were minor points to iron-out, but generally, everyone was happy with our performance. As the de-briefs filtered down through the command structure, I was told the opinion on my Minor Weapons Section. We were given a glowing report. Everything that was asked of us as a team, or of our equipment, had been achieved; my boss was a happy person, and was pleased that I was running the section professionally and competently despite only recently taking-over. My first big test had been a success...

From Portland, we headed up the North Sea towards the icy Arctic; but before we left British waters, it was decided to pay a visit to Rosyth Naval Base. Rosyth was located on the northern shores of The Firth of Forth, not far from Edinburgh in Scotland. As Invincible slowly entered the wide estuary on the approach to The Forth Road Bridge, a report was received that a WW2 mine had been seen floating nearby in the shipping lanes!

"Could we help?" they asked.

The Captain sent out a RIB with a couple of ship's divers onboard to investigate. Through the light mist, they spotted the black metal porcupine of a mine; and, from a safe distance, opened fire on it with rifles in an attempt to hit one of the spines and detonate it. When no explosion was forthcoming, a new plan-of-attack was formulated; the divers would carefully place some plastic-explosive on the mine, and it would be detonated remotely. This having been done, the whole ship's company stood on the flight-deck and patiently waited for the big bang. The sea was flat calm, hardly a ripple ruffling the surface of the water. As I watched, the sea where the mine had been, erupted into a gigantic plume of spray and debris, flying vertically into the sky. Moments later I heard the sound of the explosion; a sort of muffled fire-cracker. The seas around Edinburgh were once again safe...

Following a brief visit to Rosyth, Dunfermline, and Edinburgh, we continued our steady progress northwards to the seas around Norway. Invincible was to participate in a big annual war exercise with other navies of other nations; just as I had done aboard HMS Scylla a few years earlier. However, being an aircraft-carrier, our role would be different to that of Scylla. We were now the flagship, so we were the command-center, directing operations from a distance, and deploying our helicopters and Harrier jets to attack enemy forces. We were to stay out at sea, not entering the fjords; and we were to work in conjunction with one of the American super-carriers. When side-by-side with this vessel, it being about 130m longer than ourselves, it dwarfed us into insignificance, but we were still the *senior-ship* and took command of all battle decisions.

Being stationed away from the action meant fewer attacks on us, and fewer instances of action-stations. However, it also meant more exposure to the harshest weather conditions that Norway could throw at us, and almost constant flight operations. Day and night, the Harriers would take-off from our ski-jump runway, their jet engines rumbling through the metal decks with each launch. On landing, they would hover over the sea on the port side of the ship, before moving sideways over the flight-deck, touching-down vertically, directly above my office; the noise being deafening! And with all of these flight operations, the Harriers required constant access to their weaponry held in my deep magazine. To get this armament from the magazine to the aircraft in the hanger meant use of the two weapons lifts; thus our section had a critical role in the battle. Without the lifts, no weapons could be moved; without weapons, no aircraft could attack, and our role in the battle would be significantly reduced. All eyes were watching us; expectation intense.

According to "Sod's Law," a few days into the exercise and one of our weapons lifts decided to seize halfway up its lift-shaft!! Invincible could now only continue with the use of one lift, reducing her operational effectiveness, but not stopping her completely. The pressure was on. "Get that lift fixed immediately," was the order from above...

And so began 3 days of intense engineering; no sleep, and very little food, there was no time to waste. The two weapons lifts were renowned for their temperamental behaviour; or so my predecessor had told me. They were second-hand when they were fitted to Invincible, having been salvaged from the WW2 carrier HMS Eagle, and were past their sell-by-date even at that time. Each was identical, consisting of a metal cage about 4m long by 1m wide and 1m high. This travelled up a slightly curved lift-shaft which followed the contours of the ship's hull from the keel to the hanger-deck. It was fitted to two guide-rails, and hauled up and down by a chain mechanism connected to powerful motors.

The problem was with the locking mechanism. When the lift stopped, massive cams engaged, forcing metal teeth into the guide-rails to create a friction-lock. This was where the lift had jammed, these teeth engaging, and digging into the rail. Over the years, through normal wear-and-tear, the guides were littered with holes, dents, and other distortions, which caught on the cams as they passed, causing a locking of the system! The only way to repair the damage and free the cams was for me to stand on the roof of the lift's cage, and manually release the teeth; filing-down the damage caused as it was freed.

Having manually opened the doors at the nearest deck level, I climbed down the lift-shaft in the darkness, until I stood on the roof. It was very dangerous. There was no safety net; one sudden roll of the ship, and I would plummet to the bottom of the shaft to a certain death! Of course, being in Norway, in big seas, the ship was never stable, so I continued at my own risk. The guides were covered in thick gloopy grease which got everywhere, so within minutes, not only was I on an unstable platform with a shear drop to one side; but I was covered in grease, so if I grabbed anything to steady myself, I would slip-and-slide all over the place! Things were getting worse by the minute!

While my team raised the lift (weighing many tonnes), using a hand-operated winch, I levered the cams open, and ground-down the ridges of hardened-steel that had been left exposed on the guides by the serrated teeth. After many hours work, I thought the lift was fixed, so with me still crouched upon the roof; the lift was activated to try to get it up a level. All seemed fine until, "CRUNCH." There was a colossal shudder, a screaming of metal-on-metal, and the lift came to a sudden stop as I was plunged into darkness again. All that could be heard was my voice shouting out,

"SHIT!!!!!" followed by a stream of swear words...

The lift had ground to a halt yet again, only at a new point on the guide-rails, creating even more indentations to remove. This continued repeatedly for two days (although it seemed even longer). No sooner had I fixed one bit of damage and got the lift running, than it would catch on some new distortion on the guide rail, and lock again. The only solution was to travel the full length of the lift-shaft atop the cage, and remove *every* potential bump, hole, or bend in each rail. At least then, it should be a permanent fix; I hoped.

By day three, I was exhausted. I had not slept at all as I was the only one with technical knowledge on the section and was needed at all times; the rest of the section worked on shifts so they could at least get a little rest. But this time, I thought the job was done. I crossed my fingers, pressed the green "GO" button, and hoped for the best. The lift worked. But I could not trust it; it had done this before, then jammed after a few runs. So I tested it again and again. Eventually, I gave the WEO (weapon engineering officer) a call to say it was up-and-running again. A big sigh of relief ensued. He was mightily relieved and congratulated our section on the effort and perseverance we had shown. "Brownie-Points" to us...

By now, I was past tiredness. But a couple of days later, I was sat eating my lunch when I collapsed head-first into my meal; completely exhausted! I think I slept for 24 hours solid before recovering enough to get back to work. It just goes to show the extremes you can push yourself to when you really have to...

Despite this hiccup, the exercises had gone well. On a personal level, the trip to Norway was not so great! My brother had been getting married in September, and despite numerous attempts to get flown back to the UK for a day or two, permission had been denied! I was the only one NOT at the wedding. I was left feeling I had let him, and the rest of the family, down; even though it was through circumstances beyond my control. I had mixed feelings; annoyed at missing the wedding, coupled with elation at overcoming the weapon-lift problems (and hopefully resolving the problems for good). These feelings were short-lived though, as work has a habit of keeping you busy, and taking your mind off things. The deployment continued...

Next stop was a welcome break in the Portuguese capital, Lisbon. With the sun shining, and the warmth seeping into our frozen bones after Norway, it was an ideal opportunity for a bit of relaxation before heading through the Straits of Gibraltar, and into the Mediterranean. Having been here before on Scylla, I made a point of NOT suggesting a walk from Cascais back to Lisbon; not after underestimating the distance last time. Instead, I joined a few fellow Petty Officers visiting the tourist-sites of the castle, and the Belem Tower; and I maintained my record of running in every country visited.

As Invincible entered the Mediterranean Sea and the weather became settled, we began participating in a number of exercises with other naval forces in, and around the island of Cyprus. Our aircraft were constantly operational, taking advantage of the tranquil conditions to increase their tally of hours in the air. And between flying periods, the ship's company took advantage of the pleasant sunshine by taking part in the daily circuit-training sessions held on the flight-deck, or by running around the upper-deck; a much more pleasurable experience than on the cramped HMS Scylla. There was even a little "hill" to run up, in the form of the runway's ski-jump. Fitness on Invincible was very well catered for. Apart from the circuit-training, which could be held on the flight-deck in good weather or in the hanger if not so good; there was a well-equipped gym on the mezzanine deck within the hanger complex. Here you could run on the treadmills or steppers, or you could row on the "ergos." There were free-weights to lift, and benches or mats to use as you wished. My favourites were the rowing machines; I spent hours at a time rowing back and forth, the sweat dripping off my elbows to form puddles either side of the seat rail. It certainly whiled away the long hours at sea, at the same time, keeping me fit.

Excitement mounted as we neared our next port-of-call. We were soon to arrive at Alexandria in Egypt, and lists of available trips and excursions began to appear on the notice-boards. We were due to be here for over a week, working alternate days, but on our free days, we were encouraged to sign-up for the trips; after all, what was the point in going to these exotic places if you did not take time to explore them?

As our ship entered the port of Alexandria, the city beyond appeared to be a mass of low-level tower-blocks and sandy coloured buildings, punctuated with the odd dome or minaret-tower of the local mosque. Everywhere was bustling; people and traffic constantly on the move. A cacophony of car horns were sounding as if it was a means of greeting between friends, rather than a warning of your presence. And in the harbour were a multitude of different sized, different coloured, wooden fishing boats, gently bobbing on the litter strewn waters. Everything seemed to have a coating of pale orange sand; even the air above the city had an orange tint to the hazy cloud that enveloped it. It was a mixture of ancient and modern, sandwiched between the cooling waters of the Mediterranean, and the oppressive heat of the Sahara Desert.

Amongst the many Egyptians that inhabited this city, lived a few British Ex-Pats. They duly invited members of our crew to an evening of running and drinking, hosted by the Alexandria Hash-House-Harriers. I was keen to attend, having not encountered Hash-House-Harriers before. These groups were spread throughout the world, mainly run by British Ex-Pats, and they organised running contests that were a mixture of cross-country running, trail running, and treasure-hunting; following clues and signs laid by a *hare* that ran ahead of the group, setting the route. Despite the intense heat (even in the evening), it was great fun. However, the main aspect of these gatherings was the social side of the club; it was obligatory that you end the evening downing copious amounts of alcohol, paying "fines" set by the organiser, by drinking shots of spirits, and thoroughly enjoying yourself. From what I can remember the following day, it had been a great evening...!!

When I think of Egypt, the first image to spring-to-mind is that of the pyramids. How could I travel here and not get to see them? It was compulsory wasn't it? So I signed-up for a cultural trip, along with what seemed like half of the ship's company, to visit the sights of Cairo. It was a long day, starting early, with a dusty coach journey through the stifling heat of the desert, and into the even more stifling atmosphere of Cairo city-center. It turned-out to be a whistle-stop-tour with hardly any time to appreciate my surroundings. First stop was the Tutankhamen Exhibition in the National Museum. No time to waste, it was a case of exit the coach, form a line, and file-past the exhibits recovered from the tomb of the "Boy Pharaoh," before returning back to the bus, and onwards to the next stop.

The sight of the Pyramids of Giza, isolated in the flat desert sands should have been a jaw-dropping spectacle. In reality, they stood a few hundred meters from the edge of the cosmopolitan city limits! In one direction, you could see them silhouetted against the backdrop of the sand-dunes of the Sahara; but turn your head through 180 degrees, and you were faced with the sandstone office blocks and ever present traffic of Cairo! None-the-less, I was escorted to the foot of the main pyramid where I stood amid a line of spitting, smelly, and rather angry looking camels, to gaze in awe at the massive stone blocks with which the pyramid was built. We had been warned about the camel drivers pestering us into camel rides, and then holding us hostage until we paid them way-above-the-going-rate to let us off the beasts; they had not accounted for an ex-field-gunner in our midst though...! At 6 foot 6, and muscles everywhere, when faced with a grumpy camel that refused to let him off, he punched the camel square in the jaw, knocking it to its knees! Needless to say, its owner did not attempt to claim any money off him afterwards...!

Following a narrow, downwardly-angled tunnel, I arrived at a burial-chamber in the heart of the pyramid. I stood, marvelling at the hieroglyphics on the walls, while a couple of Wrens decided to climb into an open sarcophagus which had been roped-off as out-of-bounds to the public. Following the steep climb out, I strolled across the sand to get a closer look at The Sphinx. Its face had been worn from years of exposure to heat and wind, but its features were still discernible, and with the pyramids behind it, I had my classic picture-postcard image of Egypt; one I will remember always.

Next stop on our speedy tour of Cairo was to a quaint rural cafe on the banks of the river Nile. Here, in the shade of the trees, we were served some local delicacies of unknown origin, for lunch?! They looked like small balls wrapped in vine leaves, but they were green and festering, with an overpowering stench to them! You had to be brave (or stupid) to eat them; most did not, but the few who did regretted it next day as they expelled their stomach contents from both ends of their bodies...!

As darkness fell, we were whisked back to the pyramids to watch the "Son-et-lumière" show. Images were projected onto the face of the Sphinx to give it the impression of being alive as it narrated the history of Egypt, with the pyramids lit by dancing-lights at its rear. As impressive as it was, the overriding memory I have of this evening was the pain caused by the millions of mosquitoes that ate us alive!

After a hectic tour of the sights of Cairo, we returned to Invincible, exhausted, but having had a thoroughly entertaining time. It was a great introduction to what culture Egypt had to offer, but next time, visiting them at a slower pace would be preferable.

A couple of days later, I embarked on another day-trip. This time, I headed 66 miles west, along the coast, to the scene of the WW2 battles at El Alamein where the British 8th Army fought the German Panzer Divisions. I visited the Commonwealth War Cemetery where 6425 identified military personnel lay beside 815 unidentified ones; brothers-in-arms in death as well as life. I stood before the Cross-of-Sacrifice, and wandered among the thousands of identical white-marble gravestones, each uniformly positioned in rows and columns as the soldiers within had been in life. It was a very sombre, thought-provoking visit, but one I am glad to have made; to witness first-hand the sacrifice that my predecessors made during this conflict.

In total contrast, the second half of the day involved a relaxing trip to a nearby beach. It was a time to unwind, before setting-sail and heading to the northern parts of the Mediterranean Sea for some weapons trials, and more visits...

As I sadly departed Alexandria, my mind turned to the weapons-trials scheduled for a few days time. We were due to have a live-firing of the Goalkeeper CIWS gun system, and despite this not being part of my section; it was such a rare occurrence, that *all* weapons engineers were involved.

The Goalkeeper system was a fully automatic Gatling-gun consisting of 7 rotating barrels that fired 30mm projectiles. Each projectile was a solid tungsten bolt (penetrator) encased in a nylon sleeve (sabot), and it could fire bursts of 1000 at a speed of 4200 rounds per minute. Its purpose was to use its own target-tracking radars to locate incoming missiles or aircraft, to prioritise these targets, and then obliterate them with projectiles. It was so advanced that having destroyed a target; any incoming shrapnel (down to 5cm in size) would also be targeted, prioritised, and destroyed.

For the trial, we were to only use one of our three guns; and we would be shooting at a target towed behind an aircraft. The day before the trial, I helped the team manually load the self-contained magazine fitted to the gun. Due to the speed with which the projectiles were fired, nothing could be allowed to enter the magazine other than the rounds themselves; any foreign-objects would instantly jam the mechanism, and ruin the shoot.

On the day of the firing there was nothing much to do; all preparations having been completed the day before. I found a suitable location, and awaited the target aircraft's arrival. As it entered our range, the forward gun-mounting rotated sharply as it locked onto the target. Seconds later, there was a "Thwwwwwwwww" sound, as if someone was blowing a raspberry, only much louder. It lasted a matter of 15 seconds, during which time around 1000 projectiles shot towards the target. All that was left to see was a spiral of smoke rising from the end of the super-heated gun-barrels. That was it, it was all over...

Later, I watched the firing via the onboard camera system, magnifying the target as it was blasted from the sky. As I watched, the black object vanished in a fraction of a second; but the trailing cable then became the target. I watched as the Goalkeeper progressively destroyed the end of this cable, gradually working its way towards the aircraft that was towing it...! An uncomfortable few seconds for the pilot, I should imagine!

And so, with the trials successfully behind us, we steamed north towards the Black Sea port of Istanbul...

CHAPTER 21

Eastern Mediterranean

In October, the weather in the Mediterranean was beginning to cool-down a little, but it was still pleasant; certainly better than it was back in the UK. HMS Invincible cruised northwards, passing between Crete and Rhodes and into the Aegean Sea. At the north-eastern corner, she entered the Dardanelles Strait, a narrow stretch of water connecting the Aegean Sea to the Sea of Marmara. At approximately 1km across, I had a good view of the terraced hills to my left, covered in dark scrub-like bushes. Sat atop these hills was a tall, white obelisk; "The Helles Memorial." This was a Commonwealth War Graves Commission site commemorating those who died at the Battle of Gallipoli during WW1. As we passed by, some of the details of the battles that occurred here were relayed over the PA system. Many Australian and New Zealand troops were killed here on the 25 April 1915, and it is from this conflict that they now have ANZAC Day where they remember the fallen, as we do our departed on Remembrance Day.

Istanbul, also known as Constantinople and Byzantium at various times, was sat at the top of The Sea of Marmara, straddling the Bosphorus Strait, at the entrance to the Black Sea. It was where east meets west; Asia meets Europe. It was also where we met the rain and cooler weather conditions! Anchoring in the middle of the Bosphorus, straining against our anchor-chains in the strong current, I could see the city spread-out over the hills on both sides of the straits. Amid the mass of predominantly white, residential and office buildings, I could make-out the distinctive modern football stadium. I could see the white domed Topkapi Palace (home to many of the Ottoman Sultans for over 400 years), sat amid its own tree-filled gardens on the tip of the peninsular. To its rear, I could see the 6 minaret-towers of The Blue Mosque rising regally above the city. Behind me, to the north, the impressive 1973 Bosphorus Bridge straddled the straits, linking the east and west sides of the largest city in Europe; and at its foot, on the Asian side of the straits, stood the waterside Beylerbeyi Palace (an Imperial Ottoman summer-residence from 1860), with its many windowed facade giving the impression of a two-storey wedding cake.

We did not have a lot of time to enjoy our surroundings as this was to be a fleeting-visit; just enough time to have a single afternoon ashore, exploring the immediate vicinity. Access ashore was by "pas-boat" (passenger boat) which only ran at set times, so it was essential that our time-keeping was exact or we would miss the return trip. Whilst others chose to experience a traditional Turkish-Bath, or just sit in a bar (which they could do anywhere), a few of us decided to try and cram-in some of the tourist sites. Once ashore, we headed for the predominant tourist attraction, visible from anywhere in this sector of the city; The Blue Mosque. We meandered around the dark, damp streets, slowly getting wetter and wetter in the constant heavy drizzle; until, quite unexpectedly, we emerged into a large open square with the mosque laid-out before us. We had arrived.

The Blue Mosque, or to give it its proper name, The Sultan Ahmed Mosque, had been built between 1609 and 1616. First impressions were that it looked like a Turkish version of The Taj Mahal, with its grand forecourt lined by minarets, and its 5 main domes glinting in the damp conditions, surrounded by a further 8 secondary domes. By night, these domes would be doused in blue light, enhancing its magical appearance; but for us, this would remain a distant vision as we had to be aboard ship before nightfall. As I passed through the main gateway, I arrived at an internal courtyard lined with archways leading away to private rooms within the complex. Having removed my footwear in accordance with religious protocols, I entered the main chamber of the mosque. It was a breathtaking sight. The room was huge, the roof visible hundreds of feet above my head. The floor was covered with a plush red carpet, and the internal walls and domes were decorated with hand-painted blue ceramic tiles; giving it its name, The-Blue-Mosque. Hanging above head-height were thousands of lamps, connected in strings as if floating mid-air; these lights giving the mosque a bright and welcoming atmosphere despite there being only small windows, high-up, allowing external light to penetrate the interior. This was a working mosque; many of the local men milling around, awaiting the call-to-prayer. Having had a good look around, we decided to move on to our next attraction as time was limited.

It was still raining outside, so we thought it might be sensible to look for somewhere to go that was sheltered. We saw a sign, following it to The Basilica Cisterns, not knowing what to expect when we got there. As I descended the 52 stone steps into the bowls of the earth, anticipation rose. What would I see down there? Was it a form of underground sewer system as I had suspected? I was to be pleasantly surprised... The cistern had been built in the 6th century and was one of hundreds hidden beneath the streets of Istanbul. It was designed as a sort of underground reservoir and water-filtration system, built by over 7000 slaves. The water it contained serviced the Great Palaces nearby, until more modern methods of supply took over.

On entering the main cathedral-like chamber, my breath was taken away for the second time that afternoon. The space was vast; covering about 9800 square meters. It could hold around 100000 tons of water; although at the moment, there were only a couple of meters of water in the bottom. The ceiling was supported by a forest of ionic and Corinthian, marble pillars; each 9m high and linked to its neighbour via an intricate array of cross-shaped vaults and rounded arches. Each pillar was individually carved with ancient designs, and the whole ensemble was illuminated by multi-coloured beams of light, adding to the dramatic effect. Having never seen anything quite like this, it seemed strangely familiar?! Why did I appear to know of this place? It was then pointed-out that these cisterns had been used as a backdrop for part of the 1963 James Bond film: "From Russia with Love." Of course, that was where I had seen it before...

With time running out rapidly, we ran through the narrow streets back to the jetty, and were able to catch the boat back to Invincible. Although we had not had a lot of time ashore, this had been one of the more interesting and unexpectedly fun trips so far. However, our departure next morning beckoned, and we were to have a few more days at sea before our next visit in Europe. Where would our voyage of discovery take us next, we wondered?

As Invincible headed south into the Mediterranean Sea, we turned west, skirting the islands of Sicily and Malta, and heading into the Tyrrhenian Sea to the north and west of Italy. Whilst patrolling this area, we passed the island of Stromboli. Rising out of the sea like a perfect-cone, this was an active volcano with a town spread around its base. Although not erupting at the moment, it made you reflect on those who would choose to live in the shadow of such a dangerous place, constantly wondering if today would be the day that their home was destroyed in a flood of lava!

Next on our itinerary was Palermo in Sicily. Think "Sicily," and you automatically think "home-of-the-Mafia!" Before we even docked, rumours were rife of what the Mafia would do to us if we caused any trouble ashore (or even mentioned their name in public!). Of course, this was just scare-mongering; however, sat at the top of a hill overlooking the port of Palermo was a modern, glass-fronted villa. Who owned it? Clearly, whoever it was had money, and lots of it. In no time, stories spread that it belonged to the local *Godfather*, watching over his town in a protective manner. How true this was, I do not know, but it certainly fitted with the location, so the myth continued...

Palermo was a beautiful city, full of culture and history. It had grand piazzas and elegant opera-houses. It had narrow flag-stoned streets, and wide, modern motorways. It was a catholic country and had many churches built in a Byzantine or Norman style, as well as a huge cathedral incorporating many different architectural elements. Within the city-limits there were sections of two protective walls, one of which dated back to the Phoenicians around 734BC. It was a very interesting, and culturally diverse city.

Only being here for a couple of days, and only having one free day available, I scanned our ship's notice-boards to see what was on offer. I settled on a day-trip into the interior of Sicily, incorporating a climb up Mount Etna and a visit to some scenic fishing villages to see the *real* Sicily.

Mount Etna dominated the island of Sicily. It was a gigantic, active volcano; the tallest in Mediterranean Europe at 3329m high. Due to the fertile volcanic soil, the lower slopes were green with vineyards and orchards. But as you climbed higher up the winding summit roads, this contrasted with the barren, almost moon-like vista; pitted with craters and ancient lava-flows. We travelled by bus as far as we were allowed to up the side of Etna, and then walked a little way across the grey, rough-surfaced lava fields. I was told that we could not go right to the summit as Etna was currently active, and on the verge of an eruption. Even with my limited knowledge, I could see plumes of white steam emerging from blow-holes at a number of points further up the slopes, so I was not too disappointed to hear this news. After we left Sicily, Etna erupted for a period between 1991 and 1993, threatening the town of Zafferana with total annihilation. I was glad I had seen it in its active mode, but that was close enough for me; I left the slopes satisfied and safe, and continued on our tour of Sicily by heading to the coastal town of Messina on the northern tip, almost within touching distance of mainland Italy.

On returning to the ship, we readied ourselves for sea, preparing for the final leg of our deployment. We sailed majestically out of Palermo Harbour and headed back across the Mediterranean towards the Straits of Gibraltar.

Gibraltar was a peninsular at the southern tip of Spain, with the Straits of Gibraltar being 8 miles across at their narrowest point to Morocco. It was a British territory (whose ownership was constantly disputed by Spain), and was strategically placed to control the shipping-lanes into and out-of the Mediterranean. As such, there were permanent army regiments garrisoned here, as well as a big Royal Navy base called HMS Rooke. The peninsular was dominated by The Rock; a 426m high lump of Jurassic limestone, surrounded at sea-level by the densely populated town of Gibraltar on all sides. To the east, the Rock's slopes were shrouded by large concrete rainwater-catchment areas and a desalination plant; to the west was the main area of the town and the navy base; and to the north, the border with Spain, which was the international-airport's runway (which you had to cross to enter either country).

This was my first visit to "Gib," as it was known. It was a regular stopping-off-point for Royal Navy ships though, and they were well used to the antics of us sailors. To me, just wandering around the town was like being back in the UK. English was spoken everywhere (albeit with a bit of an accent), there were British shops, British post-boxes, British "Bobbies" (police officers); it was just like being at home. However, the main attraction from the navy's point-of-view was that it catered for tourists and sailors very well, with pubs and clubs everywhere! They were very used to dragging drunken navy personnel back to ship, having their own shore-patrol based at Rooke.

Being my first visit here, I wanted to see a bit of the Rock, other than just visiting the bars. So I headed up to the Rock's summit on the cable-car, to be greeted outside the cafe by a pack of surly-looking Barbary Apes! These were native to the Rock, living free, and protected by the army. However, they had a reputation of being quite mischievous; often stealing tourists' clothing, hats, or food, when they least expected it. They had been known to be very aggressive too, so I approached them warily to have the obligatory photograph. I took a step back the instant one of them screeched at the top of its voice at me, barring its teeth! Maybe it was just warning me to keep away, but judging by the smirk on its face, I think it was doing it on purpose to scare us tourists!

Whilst here, I took the opportunity of going on a trip *inside* the Rock. The Rock was riddled with tunnels and roads, not normally visible from the outside. Many of them were controlled and operated by the army, as at one point, it was used as a military armament-depot. A lot of the chambers and tunnels dated back to the Victorian era, or earlier, and in a number of them, they housed ancient cannons looking out over the Straits of Gibraltar to ward-off invaders. To me, it offered a lovely view across the sparkling waters, or over to mainland Spain; it was very scenic...

The other thing that Gibraltar was famous for was the infamous "Rock Race." It was tradition that visiting ship's companies attempt the run from HMS Rooke, up the narrow, winding, switchback roads, to the summit. As our visit was relatively short, we could not arrange an official "Rock

Race" challenge; however, through our PTI, a few of us attempted the run as a bit of fun. I am not sure that FUN was the right word though! As you would imagine, all of the roads had a steep uphill gradient (there was not one flat bit at all), so pacing yourself was essential. As an experienced runner, I coped pretty well; following the route up, through the army base, and eventually onto the footpath that ran across the ridge at the top of the rock. By following this path, I eventually came to the cafe that I had arrived at by cable-car the day before, and the finish-line. In all, it took me around 20-25 minutes going up, and about 10 minutes going down. But, apart from it being good fun, this was a practice session for when we returned the following year, and mounted an *official* challenge on the Rock Race record...

After leaving Gibraltar, Invincible left the Med on the final part of the deployment; we were nearly home. But this was now early November, and not wanting to miss-out on any firework-displays, our boss decided to schedule a live GAM-BO1 shoot, using tracer-rounds to simulate fireworks, to celebrate Bonfire Night. While we were preparing for this, he decided we may as well have a live-shoot of the SRBOC and Seagnat chaff launchers too. So, rather than having a nice relaxed cruise home across The Bay of Biscay, my section was working flat-out preparing the weapons for the shoot.

The chaff launch was first. Everything went smoothly, but there was nothing to see (as on Scylla when we did a similar launch). As dusk began to fall, my gun-crews prepared for their shoot. Unlike with normal 20mm rounds; every fourth tracer round is illuminated red to help the aimers see where they are shooting. Some of the ship's company came onto the flight-deck to watch the demonstration; and once the go-ahead was given, we lit the night sky with chains of red flashing ammunition. It was not quite up to the standard of a professional fireworks-display, but it was the best we could do under the circumstances. The WEO was happy, and once again, I had proven the worth of my section aboard ship.

A few days later, we prepared to return to Portsmouth Dockyard. We had been away for 4 months, and we were looking forward to a bit of time-off over Christmas and the New Year. It was a damp, drizzly morning as Invincible slipped into the dockyard conducting a Procedure-Alpha entry, with the ship's company lining the flight-deck in best uniforms. Crowding onto the jetty were our families, cheering our return; ready to whisk us away for some well-earned rest. Little did they know, but we would only be back in the UK a short time before setting-off on an even longer deployment the following year...!

CHAPTER 22

Pre-Deployment Preparations

At the start of 1992, our schedule for the rest of the year was beginning to take shape. From May onwards Invincible would have the prestigious honour of being the Admiral's Flagship on an extended tour through the middle-east and out towards the orient. In years gone by, extended tours like this were fairly common, but with cut-backs, it was now a very *rare* occurrence. Before then, I had a busy few months in Portsmouth preparing the ship to look her best, and ensuring my section was fully functional for the forthcoming tour.

As the trip was primarily going to be a PR initiative, a lot of our ammunition would not be required. Certain countries would not allow the ship to dock unless we confirmed that we were *not* carrying nuclear weapons onboard. As a result, we needed to partly de-ammunition the ship, removing anything that might cause controversy. It was Royal Navy policy to neither confirm, nor deny the presence of nuclear weapons on its ships. However, it was a known fact that some of the 500-pound-bombs carried by our Harrier jets had tactical nuclear capability. Because of this, it was decided to off-load all of these to shore before our departure. The bombs were stored in the deep magazine, and came under my section's responsibility, so it became my job to organise the de-ammunitioning; something I had never done before. Due to the nature of the weapons being removed, it was to be conducted over a weekend, and the majority of the crew would be given leave; only a skeleton-crew remaining. Armed security would be arranged for the ship, and the whole jetty would be cordoned-off, with no other ships moored near us.

The weekend arrived, and my team began lifting the bombs (in their individual, sealed canisters) up the weapons-lifts, into the hanger. Once I was satisfied that they were safe and ready for transport, we moved them onto the flight-deck to wait for lifting onto the jetty by crane. As the lifting began, tension heightened; we would not want to drop any of them, would we? Security stepped-up their game, blocking access to anyone not directly involved in the de-ammunitioning process. Everything was going well, and the area was totally sealed-off; or so I thought...! As we progressed, I became aware of a small tourist boat passing us. These boats often ran excursions around the dockyard, showing interested parties the Royal Navy's ships, but they were supposed to stop their trips during de-ammunitioning, on safety grounds. They obviously had not got the message for some reason. As it passed by, I could clearly hear the onboard commentary saying,

"If you look over to your right you'll see the aircraft-carrier, HMS Invincible. You'll notice that they are currently in the process of taking off their nuclear weapons which are in those boxes hanging from the crane!"

So much for security, eh? Not only should these civilians be unaware that we *may* carry these types of weapons; but they certainly should not be able to identify them, and then tell the general-public what we were doing...! I could not help but smile. Despite all the security restrictions in-force that I had control over, there was always the unpredictable element. They always used to say that the skippers on these tourist boats knew more about what goes on in the dockyard than we did; and so it would seem...

Imagine the Armoury aboard HMS Invincible; row-upon-row, rack-upon-rack of L1A1 SLR rifles (I forget the numbers, but there must have been 150 to 200 of them); further racks of sub-machine guns (SMG), light machine guns (LMG), and heavy machine guns (GPMG); and boxes of 9mm pistols, riot-guns, and shotguns. It was a very busy area of the ship, and one which fell under the auspices of my section.

The SLR (L1A1) rifle had been the mainstay of British personal weaponry for many years, but from 1985 it was beginning to be replaced by its successor, the SA80 rifle. The replacement started with the army, and over the following years progressed to the other UK armed forces. By the beginning of 1992, it was HMS Invincible's turn to be upgraded to the newer, supposedly better, weapon.

The SA80-A1 rifle dated back to an original design of the late 1940's, but was shelved at that time. Over the intervening years, it was redesigned and improved upon until the first prototypes were issued in 1976. By the time the Royal Navy received them, the first issue of the SA80 had been in-service for a number of years, and had gained a poor reputation! There were a number of issues with them, not least being that the barrel housings were made of plastic; when fired repeatedly, the heat generated melted these grips, distorting them or causing them to fall off! There was also an issue with the firing-pin snapping, and the magazine release-catch being on the wrong side of the weapon causing it to inadvertently drop the magazine of ammunition when you needed it most! These were to be the "upgrade" to the perfectly functional, and much loved SLR's, and we were about to receive them onboard...

While we were in Portsmouth, between deployments, I would be responsible for conducting the changeover from

SLR to SA80. Luckily, we were to do this in stages; rather than removing all of the old weapons at the same time as receiving the new ones, we would have an overlap period where we would carry both varieties onboard. So, in early '92, my section received a multitude of new weapons and associated ammunition to integrate into our small-arms magazine and armoury.

When new weapons were issued, they arrived individually wrapped, and packed in thick, protective grease. To make them fit-for-use, all of this grease had to be removed; the weapon inspected in minute detail for defects, and then it needed to be prepared for storage on the racks. This was to be The Minor Weapons Section's task for the foreseeable future. It was a long, time-consuming, and labour-intensive job; but one that every member of my section took to with great enthusiasm.

A few days later, I had a very FULL armoury, lots of sparkly new rifles; but lots of older, more reliable weapons as a back-up in case the newer SA80's proved to be as bad as their reputation suggested. We were covering both eventualities...

During the 2000's, I understand that the issues that we had relating to the SA80's were finally addressed, and a new version was developed; the SA80-A2. From all reports, this weapon was the exact opposite of its predecessor; it was light, accurate, and efficient, and all of the teething-problems that the original version had, had been ironed-out; a much better weapon all-round.

As the weeks ticked by, Invincible gradually inched towards its Flagship standard of readiness. Bit-by-bit, the upper-deck areas were stripped, cleaned, and painted; and as the Minor Weapons Section had so many external areas, it fell to us to complete quite a lot of this work. It also highlighted certain team members' deficiencies in their training and abilities...! One of my team, "Balsa" was given the task of painting a bulkhead with another mechanic.

"OK, WEM Wood, I've got a little job for you," I said. "I want you and WEM Jones to paint this bulkhead. The paint's over there with the brushes. Everything has been stripped, cleaned, and rubbed down – you just need to give it a coat of undercoat, OK?"

"Yeah, no problem PO," he replied.

"Make sure you put those sheets down on the deck to catch any drips, yeah?"

"Of course, PO."

"Remember – small amounts of paint on the brush – I don't want it to look like a pile of shit. Is that clear?"

"Yes PO, you can count on us, we've done it before loads of times."

"OK. I've gotta go check on some other stuff, but I'll be back in a little while, so crack-on with the painting till I get back."

"Will do boss."

When I returned, I could not believe my eyes! "Balsa" was putting his 3-inch paintbrush into the can of paint all the way up to the handle; then, without wiping off any excess, he was slapping it on the wall, trying to rub it in as it dripped in rivulets towards the deck. His hands were swimming in the paint, which was running up his arm and all over his uniform; and the area of deck between the wall and the tin was a mass of drips, spots, and spatter! It was utter chaos...! Surely he had enough common-sense to realise he was doing something wrong?

"Balsa, what the fuck are you doing? Didn't you listen to a word I said? Put that brush down before you make even more mess," I shouted at him.

"What's wrong PO? Isn't this what you wanted?"

"Are you stupid or something? Look at the bloody mess; there's paint everywhere!"

"It's not that bad, look, we're nearly finished. It looks fine to me."

"Really? What about the paint all over the deck, and the drips on the wall?"

"That's OK, I can smooth it out in a mo, and then I'll tidy-up when I'm finished."

To him, his work was a masterpiece!! Clearly an intense session of painting instruction was needed; not to mention hours of tidying up this scene of disarray. This rating was left in NO doubt as to his failings as I instructed him in the correct techniques; trying hard to control my temper...!!

But it was not all hard work. Invincible's Senior Rates Mess arranged a formal evening dinner aboard HMS Victory to celebrate the completion of these preparations. By day, HMS Victory was open to the public. As an 18th century ship-of-the-line, and Admiral Nelson's Flagship, she was preserved in dry-dock in Portsmouth as a museum. However, she was still part of the modern Royal Navy fleet, and as such, still retained a small crew of regular navy personnel. Outside of working hours, arrangements could be made for NCO's and Officers to visit, to have tours of the ship (the areas that the public do not get to see), and to have a meal in Nelson's Officers' Quarters onboard.

At the appropriate time, our group of Chiefs and Petty Officers wandered the short distance from Invincible to Victory; resplendent in our crisp white short-sleeved shirts, epaulettes, cummerbunds, and caps. As I stood before the gangway, I looked up to the towering masts, shrouded in black rigging, silhouetted against the dusky skies. Ducking to enter the main gun-deck, I instantly became aware of the low deckheads and the cramped conditions; I became attuned to the ghosts of the past, my predecessors, those who had lived and died aboard this ship. It was a strange situation; modern navy meets ancient navy. As we were shown the living quarters, the hammocks, the firepower that this ship possessed, each of us drifted into our own little world; considering how it would be if time were to be reversed, and we were to serve aboard such a relic of the past.

Snapping back to the present, we entered the Admiral's Quarters, and there laid before us, was a splendid selection of food. As we tucked in to this scrumptious feast, conversations returned to the modern day, to our forthcoming deployment, and to the many varied countries we were to visit. All the time, though, the ghosts of the past watched over us, listening to our discussions, and no doubt comparing their voyages of discovery to our own. Hopefully, we were not too much of a disappointment to them, we had a hard act to follow, a high standard to live up to...

CHAPTER 23

Orient 92 Begins...

"Orient 92" was the name of our 7 month deployment to the Mediterranean, the Persian Gulf, and as far east as Japan. On 12th May 1992, Invincible quietly slipped out of Portsmouth Dockyard on a dank, grey morning. As the crew lined the flight-deck in their best uniforms, and the Royal Navy band played a medley of tunes from their repertoire, we slowly glided past the few hardy souls that lined the harbour walls waving us goodbye. We were now the Royal Navy's Flagship, we had an Admiral aboard, and we were about to embark on the biggest PR trip of the modern era; flying-the-flag, representing Britain abroad. We were not alone though. With us were the warships Norfolk, Newcastle, and Boxer; and supporting us were the RFA's Fort Austin and Olwen. Each ship would have slightly different itineraries, slightly different duties, but each would follow the same basic route.

Within 3 days, the flotilla had travelled through the Bay of Biscay, past Gibraltar, and into the Mediterranean Sea. The weather was turning tropical, but navy life still continued. We conducted a RAS (replenishment-at-sea), refuelling HMS Boxer, as a pod of dolphins leapt amid the waves created between our two ships. And as the temperatures steadily increased, it became apparent that our upper-deck ammunition was getting dangerously warm! We tied thick hessian mats to the roof of each magazine, and doused them in cold sea-water hourly, in an attempt to reduce the internal temperatures. This worked fine, and so became my section's chore for the rest of the deployment (at least, for the periods when the heat dictated that it was necessary). Surprisingly, I was never short of volunteers (even from other departments). Everybody wanted to help; or could it be that they just wanted time to sunbathe? It was made abundantly clear that self-inflicted injuries (namely, sunburn) would NOT be tolerated, and would be punishable by fines...!

Throughout the initial few days in the Med, flight operations continued at a fast pace; the newly-embarked Harriers and Sea Kings taking advantage of the good weather to practice their deck landings. However, things did not always go according to plan. On one sortie, a Sea King helicopter on a routine flight failed to return to the ship! Mechanical failures were blamed, but the crew were forced to ditch the aircraft in the sea. Luckily, the design of the Sea King is such that its body is shaped like a boat at the bottom, and so it was able to float for a short while before slipping beneath the waves. The crew took advantage of this period of time to climb aboard their life-raft to await rescue. I understand that the navy managed to recover the helicopter at a later date, but as to how serviceable it was after its visit to the sea-bed, I do not know...

On another day, 4 of our Harrier jump-jets had been away from ship conducting training exercises. They all returned together, taking position off the port side of the ship, and hovering sideways across the deck to land on their designated spots. Due to the deafening noise created by their thrusters as they hovered, my section took-cover in our workshop on the port boat-deck until they had landed. One by one, the crescendo increased as each Harrier dropped with a thud onto the flight-deck, and then gradually wound-down the engine noise. As jet number four approached, my team prepared to carry on with their duties once the noise had died down; but as the thrusters' noise reached its peak, and the jet began to traverse sideways towards its landing spot, the screaming of the jet engines suddenly stopped; INSTANTLY!! We all looked at one another.

"That shouldn't have happened," I said. "Something must be wrong!"

In the split-second that it took me to open the door and step onto the boat-deck, the Harrier had hit the water and sunk. All I could see was the tip of the tail-fin as it dipped beneath the surface! As for the pilot; he became the newest member of the "Ejection-Tie-Club"; an exclusive club for those who had made use of their aircraft's ejection seat!!

This was not the best way to begin a deployment. Now short of one jet and one helicopter, we continued across the Mediterranean Sea towards our first port-of-call; Athens in Greece. To be accurate, Invincible was not docking in Athens itself, but Piraeus, 7 miles away. We berthed at the Central Port, surrounded by cruise-ships and ferries to every Greek island in the vicinity. It was a hive of activity; buzzing with the comings-and-goings of thousands of tourists and locals alike. In my pristine white "tropical-uniform," I helped to convert the hanger into a venue for the Wardroom's cocktail party; resplendent with flags and banners, and a Harrier jet sat pride-of-place. This was the first of many parties that the officers would hold to wine-and-dine local politicians and dignitaries; an opportunity to show-off the might of the Royal Navy, and to entertain the guests with music from the Royal Marines Band.

But that was the officers' responsibility; the junior and senior rates were more interested in seeing the treasures of ancient Athens. So it was, that the weapons department organised a joint-trip to see some of the sights of this glorious city. Jumping aboard the electric train (ISAP) from

Piraeus, I made the short scenic journey into the heart of Athens. I climbed the hill in the center of the city to visit The Parthenon on the Acropolis. This was an ancient temple dating back to 447BC, dedicated to the Goddess Athena (from where Athens got its name). It dominated the Athens skyline; sat atop its rocky promontory overlooking the rambling city below. I walked amid its multitude of Doric and Ionic pillars, marvelling at the skill required to build the many friezes and pediments using only basic tools. But all too soon the heat began to take effect as The Acropolis was totally exposed to the full force of the Mediterranean sun. We retreated to the shaded streets, wandering beneath the many olive trees that lined the roads in the lower part of the city. With ice-creams in hand, we stopped at the Panathenaic Stadium (aka Kallimarmaro Stadium); the scene of the first modern-day Olympics in 1896. Originally built by the Romans in the 6th century BC, it was constructed entirely out of white marble; consisting of a long narrow oval track, surrounded on three sides by steeply-banked seating, similar to an elongated amphitheatre. Having been abandoned, it was rebuilt for the opening of the modern Olympics, hosting a number of sports at the event. To me, it was like stepping-back into Roman times; images of chariot races, and "Ben Hur" flying through my mind. Then, having realised its history with the Olympics, we re-enacted the 4x100m relay final; running down the track, passing our ice-cream cone (baton) from person to person. Whether we were meant to be running on the track of an ancient monument is a different matter, one that we did not hang around to find out...!

    Next on our tour of Athens was Syntagma Square. Here, before the "Tomb of the Unknown Warrior," I watched as the Greek Presidential Guard performed their "changing-of-the-guard" ceremony. Dressed in their beige and white, frilly dress-like tunics, white tights with tassels attached, and boots with black pom-poms on the toes; they strutted in slow-motion in an exaggerated, high-knee march. They scuffed their boots on the ground as they repeatedly allowed their lower leg to pendulum from the knee; at the same time, their upper body remained rigid, holding tightly to their antique rifles held at the slope-shoulder position. Clearly proud of their history, they performed their peacock-dance before the massing crowds who stood in awe, gazing at the spectacle. Whether it was the right thing to do, I do not know, but many of our number felt *compelled* to imitate the style of marching that we had just witnessed. Yes, it was hilarious to watch, but not really fitting with the solemnity of the occasion.

With our day of freedom now complete, we headed back aboard Invincible, eager to continue on our magical-mystery-tour across the globe. Where to next? I knew we had to pass through the Suez Canal, so Egypt seemed the likely location...

As May became June, Invincible continued her cruise through the Sea of Crete, heading east towards Cyprus. Everything carried-on as usual until one evening, as darkness fell, a mysterious message was relayed over the ship's intercom.

"Until further notice, the upper-deck and flight-deck is out of bounds. Nobody is to go on the upper-deck unless performing essential duties. That is all?!?"

Rumours were rife. What was going on? Nothing had been scheduled, so what was happening? My section still had to cool down the upper-deck magazines, so on this occasion, the *whole* team congregated on the upper walkways of the island under the pretence of conducting this vital task. Out of the black, star-speckled sky, I heard the sound of a distant, "wocka-wocka;" the distinctive noise of a helicopter's rotor. But there was nothing visible; where was it?

"Can anyone see the chopper?" I asked.

"No, but it isn't far away. I think it's coming from that direction," someone said, pointing to the south.

"What's all the secrecy about anyways?" my Leading Hand asked. "Who's coming onboard that we aren't allowed to know about?"

Gradually the noise increased until I could make-out the shape of a two-rotor Chinook helicopter; but this was no ordinary Chinook, it was completely black, no markings, and no visible lights of any sort! Gracefully, it landed mid-flight-deck and from its rear cargo bay emerged a group of blackened shadows. They quickly disappeared into the ship without fuss or noise. We all looked at each other, reading one another's minds.

"That's gotta be the SAS, hasn't it?" I said.

"Yeah, must be," everyone agreed.

A short time later, I returned to the senior rates mess to see a couple of men in civilian clothes sat cleaning rifles. On talking to them, it transpired that they were SAS (special air service – Special Forces) sergeants who were catching a lift towards Cyprus. The following morning they were going to depart in their Chinook, jump into the sea a few miles away from Cyprus, and swim this distance to make a covert entry onto the island. Once ashore, their training mission was to raid a military establishment, make their escape, and swim out-to-sea to RV with a submarine at a predetermined location. I sat agog; this was like something out of James Bond, and yet this was real-life! This was what makes the SAS the best in the world, what makes them very "special" soldiers. As with when I plucked members of their regiment from the sea as they parachuted into the ranges off Falmouth, these soldiers blew-away the stereotypical image I had of what the SAS should look like. They were not your imagined killing-machines, muscles everywhere, and shaved heads; they were just ordinary super-fit people who could blend into a crowd unnoticed; as they were often required to do. But look into their eyes and you saw a focused steely stare; you certainly would NOT want to get on the wrong side of them...!

Without further disruption to our schedule, the SAS left as they had arrived; stealthily. And Invincible continued her travels south towards the Suez Canal. On arrival at Port Said, the northern entrance to the Suez Canal, we had to wait for a day until a convoy could be arranged to travel south. The Suez Canal linked the Mediterranean Sea to The Red Sea. It was only possible to travel its 193km route in one direction at a time, as it was not wide enough for two ships to pass one another, hence the need for a convoy system. Whilst waiting, those crew members who had not been to Egypt before were given the opportunity to visit Cairo, and The Pyramids, as I had done on a previous visit. The rest of us stayed on Invincible, unable to go ashore in Port Said. However, if we could not visit the town, the town would visit us. A selected few local traders were invited onboard to sell their wares from the flight-deck. Lots of haggling ensued as everyone attempted to get the best deal on a piece of fruit, or a memento from Giza. We even had a local merchant set-up a stall taking bets on which one of three cups a ball was beneath. We all knew it was a con, but with him wearing his red fez, and with his little monkey sidekick dressed in plush velvet waistcoat and hat; it was very entertaining.

  The journey south through The Suez Canal was purposely uneventful. Due to political tensions in the area, warships passing along its length were not allowed to show any signs of outward aggression. Because of this, my section trained all weapons inboard, and covered them in protective tarpaulins. Apart from those required to operate the ship during the transit, the rest of us were given the day off. We were free to sunbathe or play deck-hockey on the flight-deck. But most of us sat and watched the world go by. It seemed amazing that our aircraft-carrier could even fit in the canal; apart from The Bitter Lakes (an area mid-way along, where it was wider than normal), there only appeared to be a few meters either side of the ship's hull. As we slowly cruised down the channel in the stifling desert heat, we passed Egyptian military bases, watching our progress, training their missile launchers at us; just in case...! But overwhelmingly, the sight we saw most was sand; golden, flat, featureless sand, going on for mile after mile.

Having passed Port Suez, the southern exit, we entered The Red Sea. Little did I know, but in years to come, as a diving instructor, this area would become my regular playground. I would even live, and work, in Hurghada for about 6 months. But for now, it was merely another channel of sea to pass through before we arrived in The Indian Ocean.

To while-away the time during this section of the voyage, a "SOD's Opera" was arranged. SOD's Opera was the title given to an informal, often irreverent, concert, play, or comedy-show that was run by the ship's company, and generally took-the-mickey out of the officers. It stood for "Ship's Operatic and Dramatic Society," and dated back to Victorian times. Our version was an ad-hoc mixture of performances from the Royal Marines Band, individual singing and music groups, and lots of sketches portraying members of the ship's hierarchy in humorous situations. Remember, this was before the era of "political correctness" so most of the sketches involved swearing and abuse towards the officers, but done in a funny and non-confrontational manner. Lots of beer was downed before, and during the show; by those performing, and those watching. And a good time was had by all; it was naval tradition that those in command take the brunt of the abuse, and it was the accepted way for the junior rates to air-their-grievances whilst boosting morale throughout the entire ship.

As Invincible continued past Djibouti and the Gulf of Aden, she turned south, skirting the coast of Somalia, and headed for the equator. At exactly 0 degrees of latitude, she crossed from the northern to the southern hemisphere, and at this point, she came to a stop as the traditional "Crossing-the-Line Ceremony" was performed. A stage was constructed in the center of the flight-deck, complete with a 1.5m deep pool of icy sea-water. As the crew congregated on the upper-deck, King Neptune and his wife made their ceremonial entrance sat atop a suitably decorated aircraft-tractor, simulating a chariot from the deep. Two crew members played the role of Neptune and Mrs Neptune, dressed in mermaid's tails, silver crowns, and carrying their home-made tridents. Supporting them were Neptune's helpers in their brown sacking tunics and blackened faces, and the "Marine Police" whose job it was to round-up all of those who were making their first crossing of the equator. Amid loud cheers and jeers, each newbie was physically dragged up onto the stage where they were initiated into Neptune's realm. Having been restrained and forced to sit on a chair adjacent to the pool, they were welcomed to the equatorial region before having their entire head, face and shoulders coated in a yellow, foul-smelling, buttery mixture. This was duly scrapped-off using an oversized cutthroat razor, and then the victim was unceremoniously dunked backwards into the pool in a mock christening ceremony. Nobody was immune, even the Captain of the ship had to take his turn. I, too, became one of the many subjected to this ritual, but it was a right-of-passage that all Royal Navy personnel have to endure when crossing at this location. In due course, each of us would receive a commemorative certificate, one that I could add to my "Blue-Nose Certificate" for crossing the Arctic Circle on HMS Scylla.

As mid-June arrived, Invincible made her way through the outlying islands and mangrove forests, following the shipping-channels, into the port of Mombasa in Kenya. This was our first African visit (other than Egypt), and the conditions that the local people endured was something of a culture-shock! As we tied-up alongside the jetty, I noticed that all of the ropes connecting us to shore had massive conical protectors fitted to prevent creatures scurrying up them and boarding our ship. In my mind, this meant RATS, but the ones I saw skulking in the shadows of the dockyard were nothing like we had at home; they were the size of small dogs...! In the waters surrounding our ship, I often saw the wakes of giant crocodiles gliding just beneath the surface; and in the skies above, the graceful swooping of white-headed sea eagles as they plucked fish from the water's depths.

The dockyard's wire-mesh fence separated us from the heavily wooded forest beyond. But living beneath this shelter from the unrelenting heat of the tropical sun, was what could only be described as a "slum" of corrugated metal shacks, each built within the shadow of its neighbour. Everything was draped in plastic-sheeting to protect it from the torrential rains that they had at certain times of year; and everywhere was littered with discarded rubbish thrown to the ground, and blown against the fencing by the sea-winds. The smell was overpowering; clearly there were no such things as toilets or running-water! And living amid this chaos were hundreds of men, women and children; often seen pushed up against the fence, gazing with envy at the unattainable world of luxury that lived just beyond the barrier. Each person appeared haggard, hungry, and dirty; with a look of despair in their eyes. We were warned NOT to go ashore in small groups as they would be likely to mug us for our trainers or jeans; so clearly this would be one of those countries where going for a run would not be possible. However, I did venture ashore occasionally, en mass, to explore the town, but it was decided that most of our shore-side activities should be conducted through organised trips, with armed protection around us. Two trips sprang out at me; a day-visit to a high-class beach hotel, and a two day safari to one of Kenya's wildlife reserves.

As day-guests to the Beach Resort just north of Mombasa, we had access to all of the hotel facilities including the pristine pools, sandy private beaches, and numerous pool and beach bars. As I relaxed, leaning against the gently swaying palm trees, and dived into the crystal-clear waters, I imagined, just for a few hours, that I was a regular tourist, able to afford the type of luxury that surrounded me here.

A few days later, sat in the back of an open-topped safari 4x4 vehicle, I was driven along the wide open plains towards the gated-entrance to the Tsavo East National Park. We were about to embark on a two-day guided safari tour of the Tsavo East and West National Parks, staying overnight at a 5-star safari lodge. We were all bubbling with excitement; trips like this only happened to *rich* people, we were very lucky that this was subsidised by the navy, and discounted by the Kenyan government. Beyond the gate, tarmac roads were replaced by sun-baked dusty tracks. The terrain was flat as far as the eye could see; predominantly orange in colour, interspaced with clumps of dry savannah scrub and the odd skeletal-like tree. In the far distance, the dark purple mountains could be seen skirting the edges of the plains on which we were travelling. And beating down on us was the ever-present tropical sun, burning any exposed skin; the heat oppressive and dry.

As our vehicle progressed deeper into the wilderness, I saw family groups of lions slowly ambling down the track ahead of us, clearly in no rush to let us pass. I saw giraffes, camouflaged behind the foliage of dried-out trees, their necks reaching up to the highest branches to pluck the leaves with their enormously long tongues. Hidden amongst the beige waving grasslands I spotted ostriches; their small heads and long black necks peaking above the straw-like blades to watch our vehicles pass-by. And in the distance, I saw herds of zebra and antelopes grazing on-the-move as they traversed the flatlands.

It was sad to say, but by late afternoon the heat had taken its toll and tiredness had set in. Sarcastic comments of,

"Oh look; yet another zebra!" were commonplace. The navy's dry sense-of-humour was coming to the fore.

So it was with impeccable timing that we arrived at the Tia-Tia Safari Lodge, just in time for afternoon tea. Sat atop a small hill, it offered a panoramic view of a waterhole in the valley below, and to the plains beyond. Stood all around the tiny lake were a herd of elephants, each the colour of the orange earth on which they walked. From this distance they looked impressive, but having followed a tunnel from the lodge, I emerged into a viewing-hide at eye-level with the elephants, a mere 20m from their location. From here, it was as if I was stood next to them; I could almost touch them. It was a fitting end to an exciting, but tiring, day.

We all slept well that night, in the luxurious surroundings of the lodge. Next morning, I awoke early to the sounds of the dawn-chorus; the lions roaring in the distance, and the elephants trumpeting as they topped-up on water before marching across the cracked, parched plains. As for us, we had a repeat day of animal-spotting as we made our way back through the national park, on our way to Mombasa. It had been a once-in-a-lifetime excursion; one whose memories will stay with me forever. But for now, it was back to the real world; back to navy life, and the preparations for our return to sea...

CHAPTER 24

Across the Indian Ocean

Having left Kenya, Invincible headed east across the Indian Ocean. It was to be a long, hot cruise before reaching our midway stop-off point of Diego Garcia.
    Diego Garcia was a British-owned atoll located 2200 miles east of Tanzania, 1100 miles south of India, and 3000 miles west of Australia; almost dead-center of the Indian Ocean. Built on the exposed peak of an underwater mountain, the atoll formed a horseshoe-shaped string of land surrounding a central lagoon. Although a British Indian Ocean Territory, it was leased to the US government who built a huge naval-base, airfield, and satellite communications center on the island, and who were its *only* inhabitants. Due to its remote location, it was often referred to as, "Fantasy Island," and was used as an emergency runway for commercial aircraft, and the space-shuttle; it was used as a satellite-tracking station for the US space program, and as a listening station for subsequent military operations around the world. To us, it was simply a desert-island with an

American base on it; and a chance for a break from the monotony of life at sea.

I resumed my mission of running in every country that I could; jogging in the stifling heat, past the driftwood-littered, white sandy beaches; past the claw-like mangrove roots as they dipped into the warm salty water; and into what passed as the island's only town (a glorified naval-base, complete with beach-side Tiki-bars and cafes). Similar to Roosevelt Roads in Puerto Rico, this base had every facility that an American serviceman could dream of when away from home. It was effectively a little part of the US on foreign soil.

After a suitable period of "RnR," we returned to sea with the promise of an imminent live missile launch to look forward to. Invincible planned to fire one of its Sea Dart surface-to-air missiles. Although this did not come under my section, these were such rare occurrences that all weapons department personnel were either actively involved in the preparations and launch, or were allowed to witness the live shoot. The launcher, mounted on the bows, was capable of firing two missiles at a time (although for this exercise, only one would be launched). Each missile was 4.4m long, weighing 550kg, with an 11kg warhead that activated on contact or proximity. It could travel at a speed of mach 2, and was designed to attack aircraft or incoming missiles. It had semi-active onboard radar that tracked its target once it had been identified and illuminated by the ship's weapons radar. On the day of the launch I watched eagerly as the missile was automatically loaded onto its launcher. A target was acquired, and it spun towards the starboard side. There was a loud, "Woooooosh" sound as the missile left the ship; the vibration reverberating through the deck-plates into my bones. The missile arced into the sky following a pre-set trajectory, leaving a trail of thick acrid smoke in its wake. In a split second it was gone, vanished from sight as it headed towards the heavens. Another successful launch of the Sea Dart for HMS Invincible...

But as we progressed steadily eastwards, it was decreed that our escorts, the RFA's (Royal Fleet Auxiliaries) needed some training and practice with their *only* form of defence; their fixed-mounting GPMG machine-guns. The crews on these ships were civilians, but because they worked closely with the Royal Navy it placed them at risk, so they needed a means of defending themselves from attack. It fell to my section to provide this training as we were the Minor Weapons Section. My Chief Petty Officer and I were detailed to fly onto the Fort Austin in order to give their crews two days of training.

This was my first helicopter flight in the navy, so having donned the bright orange emergency "once-only-suit" (effectively, a diver's dry-suit, sealed at the neck and cuffs to protect from water ingress in the event of a ditching at sea), I waited for my safety briefing. This consisted of the pilot saying,

"If we go down in the water, wait until the chopper is fully submerged, then do your best to get out before inflating your life jacket. Don't inflate in the cab or you'll die...!"

With these inspiring words of confidence, I climbed aboard for my two minute flight to the Fort Austin's deck. The journey in the Sea King helicopter was short but extremely noisy (even with ear defenders on), and the vibration was extreme; rattling my very soul. Moments later, we landed with a bump, and were welcomed aboard by the civvie crew.

Life on an RFA was nothing like I had experienced before. I was given my own cabin (yes, a proper cabin; complete with en-suite, wooden fitted-bed, and office space). The food was equivalent to a hotel's, with numerous choices, and available 24/7. And the crew were extremely relaxed, with good morale, and very little of the discipline, rules, and regulations to which I was accustomed. The weapon training and live practice shoots went very smoothly. The gun-crews were well-drilled in their procedures, and from my point-of-view, it was a breath of fresh air to be able to *ask* people to operate and clean the weapons, rather than shouting and ordering them to do it, as I often had to in the Royal Navy. It was a totally different way of getting things done; one that worked brilliantly with civilian crews.

All too soon, it was time to return to Invincible, only this time we were to travel back in a Lynx helicopter, during a RAS between the two ships! The Lynx was a much smaller helicopter than the Sea King. I sat in the rear seat facing to port, with the rear sliding-doors open to the elements. The cabin was so cramped that I could touch the two pilots, and at a stretch I could have reached the controls; it was not big! The only thing holding me in was a waist-belt; if I had leaned forward without it, there was nothing to stop me falling to my death. As the helicopter lifted gently into the air, it turned sharply to port and it seemed that the blue of the sea rose to fill my whole line of sight through the open doorway. It levelled-off, and took position above, and to the rear of the two ships as they cruised side-by-side, transferring fuel and stores from one to the other. We were waiting for permission to land back on Invincible, but due to the RAS, we were ordered to hover in a holding-position until given the go-ahead. Our pilot was a fresh-faced, relatively new aviator, who got bored rather quickly with the waiting around. Over his shoulder he said,

"You don't mind if we go for a bit of a fly around while we're waiting, do you?"

It was less of a question, more of a statement of intent. Before I had a chance to reply, the Lynx shot forward and out over open sea. The engine revs increased with a whine as the helicopter flew, what appeared to me, to be vertically upwards until at the peak of its climb, it momentarily levelled-off before dropping like a stone, nose-first towards the water's surface. Through the front windows, all I could see was white-capped, royal-blue ocean, approaching at a rapid rate of knots. My knuckles were white, gripping the edge of the seat for dear life! My breathing had stopped in preparation for the impending impact. It was like being on a rollercoaster, only without the safety of the track to adhere to...! At the last minute, the Lynx pulled out of the dive, skimming the surface of the sea at some ridiculously low level; the waves flashing by the open doorway at a tremendous speed. The pilot leaned over with a sadistic grin on his face,

"You both OK? That's what we call a stall-dive. What do you think of aerobatics then?"

We were too shocked and scared to reply. We just sat there, shaking as the adrenalin worked its way through our bodies. Landing back on the stable deck of Invincible could not come too soon, and we both scurried away to the safety of our mess to regain some composure before returning to our daily duties...

By July, HMS Invincible had reached the island of Singapore for the first of her two visits. We were here for two weeks, during which time the crew would work a "tropical routine," meaning early starts, but with free afternoons and evenings (duty roster permitting). As we slid into Singapore Harbour we passed line-after-line of gigantic container ships anchored in the shipping-channels, waiting their turn to enter the second largest container port in the world. Considering we were on an aircraft-carrier, we were dwarfed by the immensity of these ships!

While the officers continued with their cocktail-parties and receptions for the Singapore nobility, the rest of us explored the city. The overwhelming impression was one of a bustling, modern city; a thriving economy, with towering, glass-fronted skyscrapers everywhere. And yet this contrasted starkly with the relics of colonial Singapore; the parliament buildings, the cricket greens, and The Raffles Hotel. Sir Thomas Stamford Raffles founded colonial Singapore in 1819 as a trading-post for the East India Company. When it collapsed in 1826, the islands were ceded to Britain as part of the establishment of the British Raj. Raffles remains the father-figure of the modern city, and as such, a visit to The Raffles Hotel was a must during our visit. Established in 1887, the hotel sat facing the waterways surrounded by its immaculate gardens. Forming a slight crescent shape, its white three-storey facade was augmented by intricately detailed balconies and a veranda. Within its many wings, it housed numerous ball rooms, billiards rooms, and the famous Long Bar; frequented by the likes of Somerset Maugham, amongst other celebrities. Renowned for only-the-highest-of-standards, its staff still wore traditional turbans and costumes from the Raj era; so it was somewhat surprising that the likes of me (resplendent in my beach-shorts and T-shirt) even managed to enter the hotel, let alone sip the over-priced national cocktail, The-Singapore-Sling, in The Long Bar.

Outside, I watched as locals and ex-pats alike, played cricket on the luxuriously plush lawns, edged by swaying palm trees; the colonial pavilion overlooked by the equally impressive government buildings. By the water's edge stood the symbol of Singapore, The Merlion. A creature with the head of a lion and the body of a fish, representing the city's fishing village roots, and its original name, Singapura, meaning "Lion City." The cosmopolitan city was a shopping Mecca, with underground shopping malls and arcades to rival America. You could buy anything your heart dreamed of, often at reduced rates compared to home, especially electronic goods imported from the Far East. But by night, the city changed. It became a sparkling cityscape, with multicoloured neon everywhere. The Chinatown area of the city came to life with street markets and food stalls. The smells of freshly cooked fish and an assortment of spices assaulted the senses. For next to nothing, you could get a freshly prepared meal from the street sellers, combining Chinese, Indian or Singaporean influences. It was here that the local people ate their meals; a sure-fire indication of the quality. But unlike in the UK, where discarded food wrappers would be thrown to the ground, Singapore was exceptionally clean. It was verging on the paranoid when it came to cleanliness, and rules were strictly enforced. Before our arrival, I had heard of how minor offences that would be overlooked at home would be punishable by arrest in Singapore. If you so much as dropped a single item of litter, spat in the street, had long hair over your collar, or jay-walked, you could be arrested on the spot! It was so strict that tourist T-shirts were produced with lists of offences depicted on them. Strict as it may have been, it did have the desired effect. Singapore was the cleanest, tidiest, and well-managed city I had ever seen; a credit to its government...

Our first visit to Singapore now complete, we sailed further east, full of information about places to visit during our return trip in a few weeks time. But before that, there was the small matter of transiting the South China Seas and the many islands of Indonesia and The Philippines. This area was rife with pirate attacks on international shipping. At first I thought it was a joke, a wind-up. But even in this modern age, pirates were commonplace around here. So it was, that our ship went to defence-watches and our upper-deck guns were manned at all times; just in case anyone was silly enough to take on the might of a British aircraft-carrier from their tiny armed speedboat...! However, we did not take this threat lightly; these pirates had shoulder-launched missiles that had been used to great effect during the Gulf War, and which, in the wrong hands, could pose a threat to our safety. Our gun-crews were primed and ready; eager to experience a fire-fight at close quarters. But as the days went by without any sightings of the "enemy," this enthusiasm dwindled until eventually, the manning of the guns in sweltering heat became a chore rather than a pleasure.

As Invincible headed north, up the coast of China, the threat level diminished; gun-crews were stood down, and normal sea routines resumed. We were on our way to Japan...

CHAPTER 25

The Far East

In July '92, our flotilla reached its furthest point east, entering the US naval-base at Yokosuka in Japan. Yokosuka was situated on the south-eastern coast of Japan, on a peninsular at the entrance to Tokyo Bay. Tokyo was a further 40 miles north, but Yokosuka was classed as part of the metropolis of Greater-Tokyo, as was its more famous neighbour Yokohama. Being a port city, it sprawled across the shorelines of the peninsular, having the iconic Mount Fuji as its backdrop. The port and US naval-base dominated the area, but the city was also renowned for its car manufacturing and other industries. To look at, it resembled any modern, international city, with tall bland-looking buildings, office blocks, and paved roads; the only features distinguishing it from others being the Japanese symbols and writing on shop-hoardings and road signs. Having had no preconceived ideas of what Japan ought to look like, I was not too disappointed. However, in the back of my mind, I had images from the past, of temples, and Samurai Warriors; surely there must be somewhere that would show the *real* Japan of old?

As luck would have it, an opportunity arose to visit the ancient Samurai capital-city of Kamakura, to the south-west of Yokosuka. I was led to believe that this was the location to see some authentic temples and shrines of the Shogun era. I was not to be disappointed. As I climbed off the coach, shaded by the juniper and cherry trees that lined the roads, I entered into a world of Shinto, Zen, and Taoist temples. Their names elude me, and one temple merged into the memory of the one before, but I saw a huge statue of Amida Buddha, serenely sitting cross-legged upon a Dias; its body streaked green by the effects of weathering on its exposed copper surfaces. I visited Tsurugaoka Hachimangū, the most important Shinto shrine in Kamakura; sat on top of a hill to the north of the city, it was approached along a 1.8km, tree-lined avenue and a great stone stairway. Along the route were a number of red wood Shinto gateways and a few intricately carved red-painted bridges straddling the canals that linked its two lakes. To the side of this ceremonial pathway stood a 1000 year old ginkgo tree which was mentioned in an urban-legend as being where a famous assassin hid before attacking his targets.

I visited other temples to see ceremonial drums and massive copper bells. I saw row-upon-row of mini Buddha statuettes lined-up like soldiers. There were literally hundreds of them, some wearing woolly-hats and scarves, others draped in colourful robes, or adorned with beautiful flowers as a sign of respect to their God from the adoring worshipers. I saw a wall of wooden caskets, uniformly lined-up and piled rank-upon-rank. Each had its own unique motif or design which I took to have a religious significance; however, it transpired that these were actually barrels of beer, for what purpose, I do not know...! Many of the shrines contained golden statues of Buddha, worn on the hands and feet from constant touching by the devotees; and everywhere was infused with the aroma of incense, the smoke drifting in the air around me.

While I was gaining an insight into Japan's culture and history, others from my ship took the famous Bullet Train from Yokosuka to Tokyo, to experience the modern side of Japanese culture. And while they were away, another group attempted the long trek up the side of Mount Fuji. Whether they made it to the summit, I do not know; but I suspect not...

Back in Yokosuka, some of us explored the area adjacent to the naval base. By the water's edge stood the British-built pre-dreadnought battleship, Mikasa. Built in the 1890's, it served in the Imperial Japanese Navy, and was flagship to Admiral Togo. It was the *only* ship of its class to be built and was preserved as a living memorial with its crew dressed in uniforms of the 1900's. With its metal-clad hull, iron masts, and powerful 45-calibre 12-inch guns, it was a formidable ship of its time.

Just outside the naval-base stood the "Club-Alliance" enlisted-men's club (open to all US and British servicemen), so it was only right that we visit for a drink or three. Nearby was the area known as "The Honch," a Mecca for shopping and nightlife and an obligatory stop-off point for all of our crew.

As the visit to Japan drew to a close, an extravagant firework-display was mounted on the shores of Yokosuka. The night sky became alive with the multicoloured explosions of rockets as they detonated way above my head; the Mikasa being draped from bow to stern in what looked like falling white fire. I like to think that this was arranged as a farewell to us; a thank-you for our visit. But somehow, I got the impression that it was actually more to do with a religious festival that just happened to coincide with our departure. Either way, in my mind, it was in *our* honour; and it was a fitting end to our cultural visit to Japan.

Whilst each ship on our deployment followed their own schedule (some heading to Australia), Invincible sailed around the southern tip of Japan and crossed the narrow straits to South Korea. To while away the time, our senior rates mess arranged an evening of song and dance in the form of a "Stars-in-their-Eyes" show. In the 90's, Stars-in-their-Eyes was a TV talent-show where members of the public performed routines imitating famous celebrities. Ours was a poor-man's-version with those members of the mess who possessed any talent, performing songs under the guise of their more famous counterparts. With makeshift costumes, and guitars in-hand, they did an admirable job of impersonating the various celebrities; memories of our SOD's Opera springing-to-mind. A good night was had by all...

Arriving at Pusan in South Korea (now re-named Busan), at the start of August, we were greeted by the second most populous city in the country after Seoul. It was modern in the most part, office blocks dominating the skyline. But tradition and religion were never far away. Exploring the city streets around the port area, I came across Yongdusan Park. This was a large public park, home to the impressive Pusan Tower; a 118m-high tower built of white stone, with a lantern-like viewing platform at the top. To me, it looked similar to an oversized gas-lamp from the streets of Victorian London. From its summit, you had the most panoramic view of Pusan and the port area spread before you, but surrounding its base were a series of immaculately maintained oriental gardens, complete with a pagoda-style temple, and a statue of the rampant Pusan Dragon. The temple, housing a big green prayer-bell, was topped by an elaborately decorated tiled roof with sweeping, upturned corners. This was sat atop 12 red-coloured pillars which surrounded the bell. It was a very serene and calming place to visit, totally in contrast to the busy hustle-and-bustle of the remainder of the city.

Nearby was Jagalchi Market. Originally a fish-market near to the port, it was now a tourist street market; a bazaar selling a variety of mementoes from Korea. In many of these stalls, the main items for sale that seemed to stand-out from the rest were soft cuddly gorilla toys! As to why gorillas were so popular in Korea, I have no idea, but everybody loved them. Most were about 1m tall, with cute expressions on their cheeky faces, and I would guess that about 80% of the ship's company bought one for themselves, or loved ones back home. On the return trip to the UK, every void aboard ship was crammed with gorillas; and when we performed our Procedure-Alpha routine during our return, a large number of gorillas made their appearance on the upper-deck, interspaced between their owners and the sailor next to them! A strange sight, I am sure...

Food in Pusan was similar to Singapore in that it was available on the streets as well as in open-fronted restaurants. A few fellow PO's and I decided to try some local delicacies, being informed that we were to have a sort of table-top BBQ. As we sat around the table, a conical brass dish was placed in the center. Beneath it was hot coal; clearly this was the cooking part of the BBQ. Plates of assorted raw meats were placed by us, and through broken English, we were invited to place our chosen piece of meat on the cone dish to cook it. It seemed easy enough, so we dived-in, eager to sample this new twist on a BBQ. The food was tasty, if a bit sweet, but it was not until part-way through that someone thought to question what it was that we were eating. On asking the staff, they smiled charmingly, and said,

"Woof, woof."

We looked at each other bemused.

"Surely not – we weren't eating DOG were we?"

It turned out that, yes, a Korean delicacy was in fact dog! Despite an initial revulsion, the meat tasted OK so we carried-on regardless. Trying new things was all part of the fun of foreign travel; or so we told ourselves...

Although we were only in South Korea for a short time, we still managed to host a visit from local businessmen and politicians, and got a taste of life in Korea. There was no feeling of tension, or worry about their northern neighbour, North Korea, whilst we were there; but as history has shown, following a change in administration, North Korea has since become much more aggressive, pursuing its nuclear-weapon policy, and making the region much less stable than it was.

With another interesting visit under our belt, we headed-off to pastures new. Next on our itinerary was Hong Kong...

Heading south-west, Invincible passed through the Taiwan Strait and on to Hong Kong. At this time, Hong Kong was still a British Territory. Following the First Opium War of 1839-42, Hong Kong Island, the Kowloon peninsula, and the New Territories became a British Colony on lease from China. During our visit in 1992, preparations were well under-way for its handing-back to China in 1997. But for the time being, it was still very much British; all-be-it with a lot of very Chinese influences.

Being one of the region's deepest natural ports, Invincible sailed into the heart of Hong Kong's Victoria Harbour, mooring alongside the city's waterside promenade, surrounded by a forest of skyscrapers. Hong Kong was one of the most densely populated cities in the world, its residents living and working so closely together that rather than the city spreading sideways; it spread up, towards the Heavens. It boasted the second highest density of high-rises in the world. This made it feel a very claustrophobic city; the tall buildings looming over the busy streets below; the sky hardly visible from street level. It also made for an exciting arrival by plane, as the commercial aircraft had to fly between these skyscrapers to land at the old airport; their wing-tips nearly touching the towers as they passed! Because of the high population, hot and humid conditions, and the enclosed environment, it meant that air pollution was a major problem at certain times of day. You could almost see the smog cloud enveloping the city as we approached, and it made for an uncomfortable time as we got used to "chewing" the air...!

Hong Kong was also a strategic British naval and military base. The army were permanently deployed here to patrol the boarders with China, stopping people entering the colony illegally. And the navy had a permanent presence in the form of HMS Tamar, a shore-base located to our west.

Our visit to Hong Kong was to be a relatively long one; a whole month. This was to be the turning-point of the deployment; a break before we headed back towards Europe, and home. As such, we were each given two weeks of "special" leave in addition to our yearly allowance. We had had prior notice of this, so some members of the crew had arranged flights back to the UK, or arranged for their wives to fly out to visit them. Others had arranged trips to Australia and other eastern countries; taking advantage of the location we were in. The crew was being slowly dispersed, but only for a short while. As for me, my parents had made the tedious flight from London to Hong Kong, via a stop-over in Singapore, and were safely ensconced in a luxury hotel, a mere 800m from where our ship was berthed; they could see Invincible from the expansive glass windows of their apartment. Often, I would run along the waterfront in the oppressive heat, stopping-off at my parent's hotel on the way back. Stood in the elegant foyer, dripping sweat all over the ornate marble floors, I am sure the immaculately dressed concierge wondered what had just walked through his front doors! Who had let the riff-raff in?

As the crew was still working a tropical routine whilst in Hong Kong, there was plenty of free time in addition to our leave entitlement, in which to explore the treasures of the city. Our regular means of travel was the famous Star Ferry which ran from Hong Kong Island to Kowloon across the harbour. These two-decked, green and white passenger boats plied the waters every few minutes, always packed with commuters and tourists alike. They were also the best place from which to view the cityscape; especially at night when the scene was alive with neon signs, floodlit skyscrapers, and often fireworks illuminating the darkness above. It was a truly magical vista; one that we got to enjoy nightly for the whole month that we were there.

Darkness also brought the start of the night-markets in Kowloon, and the Bird Market where stalls sold hundreds of small exotic birds in delicate wire cages; the area alive with the sounds of these chirping creatures. These markets were where you could buy *anything*; spices (many of which I had never seen nor heard of before), electronic goods (at vastly reduced prices), clothing (from T-shirts to fully-fitted, made-to-order suits), and food. Food was everywhere. You could buy live chickens or ready prepared meals; snake meat or cooked-to-order Chinese food. The options were endless, but all were extremely tasty; and cheap!

I visited many places in and around Hong Kong, some with other crew members, others with my parents. I had many adventures, too many to recall each one of them here, but there were certain excursions that stood out; places I visited, and experiences I had, that were more than just run-of-the-mill. I trekked to the top of Victoria Peak to the rear of Hong Kong Island. From the viewing platform, I had a perfect bird's-eye-view of the entire city spread before me, showing how compact, but densely built it was. I could see our ship, a tiny speck by the water's edge. And I could see the green hills covered in thick vegetation that marked the area known as The New Territories, bordering China. I visited the Floating Village, to the east of where our ship was berthed. Here, the poorer members of society lived, and worked, on small wooden boats, each tied to the next to form a floating pontoon of marine craft. From the outside, it looked similar to the slum I saw in Mombasa; only this one was floating amid a mass of litter on the water's surface. But those living in these conditions seemed happy. Yes, they were poor (compared to the multi-million dollar offices and hotels that surrounded them), but every one of them had a smile on their face; and with the kids playing happily in the dirty water, it seemed things were not as bad as they first appeared.

In total contrast to this, I spent an evening aboard one of the famous Floating Restaurants of Aberdeen Harbour.

Having boarded a small passenger ferry, I was transported to the elegant "Jumbo" and "Tai Pak" floating restaurants. Each was extravagantly decorated in the manner of an Imperial Chinese Palace; visible from afar, illuminated by a million lights. Having entered the world of gold and red, our group was escorted to a circular table where a feast of Chinese buffet food was laid before us on a spinning carousel. Beneath the opulent ceilings and a multitude of Chinese lanterns, we gorged on the food provided. Yes, it was clearly a tourist-trap, but one that we were all happy to experience. For that one evening, we were treated like Emperors of old...

While some of the crew visited the Ocean Park attraction (an aquarium and sealife show, rollercoaster Fun-Park, and wave-pool), my parents and I took the ferry across to Lantau Island. This was the largest of Hong Kong's islands, being twice the size of Hong Kong itself, and was often referred to as "The Lungs of Hong Kong" due to its abundance of indigenous forest and mountainous terrain. We went to Ngong Ping to visit the Po Lin Monastery, and to see the 34m bronze Tian Tan Buddha, sat cross-legged on its three layered altar on top of a hill. To reach it, we climbed the 268 stone steps to the summit, from where, on a good day, you could reportedly see Macau and mainland China. From here, we went to the fishing village of Tai O where we saw several hundred stilt-houses built over the shallow waters. The local fishermen caught, and preserved in salt, a variety of indigenous fish species; many of which were left to hang, drying in the intense heat. The smell was quite overpowering at times! In the 90's, Lantau Island was a tropical paradise, a natural environment that contrasted sharply with the man-made structures on Hong Kong Island. Whether that is still the case today, I do not know, as Lantau has become home to the world famous Hong Kong Disneyland, as well as the newly built international airport. Hopefully it has not ruined it too much...

Back in the heart of busy Hong Kong, I found the calming oasis that was known as Tiger Balm Gardens. These were a series of landscaped gardens built around the Haw Par Mansion, and were first opened to the public in the 1950's. Outside of the garden walls, city life continued in its hectic, frenzied way; a cacophony of noise, traffic, and car horns. Inside the garden walls, there was silence, calmness, and a serene stillness; only occasionally broken by the passing of butterflies or the swimming of giant terrapins in the ornate ponds. Dotted around the garden complex were a host of sculptures; tigers, dragons, Buddha's, and comic characters with cheeky grins on their faces. No doubt, each had a place in oriental history or mythology, but it was lost on me. I simply saw statues; each decorated in a rainbow-pallet of colours, from vibrant oranges and reds, to ochre yellows and azure blues. It was a very strange, but magical place which, unfortunately has since been demolished for redevelopment in this ever-changing city.

Aside from tourist activities, naval life continued as usual in Hong Kong. Cleaning was our ever-present companion, ensuring the ship was in top condition for the many visits from those ashore. One visit in particular stood out; the visit of Chris Patten, the 28th, and final, Governor of Hong Kong. He was akin to Royalty in these far reaches of the Empire, and so he was shown due reverence. On our departure from Hong Kong, it was my section's responsibility to perform a 21-Gun Salute in his honour. Mounted on the roof of the "island," our three WW1 saluting guns were prepared. Timing of each salvo was essential, so that task fell to me; the guns being operated by my team. Unfortunately, three shots into the 21-gun salute, and the Wren firing gun number-one found that her grip was insufficient to pull the ancient trigger correctly! These guns were old and temperamental, requiring a two-handed approach to pulling the trigger; quite a bit of arm-strength being essential. At the last minute, I leapt into action, taking over her position, and dealing with the timing of the salute simultaneously. Despite this minor hic-up, outwardly, nobody was aware of any disturbance, and the 21-Gun Salute went ahead perfectly.

A month had flown by; it was now time to leave Hong Kong and continue our voyage around the Far East. Little did we know that within a few days of our departure, our seamanship skills would be tested to the full...! As Invincible headed back into the South China Seas, we caught the back-end of a passing typhoon! The skies above us turned dark and foreboding. The winds increased to hurricane level, and the Heavens opened; drowning us in torrential rain! Our aircraft-carrier was over 200m long, and yet, in these conditions it was thrown around like a leaf on the water. The waves were horrendous; breaking 40m over the bows. I even saw waves flying above the height of the mast superstructure! A pipe was made,

"The upper-deck is out of bounds until further notice."

It seemed common-sense to everyone, however my section still had to conduct magazine rounds to ensure the safety of the ship! Dressed in full foul-weather gear, I donned my safety harness (normally only used for working at height) and, in company with one of the mechanics, I clipped on to the steel safety-lines strung around the upper-deck. No sooner had we stepped outside the safety of the doorway, than the rain and spray drenched us; soaking our uniforms *through* the waterproof clothing. The wind blew us off our feet, forcing us to crawl along the deck, holding onto the safety-line for dear life! Arriving at the first ready-use magazine, unable to stand up, and suddenly aware of the dangers involved in opening the magazine door in this wind, I decided to call-off the operation; the magazines would just have to fend for themselves...! We retraced our steps and dived into the relative calmness below decks. Unfortunately, for those inside, it was not quite so pleasant; many of them suffering badly with sea-sickness! The air was thick with the aroma of vomit, and people were bouncing off the metal walls, sick-bags in hand, looking extremely green in the face. It was not a good way to return to sea...

Within a day, the storm had passed, and things returned to normal. But with the ship, and its crew, battered and bruised, and feeling a little sorry for themselves, it was decided to put in to Singapore a little earlier than expected for our second visit of the deployment.

CHAPTER 26

Back to the Indian Ocean

Our initial couple of days in Singapore were marked by the torrential monsoon rains that we encountered. Moored at a jetty near a forested estuary, I watched in the humid conditions, as the rain fell vertically down from the sky; creating a sort of "rain-shadow" as it hit the overhanging canopy of trees. The tracks and roads turned to flowing rivers, and the immaculately manicured lawns and verges took on a fresh olive-green appearance. As is the way in these climes, the rain soon cleared, the floods it created dissipated, and the sun dried everything within minutes. I could now go ashore to see the places I had missed on my first visit.

From the Chinese-and-Japanese-Gardens at Jurong East, in west Singapore, to Singapore-Zoo (reputed to be the second-best zoo in the world after San Diego in the USA) in the north of the island, I travelled extensively, making good use of the efficient bus and rail networks. The foremost visit that I wanted to make was to the former POW (Prisoner-of-War) camp at Changi, in the east of the island. On arrival at the imposing concrete fortress that was the modern-day prison, I was somewhat disappointed; this was not the infamous WW2 prison camp that I had been led to believe was at this site. However, stood within the shadow of this building was a pitched-roof, open-sided, wood and bamboo chapel; a replica of the original chapel built by Australian POW's in 1944. This was a memorial to those held at this camp during WW2, and included many photographs, drawings, and mementoes of the time.

With the Fall of Singapore in February 1942, the Japanese military invaded the island, incarcerating thousands of civilians in the concrete prison. The former British Selarang Barracks outside of the prison-walls were used as a POW Camp to hold the 50,000 British, Australian, and Dutch prisoners-of-war who were interned for the duration of the conflict. Held in appalling conditions, with starvation and disease rife, over 850 POW's died at the camp; many more dying after being transferred to other camps and used as slave-labour to build the notorious Burma Railway, and the Sandakan Airfield. If the conditions did not kill them, then the sadistic beatings and torture dished-out by their captors did!

Why was it so important to me that I visited this location? Well, my grandfather, on my mother's side of the family, was one of the many forced to endure the harsh regime imposed at Changi. In some ways he was one of the lucky ones; he survived everything that was thrown at him until his liberation in 1945. However, on his return to England, he never fully recovered physically or mentally from what he experienced. He arrived in the UK with big open sores on his body, and his lungs were ruined from exposure to TB and other respiratory diseases encountered in the camp. Dying before my second birthday, I never got to know him, and he never spoke about his time at Changi, but the things he faced on a daily basis during his time in Singapore always intrigued me. It was natural that given the opportunity to visit the island, I would head to Changi to show my respects to him, and his colleagues.

Whilst in the area, I also visited the Commonwealth War Graves Commission Cemetery at Kranji. This, too, had begun life as a Japanese POW Camp, but following the end of WW2, its small cemetery was expanded to become Singapore's War Graves Cemetery; those buried at Changi (and other POW camps) being removed and re-interred here. It was the last resting place for 4394 fallen personnel from the 1942-1945 era, and 4461 burials in total. As I passed among the ranks of white-marble headstones, it crossed my mind that some of those beneath me had probably known, fought, and lived alongside my grandfather during the war. It made the experience more personal; I had a connection to these men now...

Two weeks after arriving in Singapore, our departure date loomed. I had had a great time on the island during both of my visits, but now it was time to turn my mind to thoughts of home; to the return-leg of the deployment. But that was still three months away; lots more countries to visit, and adventures to be had...

Before leaving the Far East, there was one more country to visit; Malaysia. Initially Invincible headed north from Singapore, up the east coast of Malaysia, and anchored off the island of Pulau Tioman. At 20km long and situated 32km from the mainland, this was a sparsely-populated, heavily-forested island. With our ship "dressed-overall" with small pennants draped from bow to stern, this was to be a free afternoon ashore; a celebration day, and possibly the last opportunity for us to enjoy a tropical-beach location before we returned home. Small passenger boats ferried us ashore to the nearest sandy beach. While some of our number ventured into the tropical rainforest, encountering lizards and birdlife galore, the majority of us took advantage of the deserted, white sandy beaches, and the crystal-clear waters that were sheltered by the coral reefs surrounding us. An impromptu "banyan" or beach party was organised. It was a perfect way to relax after our tourist adventures in Singapore.

It was now early October, and we set sail, passing Singapore at the tip of the Malaysian peninsular, and then north, up the western side of the country. A few days later, we arrived at the island of Penang; The Pearl of the Orient. We were based in the capital of George Town, the second-biggest city in Malaysia after Kuala Lumpur. As a former British Colony, founded by Francis Light in 1786 as part of The East India Company, it still retained a number of its historic colonial buildings, each swamped by the more modern skyscrapers, high-rise offices, and the dominant Komtar Tower (a 232m, 65-floored, cylindrical concrete monolith of 1970's design). It was a symbiotic coexistence of heritage buildings and more modern architecture. To the rear of the city was Penang Hill; accessed by its own funicular railway; and separating the city from Butterworth on the mainland was the Penang Strait, with its 8.4 mile bridge.

On leaving the confines of Invincible, I was confronted by a fleet of trishaws (three-wheeled bikes in the form of a rickshaw, with sunshade umbrella to protect the passengers); their riders keen to show me the sights of the city. For what seemed like pennies, I was driven past the modern downtown areas to "Little India," with its ornate Sri Mahamariamman Hindu Temple, and into "Chinatown." I stepped into the golden realm of the Wat Chayamangkalaram; a Thai Temple that looked like it had been transported direct from Bangkok. With its intricately-detailed gold-encrusted sea-serpent dragons guarding the entrance, to its wedding-cake tiered pagodas smothered in gold-leaf; the temple was stunning. Within one of the buildings lay a huge reclining Buddha draped in a golden sarong, its head propped on a pillow. Around the inner quadrangle were various other shrines with Buddha statues of every size and description, surrounded by pink lotus-leaf candles. But the place was swarming with tourists, the hum of their chatter adding to the busy chaotic nature of the temple. In contrast, the Dharmikarama Burmese Temple just across the road had all the peace and serenity that I would have expected to find at its more famous neighbour.

Amid the obligatory receptions aboard ship, I still found time to go on an island-tour of Penang. Aboard an ancient bus, I entered the forested hinterland. Consisting of predominantly granite-hills in the center, the southeast quarter had an abundance of rice fields and mangroves, whilst the southwest had scenic fishing villages and fruit orchards. At a place known as Sungai Kluang, I was shown a Chinese Temple called "The Snake Temple." Built in around 1850 by a Buddhist Monk called Chor Soo Kong, it was possibly the *only* temple of its sort in the world, and was originally called The Temple of the Azure Cloud. As I passed through the highly decorated porch into the main chamber, I was confronted by a number of what looked like tiered and graduated, oversized cake-stands. But instead of cupcakes adorning the various platters, there were hundreds of wriggling Pit-Vipers...! They were everywhere; on the stands, on the floor, and on the altar. The whole room had the aroma of burning incense; the sacred smoke believed to be what prevented the snakes from biting the worshipers with their venomous teeth. However, taking no risks, I was informed that they had been de-venomed as a precaution, just in case... The local devotees believed that these snakes came to the temple of their own accord, and were not brought there as a tourist attraction; I am not quite so sure...

With our visit to Penang at an end, our Far Eastern leg of the deployment was over; Invincible was to return across the Indian Ocean, and would then head into the Persian Gulf for a good-will visit in the Middle East.

With the end of our trip in sight, charity events came to mind as a means of raising money for good causes; the return crossing of the Indian Ocean being the perfect opportunity to conduct these. Our Royal Marine contingent decided to run around the flight-deck non-stop for 24 hours in a relay event. Dressed in full combat-gear, carrying packs and rifles, they endured extremely high temperatures. They were even joined by a Wren from our ship's company who managed to sustain their relentless pace for the entire day (she was the navy's first, and only, female qualified diver at the time, and extremely fit).

While this was going on, a group of die-hard gym-monkeys, including me, decided to use the two "ergo" rowing-machines to row-across-the-Indian-Ocean, 24 hours a day, for as long as it took to reach the Gulf. On paper, it sounded simple enough; just get enough bodies involved to complete 30 minute sessions on the rowers, and repeat it day and night until our arrival. Volunteers were sought, schedules were arranged, and the rowing began. The machines were moved from the enclosed hanger to the quarterdeck at the rear of the ship so that there was a view to keep us motivated, and to allow a bit of a breeze to keep us cool. Some of the crew made a token effort, doing only a single session throughout the entire week or more that it took. Others, like me, opted to do two or more sessions per day, every day (including at least one in the early hours).

By the time we had reached the Gulf of Oman, Invincible had clocked-up over 3000 nautical miles of travel since leaving Penang. As to how many miles we had completed on the rowing machines, I have no idea; records were kept, and I had the honour of having completed the most number of sessions on the rowers, as well as the greatest individual distance covered. But the main achievement was the amount of money raised for our local charities in Portsmouth.

Money was also raised by means of an onboard lottery. Each of us donated a pound per person, per week; so the amount collected was quite substantial. As our deployment was quite high-profile, lots of well known companies were keen to be associated with it. They donated prizes for our lottery; the main prize being a brand new Land

Rover Discovery! Needless to say, I did not win, but the prizes were such that it was well worth entering.

As we passed Mumbai in India, it was decided that we would have a free-day at sea. A "Village Fair" was arranged on the flight-deck, with clay-pigeon-shooting, human-skittles, deck-hockey, and a fun BBQ. Officers were placed in a make-shift set of stocks, and we pelted them with soaked sponges. And as the sun set on the tranquil Indian Ocean, The Royal Marines Band gave a floodlit evening concert, culminating in the ceremonial lowering of the flag to the soulful tones of a lone bugler. A fitting end to a lovely relaxing day at sea...

CHAPTER 27

The Middle East

November 1992.

Having crossed the Indian Ocean, HMS Invincible arrived off the coast of Oman. She was heading into the Persian Gulf to link-up with other British warships of The Armilla Patrol. Since the end of the First Gulf War in 1991, the region had settled into an uneasy peace. Although there were no outwardly hostile activities at this time, tensions were high amongst all of the Gulf States. To try to have a calming influence and to be present should any fighting break-out, NATO naval forces were routinely required to patrol the Persian Gulf, and as we were in the area, it was decided that the presence of the British Flagship would be a welcome addition to the patrol, and a show-of-force to any factions with hostile intent.

In order to enter the Gulf, we needed to pass through The Straits of Hormuz; a strategically important choke-point, 29 nautical miles wide at its narrowest point, with Iran to the north and UAE (United Arab Emirates) to the south. About 20% of the world's petroleum passed through these straits making it essential that there remained free access to all shipping. However, due to its position and importance, Iran watched over it like a hawk; multiple missile complexes were situated in the hills to the north, actively tracking all shipping (military and civilian). As a result, all Royal Navy ships entering the Gulf's waters were effectively on a "war-footing." We closed-up in defence-watches; all guns armed and manned, and all missile systems active, ready to go to action-stations at a moment's notice. As we passed through the straits, small Iranian fast-patrol-boats were seen leaving home waters to investigate the huge aircraft-carrier passing their shores. They were monitored closely, but with the heightened tensions, neither side wanted an international incident. Our sensors could detect the Iranian missiles' tracking-radar following us; reports were even heard of their missile launchers pointing in our direction (itself being an aggressive action), but no contact was received. We passed safely through the straits and joined our colleagues to patrol the Persian Gulf.

Over the following days, our ship patrolled the waters past Qatar and Bahrain, as far north as Kuwait. We conducted naval exercises with our fellow ships, and with a British nuclear submarine; reminding us that we were *still* a fully-functioning warship and not just a source of PR during visits around the globe. All the time, we were alert to potential threats, remaining in defence-watches, and ensuring our ship was ready for combat should it be required.

Finally, we moored alongside at Abu Dhabi in the UAE for a welcome break from patrolling, and a chance for the officers to mingle with the leaders of some of the politically-friendly states in this area.

Abu Dhabi was built on a T-shaped island jutting out into the Persian Gulf, joined to the mainland a mere 250m away by a series of modern multi-levelled bridges. Although, at the time, it was an oil-rich state with towering skyscrapers and high-rise buildings, it was nothing compared to the extremely affluent, center of culture and business that it is nowadays. In the 90's it was still in its infancy.

Continuing my running theme; when we arrived, the large British Ex-Pat community invited us to a Hash-House-Harriers social event. As afternoon arrived, our hosts collected us from the ship's gangway and whisked us away, out into the flat, endless desert sands where a cross-country trail had been set for us to follow. As the oppressive heat dissipated during the early evening, we raced across desert scrubland, through copses of dried-out trees, following gullies and ancient water-courses until we arrived at a small tented area. As is customary after Hash-House-Harriers events, alcohol flowed freely. But that cannot be right; surely it was illegal to drink alcohol in Arabic countries? That was what we had been told on the ship. Well, this was true; it was certainly arrestable if seen in public. But the Ex-Pat community seemed to have rules of their own (hence the reason why we were in such a remote location), and sources of alcohol were available freely on the black-market. After a few drinks in my dehydrated state, the alcohol went straight to my head. Mention was made of taking us to some underground, illegal club to continue the festivities, but from that point on, my mind was a blank! The next thing I remember is waking-up, sat on the jetty in front of our ship, holding a burger. How I got there, and what happened the night before, I have no memory of; even to this day! It was quite scary to lose a part of a day; especially in a foreign country, with people you do not know, and in a State renowned for its harsh disciplinary regulations. I was lucky. I got back to the ship safely, unharmed; but anything could have happened! I assume that I have the Ex-Pats to thank for my safe return, but equally, I have the same people to thank for getting me in that state in the first place! Never again...!

A couple of days later, I joined a trip to the neighbouring emirate, and city of Dubai. The minibus drove past various mosques nestled beneath the towering high-rises on the streets of Abu Dhabi, before it emerged into the featureless desert separating the two metropolises. With the sea to my left, the essentially flat desert landscape on my right was littered with enormous sand-dunes. Nowadays, "Off-Roading" with 4-wheel-drive vehicles over these dunes is a major tourist activity, but back then it had never been heard of. We sufficed with a quick jog up the steep slopes in the midday sun, before continuing our journey north.

Arriving in Dubai, the colossal cityscape was spread before us. As with Abu Dhabi, Dubai was a rich city, benefitting from the oil industry and the gold markets. But as with its neighbour, it too was in its infancy; it was hard to compare it to the modern-day city. There was no Burj Khalifa, no Palm Jumeirah, and no "World's Islands" complex. Instead, we watched as the ancient dhow fishing boats, and the abras (water taxis) sailed back and forth across the expansive Dubai Creek. We visited the Dubai Museum with its traditional tented-entrance and obligatory camel. And we visited the Jumeirah Mosque with its white domes and two minaret towers. But the main purpose of our visit was to go to the large shopping malls, with promises of gold galore, and counterfeit copies of the most recent Hollywood films and CD's, at unbelievably cheap prices. We were not disappointed... We stocked-up on as many discs as we could afford, before making our return back to the confines of Invincible in Abu Dhabi.

With our shopping needs fulfilled, and our political obligations to the Gulf States complete, we resumed defence-watches as Invincible returned through the Straits of Hormuz; bidding farewell to the Persian Gulf, and heading south to re-enter The Red Sea, and ultimately The Suez Canal.

On November the 5th, Bonfire Night, we slowly sailed north up the Suez Canal. As with our southern journey, guns were turned inboard and covered-up. Those not on duty were given the day-off to sunbathe, and watch the world go by. But unlike our previous transit, things were a bit more subdued on our way back. Many of us were contemplating our return to Portsmouth; thinking of the adventures we had already had in the Far East, and looking forward to Christmas at home. The Suez Canal marked a symbolic key-point in our deployment; the return to the Med. We were within touching-distance of home; and for some, this could not come soon enough...

CHAPTER 28

The Holy Land and our homeward journey

On exiting the Suez Canal, Invincible travelled north to the city of Haifa, in Israel. It was very rare for UK ships to go to Israel at this time, but it gave us the opportunity to visit some of the sites of religious significance mentioned in the Bible. However, this was only *after* we had performed a formal parade and "Divisions" on Invincible's flight-deck. The whole ship's company was formed-up in best uniforms, and led by the Royal Marines Band and the Guard-of-Honour, we all marched past the Admiral and ship's Captain. This formality out of the way, we were free to explore the city, and to go on organised trips into the center of Israel.

The port of Haifa was the third-largest city in Israel, situated 56 miles north of Tel Aviv. Built on the sprawling northern slopes of Mount Carmel, it had three distinct levels. The lower level, nearest the water's edge, was the center for business and commerce. The middle level was made-up of older residential communities, and the upper level was dominated by the more modern residential areas, overlooking the lower tiers. With the ongoing conflicts between the Arab and Jewish communities in Israel, it was somewhat surprising to find that in Haifa, both groups seemed to live in relative harmony. The people went about their daily business as they would in any other cosmopolitan city. The one thing that stuck-out as strange, compared to Europe, was the prevalence of young Israelis wandering around the streets carrying rifles (some as young as 12 or 13). Quite often, I would see teenagers queuing-up for a bus, their assault-rifle slung over their shoulder like a handbag! Nobody seemed to take any notice of them; it was "normal"...! The sight of conscripted military personnel on the streets (also armed) was also a bit of a shock; in the UK you rarely saw forces-personnel in uniform walking the streets as it posed such a high security risk. Talking to some of these conscripts, they were just normal people in a difficult situation. None of them wanted to do national service, but they had no choice. They had an acceptance of their fate, and the fact that they may well be required to fight at some point, in the conflict between Israel and those occupying Palestinian and Lebanese territories.

Before we left Israel, an opportunity arose for a day-trip through the Israeli desert to Jerusalem, Bethlehem, Masada, and the Dead Sea. I jumped at the once-in-a-lifetime chance to see these places; especially at this time of year, on the run-up to Christmas.

Our coach headed southeast, into the Judean Desert. But unlike the sandy deserts we had encountered in the UAE, this one was mountainous, and instead of soft fine sand, it was strewn with rough boulders and rubble. Passing the occasional oasis of palm trees and bushes, we entered the perfectly flat lands on the shores of the Dead Sea, and the border with Jordan. To the west was a ridge of mountains, and isolated at one end was a lone rock plateau, akin to a Mesa. This was the fortress of Masada; a UNESCO World Heritage Site. Built around 35BC by King Herod the Great, a fortified palace was placed on the flat top of this plateau, accessed by a winding footpath, now known as Snake Path.

From the top, he had a commanding view of the plains leading to the Dead Sea, 20km to the east. During the First Jewish-Roman War, Masada was taken-over by a group of rebels called the Sicarii. The Romans laid siege to the fortress in 73AD, surrounding the base and building a gigantic battle-ramp up the western slopes. Using a siege tower and battering ram, the Romans finally breached the fortress, only to find that the 960 men, women, and children had committed mass suicide...! In subsequent years, archaeological digs have only located 28 bodies, casting doubt on the accuracy of the legend, however, it was clear that some sort of siege took place resulting in the destruction of the palace and a number of deaths.

On arriving, in the blistering desert heat, I decided to pass on the long climb to the summit up Snake Path; opting instead to take the easy route via the cable-car. At the top, I wandered amid the remains of the once magnificent palace, and its adjacent Byzantine Church. I saw a stepped Herodian swimming pool, once used for ritualistic immersions. And I looked in awe at the unending views from my 400m high perch.

We had a lot of places to visit on our day-trip, so without delay, we descended the rocky outcrop, boarded our bus, and made the short drive to the shores of The Dead Sea. At 430.5m below sea level, the Dead Sea was the earth's lowest elevation on land. With 34.2% salinity, it was also the world's deepest hypersaline lake; 9.6 times more salty than the ocean. This had a number of effects. Firstly, nothing much could live in its water, making it very clear. And secondly, the salt made it very floaty. We had no choice; we had to strip-off and jump-in to test this theory. The theory proved correct; no matter how hard I tried, I could NOT sink. I lay on my back, arms and legs clear of the water, floating as securely as if I was wearing a life jacket.

After a quick dry-off in the roasting sun, it was back on the bus, and the journey to Jerusalem. This city was one of the oldest in the world, and was considered a Holy City for the religions of Christianity, Judaism, and Islam. It was also one of the core issues in the Israeli-Palestinian conflict, being partly in Israel and partly in the Palestinian West Bank.

As we approached from the hills above, I looked down on the ancient walled city. From a distance, it looked like a low-level sprawling urbanisation spreading over the gently undulating hills beneath. At its center, the Temple Mount (the holiest site in Judaism), standing proud with the sun glinting off its golden domed roof.

We entered the Old City of Jerusalem, and in true tourist fashion, formed a single-file human-chain as we wandered through the crowded, claustrophobic streets; the hawkers trying to sell us bottles of Holy-Water or parts of the Cross-of-Jesus...! We followed the alleged route that Jesus took when he carried his cross, until finally we arrived at the Temple Mount, sat atop a hill believed to be Mount Zion (from the Hebrew Bible). At this point, things got very confusing. Temple Mount was believed to be the site of various temples and mosques mentioned in Christian, Islamic, and Jewish holy books; but it was clearly a site of religious significance whatever your beliefs.

Our group moved-on to The Church of the Holy Sepulchre; a church that was said to house the site of Jesus' crucifixion, as well as the tomb in which He was interred. The most lavishly decorated area was reserved for the site of Calvary, where the crucifixion took place. With its image of Jesus on the cross, surrounded by gold-and-glass decoration, and with images of angels watching-on, it was in stunning contrast to the bland, sand coloured exterior of the church. Beneath the glass altar was the Rock of Calvary from the Greek Orthodox religion, to its side a Roman Catholic altar, and beneath it, a chapel believed to house the skull of Adam. Everywhere was decorated with images; paintings of scenes from the Bible. And everyone spoke in hushed tones, showing reverence to those visiting as part of a pilgrimage. To me, it seemed a very strange place; a myriad of stories from different religions intermixed with one another. Some parts I recognised from the Bible, others becoming part of the same story even though they came from other sources! But it was miraculous that all of these different beliefs could co-exist in such close proximity; sharing the same location despite being at odds with one another. Religion is very confusing...

Next on the itinerary was The Western Wall, at that time, also known as The Wailing Wall; although that term is now considered derogatory. Originally believed to be part of the second temple built by Herod the Great in 19BC, what remains is one of the most Holy sites in the Jewish faith. Built of huge irregular sandstone blocks, it towered 19m above the Temple Mount Plaza, and the exposed section was about 57m long. Many Jewish people were here to pray, often writing their prayers on slips of paper that were folded and placed into cracks between the large stone blocks. As a non-Jew, I was allowed to approach the wall, only entering the cordoned-off area after I had donned a traditional Kippah (brimless cloth cap, satisfying orthodox religious beliefs). Touching the wall, I was dwarfed by its immensity. We moved-on quickly as we were short of time on our crammed schedule, and we were keen not to upset or offend any of the devout religious believers with our tourist activities.

Last on our list of "must-sees" was the town of Bethlehem, situated in the West Bank, 10km south of Jerusalem. We were here for one purpose, to visit The Church of the Nativity, the site of Jesus' birth. As it was approaching the Christmas period, I expected to see lavish decorations to celebrate, but on arrival at the square that housed this church, there was nothing monumental to distinguish it as a place of religious significance. There was a three-sided plaza surrounded by plain-looking rectangular buildings; a minaret towering above the right-hand side. To the rear of this square stood a statue on a column indicating the entrance to the Church of the Nativity. To enter, I had to crouch to pass through a very low door called the "Door of Humility," but once inside the Basilica, the Corinthian-columned nave and aisles led to the lavishly decorated altar. This was known as an iconostasis; an array of icons and religious paintings. Beneath the Basilica was The Grotto of the Nativity. This is where Jesus was believed to have been born; in a cave, as opposed to the widely held belief of a stable. Granted, the cave may well have been used as a stable at the time. The exact spot was marked by a 14-pointed metal star embedded into a marble surround; a number of lit candles turning the location into a shrine, or altar to the birth.

Now full-to-the-brim with religious knowledge and culture, we emerged into the bright sun of Manger Square, and headed back to our ship in Haifa. It had been a long, tiring day; but one full of monumental experiences. We had visited places and seen things that many of us would never see again in our lifetimes...

Having left Haifa, Invincible sailed west into the Mediterranean Sea, heading ever nearer to home. After a couple of days of intense cleaning throughout the entire ship, we had a special guest arrive to spend the day with us before our return. As the flight-deck was cleared, a distinctive, bright-red helicopter in the livery of the Royal Family's flight, landed sedately onboard. From its rear, The Princess Royal, Princess Anne, emerged; followed closely by her entourage. She was greeted by the ship's Captain and senior officers, and escorted beneath decks to begin a whistle-stop tour of the ship. A little later, she was shown to the upper-deck where the rest of our fleet of warships and RFA's conducted a ceremonial sail-past, and helicopters and Harriers performed a synchronised fly-by. From the look on her face, she appeared suitably impressed by the show, and shortly before departing, addressed the ship's company in the hanger; congratulating us on our deployment, and in representing the UK abroad.

Life at sea continued as normal, broken only by a very special meal arranged for the senior rates mess one evening. Dressed in full evening-rig (including cummerbunds), we took-over the officer's Wardroom for the night. We were to have a formal silver-service dinner, with all the pomp and ceremony that that entailed. For many of us, this would be the first, and only, experience of such an event, and something to savour; being part of naval tradition.

On entering the Wardroom, we were faced with a long communal table bedecked with the officers' ceremonial silver table-decorations and cutlery. With seating allocated by name-plates, we located our places and awaited the order to sit down from the head-of-the-table. The head-of-the-table controlled everything; from the timing of the various stages of the meal, to toasts, to giving permission for members to leave the table for a toilet-break. Everything was governed by tradition and etiquette. We were served the many courses of the meal by the Wardroom Stewards, seconded from looking after the officers to look after us for the evening. The meal progressed slowly, and towards the end, toasts were made, beginning with one to the Queen. As naval tradition dictates, we were NOT required to stand during this toast. All other services were, but not the Royal Navy; we had special dispensation due to the fact that ships-of-old had such low ceilings, making standing difficult (or so I am led to believe). Others say that it was simply because we were the "Senior Service." After this, the port was passed around the table. Again, naval tradition dictated that it should be passed to the left *only*, and that the glass decanter, with its wide flat base, should never be lifted off the surface of the table (even when pouring it into your glass). Great fun was had trying to manoeuvre the decanter near the table's-edge in order to pour its contents into a glass held below table height. Of course, any spillage was greatly frowned upon; punishable at the head-of-the-table's discretion...! The formalities and the meal out of the way, the evening reverted into a normal mess-social, and the officers were invited to join us (after all, it was held in their Wardroom).

A few days later, and our final visit of the deployment was upon us; we stopped one last time at Gibraltar. Despite it being December, the weather was kind to us, being similar to a UK summer's day. The time had arrived for our *official* ship's company attempt at The Rock Race. A few of us had had a practice on a previous visit, but this time, everyone not on-duty was expected to have a go. Whilst most treated it as a fun-run, wearing fancy-dress costumes, some of us fitness-freaks decided to attempt the race record. I am not sure of the times involved, but we had a good try at beating it, coming close. Once completed, we sat at the finish line watching as the hundreds of less-fit personnel completed their run (or more accurately, "walk") up the hill; watching as Neptune and his "wife" passed us, along with a number of fairies, and some unknown characters in their make-shift costumes. It was a fun way to end our last trip ashore...

All that was left now was for us to transit the Bay of Biscay, and to completely clean and tidy the ship, top-to-bottom, in readiness for our arrival in Portsmouth Dockyard.

As Invincible entered the English Channel, the aircraft, and most of their support crew, disembarked for their return to RNAS Culdrose. The rest of us continued along the channel in the rain and mist, slowly getting nearer to Portsmouth. Unfortunately, we were not due to dock until the following morning, so it meant one last night afloat, within touching-distance of our home port. One last chance for a few drinks before we all went our separate ways the following morning.

Our last day of deployment dawned to an overcast, chilly morning; a typical December day in the UK. In our best uniforms, gorilla toys not far from our hands, we mustered on the flight-deck for our final Procedure-Alpha entry into port. With bright orange tugs ahead and astern of us, we glided majestically into Portsmouth. On our approach, the harbour-walls in Southsea were lined with cheering crowds, and when we reached our jetty, they must have been 5 or 6 deep; held back by flimsy looking barriers. Amid the throng were a selection of banners and Union Jack flags.

Each of us was straining to see our family and friends; many claimed that they saw them, but with the vast numbers waiting, it was hard to identify individuals.

Once the gangways were safely erected, the crew was allowed ashore to greet those who had come to see our return. My parents made the journey down from Norfolk, and having found them, we all went back onboard for a brief guided-tour of the ship. This was followed shortly afterwards by some well-earned leave over the Christmas and New Year period.

"Orient 92" had come to an end...

CHAPTER 29

The beginning of the end...

With my return to HMS Invincible at the start of '93, things settled into the normal routines associated with life in our home port. Little did I know at this point that I was only destined to be part of Her Majesty's Royal Navy for a matter of three more months! Things were about to change drastically; and rapidly...!

Approximately 10 months earlier, around the start of Orient '92, I had gained a new boss; a new Weapons Engineering Officer (WEO) had been appointed to HMS Invincible. Compared to the previous WEO (who was friendly and helpful towards everyone in the department), this one seemed "stand-off-ish," aloof, and outwardly formal in his dealings with us. I did not think anything of it; putting it down to him being new to the ship. Up until his joining, all of my annual appraisals had been good; above-average in every respect. Remember, I had been recommended as a leadership instructor immediately prior to joining Invincible, and I had been promoted to Leading Hand early due to good conduct. I had also received my first "Long-Service-and-

Good-Conduct-Badge" at the recommended time. So, when my yearly report was due in '92, it came as a bit of a shock to find that this new WEO had marked me down slightly, compared to previous reports! I was still in the "OK" banding, with at least two levels lower before action needed to be taken, so I was not too worried. As the WEO had only recently joined, and he did not really know me yet, I put it down to him just setting-the-boundaries in his department; giving me a kick-up-the-arse to make sure I was working at the top of my game. No specific areas of improvement were mentioned, and no specific failings of equipment or leadership command-and-control had been highlighted, so I had nothing with which to base his actions on. As the WEO had not given me any warnings, and no action-plan to improve, I took it that he was happy overall with the way I was running the section. For the rest of the deployment I continued, safe in the knowledge that everything was fine, my section was functioning perfectly, and that my boss was pleased with the way I was running things. He had not said anything to me to the contrary so that was all that I could assume.

Towards the end of January '93, I was summoned to the WEO's office; something about my annual appraisal was mentioned.

"That couldn't be right," I thought, "it's not due until May!"

Having been asked to sit down, I was completely oblivious to what was about to happen. The WEO seemed to be fumbling-around, shuffling papers, and not looking me in the eyes. He looked uncomfortable, embarrassed, almost ashamed of what he was about to say.

"We've been looking at your section, and your reports," he said.

There was a pause as he looked for the right words to use.

"We've decided to let you go. You are going to be discharged to shore as of March!"

I was in total shock. This had come out-of-the-blue; no prior warning at all. My head was buzzing. What did this mean? What had I done wrong? Surely, if I was getting kicked-out of the navy there had to be a reason why? Why had nobody bothered to tell me in advance? Oh, and who was this "we" that had been looking at my reports and section?

I had a hundred questions flying around in my head, but as I was in shock, all that came out was,

"Oh! Why is that, Sir?"

The WEO huffed, and said something to the effect of,

"It just is. We'll give you more information later, but for now, just accept what is happening. I suggest you start thinking of what you are going to do in a couple of month's time..."

And with that, I was ushered out of the office; confused, dazed, and with a feeling of anger brewing-up inside me! Was it just a conflict of personalities; the WEO just did not like me? Or was there more going-on behind the scenes that I did not know about? I went away to think about what to do.

Having spoken to a few other people, and dug around to see if I could find what was going on, the recurring phrase that was mentioned was, "OPTIONS-FOR-CHANGE." This was the government's restructuring of the British defence forces which was started in 1990 and was ongoing at this time. For the Royal Navy, officially, it was to reduce the number of ships from about 50 to 40, but for quite a while they had been crying-out for volunteer redundancies as well. When that target was not met, compulsory redundancies were implemented. Clearly, they were targeting a set figure for naval personnel too. It was all about cost-cutting, budgets, and fitting everything into the defence reviews. HMS Scylla, my first ship, became one of these cost-cutting measures, and from all indications, so was I.

The contract-of-employment that I was subject to stated that I had to complete an eight year return-of-service as part of my apprenticeship. Within that period, the Royal

Navy could terminate my employment at their discretion. I had completed seven years, and had I done more than the eight required, the navy would have had to offer me a full redundancy package; including paying-me-off with somewhere in the region of £25000, as well as providing resettlement training in order to fit back into civilian life. As it was, with less than eight years service, they could terminate my employment without paying me anything, and without any resettlement. It would save them quite a bit of money!

    I could fully understand this, but what annoyed me was that nobody in authority, the WEO included, would openly admit that this was what was happening. It had crossed my mind that the WEO had been appointed to Invincible with the hidden-agenda of looking for money-saving cuts that he could implement. Whether this was the case, I will never know; but it certainly fitted with the way he had acted since his arrival.

    A few days later, I booked an appointment to see the WEO again. Questions were asked as to why I was being effectively "sacked." But, as with our first meeting, he was extremely vague; committing to nothing, and admitting nothing. As some consolation, all he said was,

    "Don't worry, it's not a sacking. You won't be dishonourably discharged. You have an exemplary record, and that will be highlighted in your references and documents when you leave."

    My reply was simply,

    "If my record is so exemplary, then why am I being let go, Sir?"

    But that was met with a silence and a hard stare. I had considered other options other than being kicked-out, and said to the WEO,

    "Well, how about I just get transferred instead of being discharged? I was recommended as an instructor at Royal Arthur; why can't I go there? Or even change jobs to join the Marines, or as a PTI?"

"No. That's not possible. We've spent so much money on your training that it would not be cost-effective to let you transfer," he replied.

"But surely, having spent all that money to train me, the worst thing to do would be to waste it entirely by binning me? It would make more sense to use my skills and experience by keeping me in the forces in a different role, wouldn't it Sir?"

"No!! That's not going to happen. Get used to the idea..." he said.

I was not impressed. It was like banging my head against a brick wall. Clearly things had been set in motion; decisions made, and no matter how much I protested, nothing was going to alter. I made my feelings known, and lodged a *formal* objection, but that was dismissed without thought. We had no trades-union; no representatives to wield the sword of power. It was not like I could go to a tribunal, go on-strike, or do anything that may have been an option in the civilian world. In the forces you are trained to follow orders, this was just another order that ended my career. Decisions were absolute!

Over the following weeks, I accepted my fate, reluctantly. The Royal Navy was good to its word. I received a glowing report, highlighting my exemplary record and my experiences aboard ship. I received my naval-records as part of my leaving package which proved to be everything that any prospective civilian employer would love to see; adding to my CV and internationally-recognised engineering qualifications. But nowhere on the paperwork did anybody give a reason for discharge; it was ambiguously left open, almost as if I had decided of my own accord to leave. To this day, nobody has officially given me a written or verbal explanation of why I was discharged, which I think is disgraceful! All they had to say was, "Options-for-Change," but, no, nothing was said!

With the leave that was owing to me, I was posted to HMS Nelson, the shore-base at Portsmouth Dockyard, on the

12th March 1993; for one day. I returned all of the uniform that was asked for; which consisted of my respirator and my filthy sea-boots. Everything else, I could take with me. I was given my discharge paperwork. Some unknown senior rate who I had never seen before, thanked me for my service. And I was shown to the front gate...

I was offered no resettlement package. Normally, anyone leaving with exemplary service is given months' of advance notice, and given various training-courses before they leave. I got nothing!! I was told that I would not be required to go onto the naval reserve list, where normally you would expect to be on-call for a few years. I was given one month's pay in compensation. Nothing more.

And on the 10th April 1993, I became a civilian...

CHAPTER 30

Postscript

Did I feel bitter about how my career in the Royal Navy ended? YES...!! For the first year I felt very bitter; angry that the career I loved had been ended due to "politics." But I was even angrier about how it had been implemented; how I was never given a full explanation (or any explanation at all!). Angry about how the WEO had not used any man-management skills when talking to me, and had not even considered any other options.

With hindsight, there were other pointers suggesting that my theory (because that is all it can be without any proper explanation) was correct. In the weeks between the time it was announced that I was to leave, and the actual date of my departure, there were NO efforts made on the part of my superiors to get a replacement for my section. When I left, the Minor Weapons Section was left in limbo with no senior rate in-charge of it! From talking to others who remained onboard after I was gone, it seems that the section was broken into smaller parts; each weapon-system or piece of equipment being allocated to other weapons engineering senior rates to incorporate into their own sections. To me, this is the definition of "redundancy;" only in this case, the navy managed to avoid any redundancy payouts.

The other thing that was annoying, like a kick-in-the-teeth, was that in the same week that I was discharged as a money-saving exercise, the Royal Navy was recruiting in the media for new-joiners in the exact same role that I had just left. To me, they were saying that they could not afford a senior rate's pay in the role, but a new recruit would be a lot cheaper. Over the years, this is something that I have seen a number of times. A budget-review or series of cut-backs is followed by redundancies, which is followed by a new recruitment campaign! Maybe this is some form of ongoing policy...?!

However, I believe in FATE; everything happens for a reason. You may not know, or understand what that reason is at the time, but long-term, the reason will become clear. Although I was not happy about leaving the navy when I did, if I had not done so, I would not have walked into a civilian engineering job within a couple of weeks. The skills I had learnt in the navy and the references I had received meant that the first job I applied for, I got. If I had not gone into civilian engineering, then I would never have found-out that I hated the monotony of it compared to naval engineering, and I would never have applied to join the police force as an alternative. With my experience in the navy, the police jumped at the chance of offering me a career; around half of my intake was ex-forces personnel. And the experience I had of looking after my section, dealing with their personal issues, and my organisational abilities, helped enormously throughout my police career. Clearly, fate dictated that one opportunity lead on to another, and that the skills acquired in one role could be transferred over into another role. Everything was linked to everything else...

So, what did I gain from my years in the Royal Navy? Well, I grew-up rapidly. Quick promotions, and subsequent responsibility, have a habit of doing this. I learnt a lot of self-discipline. I learnt what my limits were, both physically and mentally, and I learnt to push beyond those boundaries. I learnt to be well-organised and tidy in everything I do. My wife would probably argue that it is more a case of OCD; but I plan ahead with everything, I have routines, I still do all the ironing (to navy standards), and so on...

Fitness was a big bonus. When I joined-up, I was the most unfit person in the intake. When I left, I was virtually addicted to training, be it the gym or running, and in subsequent years, I have completed fast marathons; going from one extreme to the other!

Confidence and leadership; yes, I did gain in both. But I was still pretty naive when I left the navy. It was not until I joined the police and was dealing with violence and conflict on a daily basis, on my own, that I truly learnt the art of these two skills.

Life in the Royal Navy gets into your blood; there were many aspects of navy life that infused into civilian life after I left. The love of the sea and the travel-bug way of life, were some. In my case, I went on to become a SCUBA Instructor, travelling and working throughout the world, before settling down in the Canary Islands as an Ex-Pat for a few years. Clearly this aspect of navy life lives-on in me. Beyond that, the distinct terms used in navy life became embedded in the way I spoke in civilian life. Every now and then, words of navy-slang origin slip into everyday conversations. References to "the ogin" (sea or water), "scran" (food), "gash" (rubbish), and getting "goffered" (spray) can often be heard hiding in my sentences.

But on a more serious note, the navy taught me loyalty; loyalty to friends and colleagues, and loyalty to the company or organisation that you work for. In the police, loyalty was a given; you backed-up your mates, and vice versa. Without it, you trod a very dangerous line, and you would end-up getting hurt. You needed your mates around you. Loyalty to your employer was a different matter though.

Yes, in principal, you were loyal to them, but as I found out with the Royal Navy, they were not necessarily going to reciprocate. I have learnt to treat their loyalty to you with a-pinch-of-salt. When it suits them, they are loyal, but when it comes to budgets and politics, they will look after themselves first regardless of how it affects individuals.

Tolerance was something that the navy taught you, or rather, you learnt through experience in the navy. Having to live in close proximity, in confined quarters for months at a time, with people of every background, religion, belief, character and attitude; you learnt very quickly to get-along with people. Throughout my time in the navy, I was known for being very laid-back in my attitude to others. For the words "laid-back" you could substitute "tolerant." When I joined the police, this ability became crucial. You have to deal with every aspect of human-life as a *copper,* and personal thoughts or opinions need to be suppressed. You need to tolerate people's aggression towards you as part-of-the-job without being goaded into retaliation. But equally, you have to know where the limits are. As soon as someone steps over that line, "Mr Nice-Guy" suddenly turns into "Mr Enforcer." It is like having a split personality! Maybe it is because I am getting older, or maybe it is due to the constant suppression of my opinions in the police, but my once calm, tolerant persona is getting progressively less tolerant as time goes by...! I am much more opinionated and vocal nowadays than I once was.

All in all, the Royal Navy experience left me with many more positive attributes than it did negative ones. I enjoyed my time serving Queen-and-Country, and I enjoyed my travel adventures. But this was just one chapter in my life. To discover how I fared in the police, and as a diving instructor travelling the world, you will need to read my next two memoirs.

How I continued after leaving the Royal Navy is now quite evident, but what about the ships and bases that I served on?

HMS Raleigh is still the navy's new-recruit training establishment. I drove past it the other year, seeing a squad of newbie's running in the lanes nearby. It certainly brought back fond memories of my time there.

HMS Collingwood is still the navy's weapon engineering school, but has taken on responsibility for Maritime Warfare, Fleet Intelligence, and Leadership training. It is currently the largest Royal Navy establishment in the UK.

HMS Scylla was scrapped under "Options-for-Change" in 1993, and was sunk off Plymouth as an artificial reef, and a dive-site in March 2004.

HMS Invincible was decommissioned in August 2005, and sold to Turkey as scrap, where she is currently being destroyed.

HMS Royal Arthur was decommissioned in 1993, and was left to rot! It is currently heavily vandalised, and looking like a ghost-town!

RNAS Culdrose is still in operation as one of the biggest helicopter bases in Europe. I assume that ARE Helston is still located there, and functions in some form or another from its confines.

HMS Rooke in Gibraltar was converted to a Joint-Services Base in 1990, and was subsequently paid-off in 1996.

HMS Tamar in Hong Kong was moved prior to the handing-over of Hong Kong to China. Its new location was on the British-owned Stonecutter's Island, off Kowloon, nearby. It has since been down-graded to a government marine facility. The original HMS Tamar site was converted into the new Hong Kong's central government complex.

<u>The End.</u>

Multimedia Bonus

For those readers who were enthralled by the stories that occurred during the "Orient 92" chapters of my memoir, here is an added bonus. During that particular deployment, the ship's crew filmed many of the visits and the antics of its personnel. These films were compiled into an "official" record of the trip which was then posted on "You-Tube."

For those interested in seeing a visual account of "Orient 92," check-out the address below to watch this "You-Tube" film.

https://www.youtube.com/watch?v=LuJofrrrW2k

Credits to those who filmed it:-
Editors – Lt Grindel and CPO Gumbley
Producer – Rev Wishart
Thanks to the School of Maritime Operations Video Production Unit at HMS Mercury.

Apologies for the annoying soundtrack...

For a selection of photos from my time in the RN, be sure to visit my Website and Facebook pages.

About the Author

Andrew Heasman was born in London, but has always had the travel-bug. Having joined the Royal Navy at the age of 20, he travelled the world, rising through the ranks to become a Petty Officer aboard the aircraft carrier, HMS Invincible.

His next career path saw him become a police officer in rural Lincolnshire, and finally, he gave it all up to become a SCUBA diving instructor, following the sun as he worked his way around the globe.

Currently living in Staffordshire, he has put his experiences down in writing.

Follow his adventures, and read his books – visit:

https://ajheasman.wixsite.com/author

Contact the Author

Contact **Andrew Heasman** at the following email address:
andrewheasman.author@Gmail.com

Follow **Andrew Heasman** on Facebook
https://www.facebook.com/AJHeasmanauthor/

Follow **Andrew Heasman** on Twitter
https://twitter.com/HeasmanAuthor

For updates on future books, release dates, and **Andrew Heasman's** Blog, sign-up for his Mailing List at the following website:-
https://ajheasman.wixsite.com/author

Future Releases

Book Two in *"The Memoir Series"* focuses on the author's experiences during his eight years working as a Police Constable in The Lincolnshire Police during the 1990's and early 2000's.

It explores the author's police training at Ryton (in the Midlands), through on-the-job training on the streets of rural Boston, and culminating in a period of city-policing in Lincoln.

Often working alone, and with very little support, this is the story of real-life policing in Britain. Violence, aggression, and personal danger were a daily risk, but along the way, there were also many lighter moments; the police's "dark humour" coming to the fore.

For updates regarding this, and other projects, be sure to visit the author's website and sign-up to his **Mailing List**. Read his regular blog updates, or follow him on **Facebook** or **Twitter**.

Beyond the Waves: My Royal Navy Adventures

Beyond the Waves: My Royal Navy Adventures

Printed in Poland
by Amazon Fulfillment
Poland Sp. z o.o., Wrocław